Historic Oddities and Strange Events.

S Baring-Gould

The BiblioLife Network

This project was made possible in part by the BiblioLife Network (BLN), a project aimed at addressing some of the huge challenges facing book preservationists around the world. The BLN includes libraries, library networks, archives, subject matter experts, online communities and library service providers. We believe every book ever published should be available as a high-quality print reproduction; printed on- demand anywhere in the world. This insures the ongoing accessibility of the content and helps generate sustainable revenue for the libraries and organizations that work to preserve these important materials.

The following book is in the "public domain" and represents an authentic reproduction of the text as printed by the original publisher. While we have attempted to accurately maintain the integrity of the original work, there are sometimes problems with the original book or micro-film from which the books were digitized. This can result in minor errors in reproduction. Possible imperfections include missing and blurred pages, poor pictures, markings and other reproduction issues beyond our control. Because this work is culturally important, we have made it available as part of our commitment to protecting, preserving, and promoting the world's literature.

GUIDE TO FOLD-OUTS, MAPS and OVERSIZED IMAGES

In an online database, page images do not need to conform to the size restrictions found in a printed book. When converting these images back into a printed bound book, the page sizes are standardized in ways that maintain the detail of the original. For large images, such as fold-out maps, the original page image is split into two or more pages.

Guidelines used to determine the split of oversize pages:

• Some images are split vertically; large images require vertical and horizontal splits.
• For horizontal splits, the content is split left to right.
• For vertical splits, the content is split from top to bottom.
• For both vertical and horizontal splits, the image is processed from top left to bottom right.

HISTORIC ODDITIES

AND

STRANGE EVENTS

HISTORIC ODDITIES

AND

STRANGE EVENTS

BY

S. BARING GOULD, M.A.

AUTHOR OF "MEHALAH," "OLD COUNTRY LIFE," ETC.

SECOND SERIES

London

METHUEN & CO.

18 BURY STREET, W.C.

1891

CONTENTS.

———◆———

PREFACE.

TWO of the articles in this Series are concerned with the history of mysticism, a phase of human nature that deserves careful and close study. It is the outbreak in man of a spiritual element which cannot be ignored, cannot be wholly suppressed. It is capable of regulation, but unregulated, it is a most mischievous faculty.

"The Patarines of Milan" appeared in *Fraser's Magazine* in 1874. It is a curious episode in the history of religious fanaticism, that has, I believe, never before been worked out so completely from the contemporary historians. When the Jews are menaced with expulsion from Russia, and regarded with bitter hostility in other parts of Eastern Europe, the article on the accusations brought against them may prove not uninstructive reading.

S. BARING GOULD.

Lew Trenchard, Devon,
Sept. 27th, 1890.

A Swiss Passion Play.

WE are a little surprised, and perhaps a little shocked, at the illiberality of the Swiss Government, in even such Protestant cantons as Geneva, Zürich, and Berne, in forbidding the performances on their ground of the "Salvation Army," and think that such conduct is not in accordance with Protestant liberty of judgment and democratic independence. But the experiences gone through in Switzerland as in Germany of the confusion and mischief sometimes wrought by fanaticism, we will not say justify, but in a measure explain, the objection the Government has to a recrudescence of religious mysticism in its more flagrant forms. The following story exemplifies the extravagance to which such spiritual exaltation runs occasionally—fortunately only occasionally.

About eight miles from Schaffhausen, a little way on one side of the road to Winterthür, in a valley, lies the insignificant hamlet of Wildisbuch, its meadows overshadowed by leafy walnut trees. The hamlet is in the parish of Trüllikon. Here, at the beginning of this century, in a farmhouse, standing by itself, lived John Peter, a widower, with several of his children. He had but one son, Caspar, married in 1812, and divorced from his wife; he was, however, blessed with five daughters—Barbara, married to a blacksmith in Trüllikon; Susanna, Elizabeth, Magdalena married to

A

John Moser, a shoemaker; and Margaretta, born in
1794, his youngest, and favourite child. Not long
after the birth of Margaretta, her mother died, and
thenceforth the child was the object of the tenderest
and most devoted solicitude to her sisters and to her
father.   Margaretta grew up to be a remarkable
child.   At school she distinguished herself by her
aptitude in learning, and in church by the devotion
with which she followed the tedious Zwinglian
service.   The pastor who prepared her for confirmation was struck by her enthusiasm and eagerness to
know about religion.   She was clearly an imaginative
person, and to one constituted as she was, the barn-
like church, destitute of every element of beauty,
studiously made as hideous as a perverse fancy
could scheme, and the sacred functions reduced to
utter dreariness, with every element of devotion
bled out of them, were incapable of satisfying the
internal spiritual fire that consumed her.

There is in every human soul a divine aspiration,
a tension after the invisible and spiritual, in some
more developed than in others, in certain souls ex-
isting only in that rudimentary condition in which, it
is said, feet are found in the eel, and eyes in the
oyster, but in others it is a predominating faculty, a
veritable passion.   Unless this faculty be given
legitimate scope, be disciplined and guided, it breaks
forth in abnormal and unhealthy manifestations.   We
know what is the result when the regular action of
the pores of the skin is prevented, or the circulation
of the blood is impeded.   Fever and hallucination
ensue.   So is it with the spiritual life in man.   If

that be not given free passage for healthy discharge of its activity, it will resolve itself into fanaticism, that is to say it will assume a diseased form of manifestation.

Margaretta was far ahead of her father, brother and sisters in intellectual culture, and in moral force of character.

Susanna, the second daughter of John Peter, was an amiable, industrious, young woman, without independence of character. The third daughter, Elizabeth, was a quiet girl, rather dull in brain; Barbara was married when Margaretta was only nine, and Magdalena not long after; neither of them, however, escaped the influence of their youngest sister, who dominated over their wills almost as completely as she did over those of her two unmarried sisters, with whom she consorted daily.

How great her power over her sisters was may be judged from what they declared in after years in prison, and from what they endured for her sake.

Barbara, the eldest, professed to the prison chaplain in Zürich, in 1823, "I am satisfied that God worked in mighty power, and in grace through Margaret, up to the hour of her death." The father himself declared after the ruin of his family and the death of two of his daughters, "I am assured that my youngest daughter was set apart by God for some extraordinary purpose."

When Margaret was six, she was able to read her Bible, and would summon the family about her to listen to her lectures out of the sacred volume. She would also at the same time pray with great ardour, and exhort her father and sisters to lead God-fearing lives. When she read the narrative of the Passion, she was unable to refrain from tears; her emotion communicated itself to all assembled round her, and the whole family sobbed and prayed aloud. She was a veritable " ministering child " to her household in all things spiritual. As she had been born at Christmas, it was thought that this very fact indicated some special privilege and grace accorded to her. In 1811, when aged seventeen, she received her first communion and edified all the church with the unction and exaltation of soul with which she presented herself at the table. In after years the pastor of Trüllikon said of her, " Unquestionably Margaretta was the cleverest of the family. She often came to thank me for the instructions I had given her in spiritual things. Her promises to observe all I had taught her were most fervent. I had the best hopes for her, although I observed somewhat of extravagance in her. Margaretta speedily obtained an absolute supremacy in her father's house. All must do what she ordered. Her will expressed by word of mouth, or by letter when absent, was obeyed as the will of God."

In personal appearance Margaretta was engaging. She was finely moulded, had a well-proportioned body, a long neck on which her head was held very upright; large, grey-blue eyes, fair hair, a lofty, well-arched brow. The nose was well-shaped, but the chin and mouth were somewhat coarse.

In 1816, her mother's brother, a small farmer at Rudolfingen, invited her to come and manage his house for him. She went, and was of the utmost assistance. Everything prospered under her hand. Her uncle thought that she had brought the blessing of the Almighty on both his house and his land.

Whilst at Rudolfingen, the holy maiden was brought in contact with the Pietists of Schaffhausen. She attended their prayer-meetings and expositions of Scripture. This deepened her religious convictions, and produced a depression in her manner that struck her sisters when she visited them. In answer to their inquiries why she was reserved and melancholy, she replied that God was revealing Himself to her more and more every day, so that she became daily more conscious of her own sinfulness. If this had really been the case it would have saved her from what ensued, but this sense of her own sinfulness was a mere phrase, that meant actually an overweening self-consciousness. She endured only about a twelve month of the pietistic exercises at Schaffhausen, and then felt a call to preach, testify and prophesy herself, instead of sitting at the feet of others. Accordingly she threw up her place with her uncle, and returned to Wildisbuch, in March, 1817, when she began operations as a revivalist.

The paternal household was now somewhat enlarged. The old farmer had taken on a hand to help him in field and stable, called Heinrich Ernst, and a young woman as maid called Margaret Jäggli. Ernst was a faithful, amiable young fellow whom old Peters thoroughly trusted, and he became devoted heart and soul to the family. Margaret Jäggli was a person of very indifferent character, who, for her immoralities,

had been turned out of her native village. She was
subject to epileptic fits, which she supposed were possession by the devil, and she came to the farm of the
Peter's family in hopes of being there cured by the
prayers of the saintly Margaretta.

Another inmate of the house was Ursula Kündig,
who entered it at the age of nineteen, and lived there
as a veritable maid-of-all-work, though paid no wages.
This damsel was of the sweetest, gentlest disposition.
Her parish pastor gave testimony to her, " She was
always so good that even scandal-mongers were unable to find occasion for slander in her conduct." Her
countenance was full of intelligence, purity, and had
in it a nobility above her birth and education. Her
home had been unhappy; she had been engaged to be
married to a young man, but finding that he did
not care for her, and sought only her small property,
she broke off the engagement, to her father's great
annoyance. It was owing to a quarrel at home relative to this, that she went to Wildisbuch to entreat
Margaretta Peter to be "her spiritual guide through life
into eternity." Ursula had at first only paid occasional
visits to Wildisbuch, but gradually these visits became
long, and finally she took up her residence in the
house. The soul of the unhappy girl was as wax in
the hands of the saint, whom she venerated with in-
tensest admiration as the Elect of the Lord ; and she
professed her unshaken conviction " that Christ revealed Himself in the flesh through her, and that
through her many thousands of souls were saved."
The house at Wildisbuch became thenceforth a great
gathering place for all the spiritually-minded in the

neighbourhood, who desired instruction, guidance, enlightenment, and Margaretta, the high priestess of mysticism to all such as could find no satisfaction for the deepest hunger of their souls in the Zwinglian services of their parish church.

Man is composed of two parts; he has a spiritual nature which he shares with the angels, and an animal nature that he possesses in common with the beasts. There is in him, consequently, a double tendency, one to the indefinite, unconfined, spiritual; the other to the limited, sensible and material. The religious history of all times shows us this higher nature striving after emancipation from the law of the body, and never succeeding in accomplishing the escape, always falling back, like Dædalus, into destruction, when attempting to defy the laws of nature and soar too near to the ineffable light. The mysticism of the old heathen world, the mysticism of the Gnostic sects, the mysticism of mediæval heretics, almost invariably resolved itself into orgies of licentiousness. God has bound soul and body together, and an attempt to dissociate them in religion is fatally doomed to ruin.

The incarnation of the Son of God was the indissoluble union of Spirit with form as the basis of true religion. Thenceforth, Spirit was no more to be dissociated from matter, authority from a visible Church, grace from a sacramental sign, morality from a fixed law. All the great revolts against Catholicism in the middle-ages, were more or less revolts against this principle and were reversions to pure spiritualism. The Reformation was taken advantage of for the mystic aspirations of men to run riot. Individual

emotion became the supreme and sole criticism of
right and wrong, of truth and falsehood, and sole
authority to which submission must be tendered.

In the autumn of 1817, Margaretta of Wildisbuch
met a woman who was also remarkable in her way,
and the head of another revivalist movement. This
was Julianne von Krüdner; about whom a word must
now be said.

Julianne was born in 1766, at Riga, the daughter
of a noble and wealthy family. Her father visited
Paris and took the child with him, where she made
the acquaintance of the rationalistic and speculative
spirits of French society, before the Revolution. In a
Voltairean atmosphere, the little Julianne grew up
without religious faith or moral principle. At the
age of fourteen she was married to a man much older
than herself, the Baron von Krüdner, Russian Ambassador at Venice. There her notorious immoralities
resulted in a separation, and Julianne was obliged to
return to her father's house at Riga. This did not
satisfy her love of pleasure and vanity, and she went
to St. Petersburg and then to Paris, where she threw
herself into every sort of dissipation. She wrote a
novel, " Valérie," in which she frankly admitted that
woman, when young, must give herself up to pleasure,
then take up with art, and finally, when nothing else
was left her, devote herself to religion. At the age of
forty she had already entered on this final phase.
She went to Berlin, was admitted to companionship
with the Queen, Louise, and endeavoured to " convert"
her. The sweet, holy queen required no conversion,
and the Baroness von Krüdner was obliged to leave

Berlin. She wandered thenceforth from place to place, was now in Paris, then in Geneva, and then in Germany. At Karlsruhe she met Jung-Stilling; and thenceforth threw herself heart and soul into the pietistic revival. Her mission now was—so she conceived—to preach the Gospel to the poor. In 1814 she obtained access to the Russian Court, where her prophecies and exhortations produced such an effect on the spirit of the Czar, Alexander I., that he entreated her to accompany him to Paris. She did so, and held spiritual conferences and prayer meetings in the French capital. Alexander soon tired of her, and she departed to Basel, where she won to her the Genevan Pastor Empeytaz and the Basel Professor Lachenal. Her meetings for revival, which were largely attended, caused general excitement, but led to many domestic quarrels, so that the city council gave her notice to leave the town. She then made a pilgrimage along the Rhine, but her proceedings were everywhere objected to by the police and town authorities, and she was sent back under police supervision first to Leipzig, and thence into Russia.

Thence in 1824 she departed for the Crimea, where she had resolved to start a colony on the plan of the Moravian settlements, and there died before accomplishing her intention.

It was in 1817, when she was conducting her apostolic progress along the Rhine, that she and Margaretta of Wildisbuch met. Apparently the latter made a deeper impression on the excitable baroness than had the holy Julianne on Margaretta. The two aruspices did not laugh when they met, for they were both in deadly earnest, and had not the smallest suspicion that they were deluding themselves first, and then others.

The meeting with the Krüdner had a double effect. In the first place, the holy Julianne, when forced to leave the neighbourhood by the unregenerate police, commended her disciples to the blessed Margaret; and, in the second place, the latter had the shrewdness to perceive, that, if she was to play anything like the part of her fellow-apostle, she must acquire a little more education. Consequently Margaret took pains to write grammatically, and to spell correctly.

The result of the commendation by Saint Julianne of her disciples to Margaret was that thenceforth a regular pilgrimage set in to Wildisbuch of devout persons in landaus and buggies, on horse and on foot.

Some additional actors in the drama must now be introduced.

Magdalena Peter, the fourth daughter of John Peter, was married to the cobbler, John Moser. The influence of Margaret speedily made itself felt in their house. At first Moser's old mother lived with the couple, along with Conrad, John Moser's younger brother. The first token of the conversion of Moser and his wife was that they kicked the old mother out of the house, because she was worldly and void of " saving grace." Conrad was a plodding, hard-working lad, very useful, and therefore not to be dispensed with. The chosen vessels finding he did not sympathise with them, and finding him too valuable to be done without, starved him till he yielded to their fancies, saw visions, and professed himself " saved." Barbara, also, married to the blacksmith Baumann, was next converted, and brought all her spiritual artillery to bear on the black-smith, but in vain. He let her go her own way, but he would have nothing himself to say to the great spiritual revival in the house of the Peters. Barbara, not finding a kindred soul in her husband, had taken up with a man of like soaring piety, a tailor, named Hablützel.

Another person who comes into this story is Jacob Ganz, a tailor, who had been mixed up with the movement at Basel under Julianne the Holy.

Margaret's brother Caspar was a man of infamous character; he was separated from his wife, whom he had treated with brutality ; had become the father of an illegitimate child, and now loafed about the country preaching the Gospel.

Ganz, the tailor, had thrown aside his shears, and constituted himself a roving preacher. In one of his apostolic tours he had made the acquaintance of Saint Margaret, and had been deeply impressed by her. He had an elect disciple at Illnau, in the Kempthal, south of Winterthür. This was a shoemaker named Jacob Morf, a married man, aged thirty ; small, with a head like a pumpkin. To this shoemaker Ganz spoke with enthusiam of the spiritual elevation of the holy Margaret, and Morf was filled with a lively desire of seeing and hearing her.

Margaretta seems after a while to have wearied of the monotony of life in her father's house, or else the spirit within her drove her abroad to carry her light into the many dark corners of her native canton. She resolved to be like Ganz, a roving apostle. Sometimes she started on her missionary journeys alone, sometimes along with her sister Elizabeth, who submitted to her with blind and stanch obedience, or else with Ursula Kündig. These journeys began in 1820, and extended as far Zürich and along the shores of that lovely lake. In May of the same year she visited Illnau, where she was received with enthusiasm by the faithful, who assembled in the house of a certain Ruegg, and there for the first time she met with Jacob Morf. The acquaintance then begun soon quickened into friendship. When a few weeks later he went to Schaffhausen to purchase leather, he turned aside to Wildisbuch. After this his visits there became not only frequent, but were protracted.

Margaret was the greatest comfort to him in his troubled state of soul. She described to him the searchings and anxieties she had undergone, so that he cried "for very joy that he had encountered one who had gone through the same experience as himself."

In November, 1820, Margaret took up her abode for some time in the house of a disciple, Caspar Notz, near Zürich, and made it the centre whence she started on a series of missionary excursions. Here also gathered the elect out of Zürich to hear her expound Scripture, and pray. And hither also came the cobbler Morf seeking ease for his troubled soul, and on occasions stayed in the house there with her for a week at a time. At last his wife, the worthy Regula Morf, came from Illnau to find her husband, and persuaded him to return with her to his cobbling at home.

At the end of January in 1821, Margaret visited

Illnau again, and drew away after her the bewitched
Jacob, who followed her all the way home, to Wildisbuch, and remained at her father's house ten days
further.

On Ascension Day following, he was again with
her, and then she revealed to him that it was the will
of heaven that they should ascend together, without
tasting death, into the mansions of the blessed, and
were to occupy one throne together for all eternity.
Throughout this year, when the cobbler, Jacob,
was not at Wildisbuch, or Saint Margaretta at Illnau,
the pair were writing incessantly to each other, and
their correspondence is still preserved in the archives
of Zürich. Here is a specimen of the style of the holy
Margaret. "My dear child! your dear letter filled
me with joy. O, my dear child, how gladly would I
tell you how it fares with me! When we parted, I
was forced to go aside where none might see, to
relieve my heart with tears. O, my heart, I cannot
describe to you the distress into which I fell. I lay
as one senseless for an hour. For anguish of heart I
could not go home, such unspeakable pains did I
suffer! My former separation from you was but a
shadow of this parting. O, why are you so unutterably
dear to me, &c.," and then a flow of sickly, pious
twaddle that makes the gorge rise.

Regula Morf read this letter and shook her head
over it. She had shaken her head over another letter
received by her husband a month earlier, in which the
holy damsel had written: "O, how great is my love!
It is stronger than death. O, how dear are you to me.
I could hug you to my heart a thousand times." And

had scribbled on the margin, "These words are for your eye alone." However, Regula saw them, shook her head and told her husband that the letter seemed to her unenlightened mind to be very much like a love-letter. "Nothing of the sort," answered the cobbler, "it speaks of spiritual affection only."

We must now pass over a trait in the life of the holy maid which is to the last degree unedifying, but which is merely another exemplification of that truth which the history of mysticism enforces in every age, that spiritual exaltation runs naturally, inevitably, into licentiousness, unless held in the iron bands of discipline to the moral law. A mystic is a law to himself. He bows before no exterior authority. However much he may transgress the code laid down by religion, he feels no compunction, no scruples, for his heart condemns him not. It was so with the holy Margaret. Her lapse or lapses in no way roused her to a sense of sin, but served only to drive her further forward on the mad career of self-righteous exaltation.

She had disappeared for many months from her father's house, along with her sister Elizabeth. The police had inquired as to their whereabouts of old John Peter, but he had given them no information as to where his daughters were. He professed not to know. He was threatened unless they were produced by a certain day that he would be fined. The police were sent in search in every direction but the right one.

Suddenly in the night of January 11th, 1823, the sisters re-appeared, Margaret, white, weak, and prostrate with sickness.

A fortnight after her return, Jacob Morf was again at Wildisbuch, as he said afterwards before court, "led thither because assured by Margaret that they were to ascend together to heaven without dying."

From this time forward, Margaretta's conduct went into another phase. Instead of resuming her pilgrim's staff and travelling round the country preaching the Gospel, she remained all day in one room with her sister Elizabeth, the shutters closed, reading the Bible, meditating, and praying, and writing letters to her "dear child" Jacob. The transgressions she had committed were crosses laid on her shoulder by God. "Oh! why," she wrote in one of her epistles, "did my Heavenly Father choose *that* from all eternity in His providence for me? There were thousands upon thousands of other crosses He might have laid on me. But He elected that one which would be heaviest for me, heavier than all the persecutions to which I am subjected by the devil, and which all but overthrow me. From the foundation of the world He has never so tried any of His saints as He has us. It gives joy to all the host of heaven when we suffer to the end." Again, "the greater the humiliation and shame we undergo, and have to endure from our enemies here below"—consider, brought on herself by her own scandalous conduct—"the more unspeakable our glorification in heaven."

In the evening, Margaretta would come downstairs and receive visitors, and preach and prophesy to them. The entire house was given over to religious ecstasy that intensified as Easter approached. Every now and then the saint assembled the household and exhorted them to watch and pray, for a great trial of their faith was at hand. Once she asked them whether they were ready to lay down their lives for Christ. One day she said, in the spirit of prophecy, "Behold! I see the host of Satan drawing nearer and nearer to encompass me. He strives to overcome me. Let me alone that I may fight him." Then she flung her arms about and struck in the air with her open hands.

The idea grew in her that the world was in danger, that the devil was gaining supremacy over it, and would carry all souls into captivity once more, and that she—and almost only she—stood in his way and was protecting the world of men against his power.

For years she had exercised her authority, that grew with every year, over everyone in the house, and not a soul there had thought of resisting her, of evading the commands she laid on them, of questioning her word.

The house was closed against all but the very elect. The pastor of the parish, as "worldly," was not suffered to cross the threshold. At a tap, the door was opened, and those deemed worthy were admitted, and the door hastily barred and bolted behind them. Everything was viewed in a spiritual light. One evening Ursula Kündig and Margaretta Jäggli were sitting spinning near the stove. Suddenly there was a pop. A knot in the pine-logs in the stove had exploded. But up sprang Jäggli, threw over her spinning-wheel, and shrieked out—"Hearken! Satan is banging at the window. He wants me. He will fetch me!" She fell convulsed on the floor, foaming at the mouth.

Margaret, the saint, was summoned. The writhing girl shrieked out, "Pray for me! Save me! Fight for my soul!" and Margaretta at once began her spiritual exercises to ban the evil spirit from the afflicted and possessed servant-maid. She beat with her hands in the air, cried out, "Depart, thou murderer of souls, accursed one, to hell-fire. Wilt thou try to rob me of my sheep that was lost? My sheep—whom I have pledged myself to save?"

One day, the maid had a specially bad epileptic fit. Around her bed stood old John Peter, Elizabeth and Susanna, Ursula Kündig, and John Moser, as well as the saint. Margaret was fighting with the Evil One with her fists and her cries, when John Moser fell into ecstasy and saw a vision. His account shall be given in his own words: "I saw Christ and Satan, and the latter held a book open before Christ and bade Him see how many claims he had on the soul of Jäggli. The book was scored diagonally with red lines on all the pages. I saw this distinctly, and therefore concluded that the account was cancelled. Then I saw all the saints in heaven snatch the book away, and tear it into a thousand pieces that fell down in a rain."

But Satan was not to be defeated and driven away so easily. He had made himself a nest, so Margaret stated, under the roof of the house, and only a desperate effort of faith and contest with spiritual arms could expel him. For this Armageddon she bade all prepare. It is hardly necessary to add that it could not be fought without the presence of the dearly beloved Jacob. She wrote to him and invited him to come to the great and final struggle with the

B

devil and all his host, and the obedient cobbler
girded his loins and hastened to Wildisbuch, where
he arrived on Saturday the 8th March, 1823.

On Monday, in answer, probably, to her summons,
came also John Moser and his brother Conrad. Then
also Margaret's own and only brother, Caspar.

Before proceeding to the climax of this story we
may well pause to ask whether the heroine was in
her senses or not; whether she set the avalanche in
motion that overwhelmed herself and her house, with
deliberation and consciousness as to the end to which
she was aiming. The woman was no vulgar impostor; she deceived herself to her own destruction.
In her senses, so far, she had set plainly before
her the object to which she was about to hurry her
dupes, but her reason and intelligence were smothered
under her overweening self-esteem, that had grown
like a great spiritual cancer, till it had sapped
common-sense, and all natural affection, even the
very instinct of self-preservation. Before her diseased
eyes, the salvation of the whole world depended on
herself. If she failed in her struggle with the evil
principle, all mankind fell under the bondage of
Satan; but she could not fail—she was all-powerful,
exalted above every chance of failure in the battle,
just as she was exalted above every lapse in virtue, do
what she might, which to the ordinary sense of mankind is immoral. Every mystic does not go as far
as Margaret Peter, happily, but all take some strides
along that road that leads to self-deification and
anomia. In Margaret's conduct, in preparation for
the final tragedy, there was a good deal of shrewd

calculation; she led up to it by a long isolation and envelopment of herself and her doings in mystery; and she called her chosen disciples to witness it. Each stage in the drama was calculated to produce a certain effect, and she measured her influence over her creatures before she advanced another step. On Monday all were assembled and in expectation; Armageddon was to be fought, but when the battle would begin, and how it would be carried through, were unknown. Tuesday arrived; some of the household went about their daily work, the rest were gathered together in the room where Margaret was, lost in silent prayer. Every now and then the hush in the darkened room was broken by a wail of the saint: " I am sore straitened! I am in anguish!—but I refresh my soul at the prospect of the coming exaltation!" or, " My struggle with Satan is severe. He strives to retain the souls which I will wrest from his hold; some have been for two hundred, even three hundred years in his power."

One can imagine the scene—the effect produced on those assembled about the pale, striving ecstatic. All who were present afterwards testified that on the Tuesday and the following days they hardly left the room, hardly allowed themselves time to snatch a hasty meal, so full of expectation were they that some great and awful event was about to take place The holy enthusiasm was general, and if one or two, such as old Peter and his son, Caspar, were less magnetised than the rest, they were far removed from the thought of in any way contesting the will of the prophetess, or putting the smallest impediment in the way of her accomplishing what she desired.

When evening came, she ascended to an upper room, followed by the whole company, and there she declared, " Lo! I see Satan and his first-born floating in the air. They are dispersing their emissaries to all corners of the earth to summon their armies together." Elizabeth, somewhat tired of playing a passive part, added, " Yes—I see them also." Then the holy maid relapsed into her mysterious silence. After waiting another hour, all went to bed, seeing that nothing further would happen that night. Next day, Wednesday, she summoned the household into her bedroom ; seated on her bed she bade them all kneel down and pray to the Lord to strengthen her hands for the great contest. They continued striving in prayer till noon, and then, feeling hungry, all went downstairs to get some food. When they had stilled their appetites, Margaret was again seized by the spirit of prophecy, and declared, " The Lord has revealed to me what will happen in the latter days. The son of Napoleon " (that poor, feeble mortal the Duke of Reichstadt " will appear before the world as anti-Christ, and will strive to bring the world over to his side. He will undergo a great conflict ; but what will be the result is not shown me at the present moment ; but I am promised a spiritual token of this revelation." And the token followed. The dearly-loved Jacob, John Moser, and Ursula Kündig cried out that they saw two evil spirits, one in the form of Napoleon, pass into Margaret Jäggli, and the other, in that of his son, enter into Elizabeth. Whereupon

Elizabeth, possessed by the spirit of that poor, little, sickly Duke of Reichstadt, began to march about the room and assume a haughty, military air. Thereupon the prophetess wrestled in spirit and overcame these devils and expelled them. Thereat Elizabeth gave up her military flourishes.

From daybreak on the following day the blessed Margaret "had again a desperate struggle," but without the assistance of the household, which was summoned to take their share in the battle in the afternoon only. She bade them follow her to the upper chamber, and a procession ascended the steep stairs, consisting of Margaret, followed by Elizabeth and Susanna Peter, Ursula Kündig and Jäggli, the old father and his son, Caspar, the serving-man, Heinrich Ernst, then Jacob Morf, John Moser, and the rear was brought up by the young Conrad. As soon as the prophetess had taken her seat on the bed, she declared, " Last night it was revealed to me that you are all of you to unite with me in the battle with the devil, lest he should conquer Christ. I must strive, lest your souls and those of so many, many others should be lost. Come, then ! strive with me ; but, first of all, kneel down, lay your faces in the dust and pray." Thereupon, all prostrated themselves on the floor and prayed in silence. Presently the prophetess exclaimed from her throne on the bed, " The hour is come in which the conflict must take place, so that Christ may gather together His Church, and contend with anti-Christ. After Christ has assembled His Church, 1260 days will elapse, and then anti-Christ will appear in human form, and with sweet and enticing words will strive to seduce the elect; but all true Christians will hold aloof." After a pause, she said solemnly, "In verity, anti-Christ is already among us."

Then with a leap she was off the bed, turning her eyes about, throwing up her hands, rushing about the room, striking the chairs and clothes-boxes with her fists, crying, " The scoundrel, the murderer of souls!" And, finding a hammer, she began to beat the wall with it.

The company looked on in breathless amaze. But the epileptic Jäggli went into convulsions, writhed on the ground, groaned, shrieked and wrung her hands. Then the holy Margaretta cried, "I see in spirit the old Napoleon gathering a mighty host, and marching against me. The contest will be terrible. You must wrestle unto blood. Go! fly! fetch me axes, clubs, whatever you can find. Bar the doors, curtain all the windows in the house, and close every shutter."

Whilst her commands were being fulfilled in all haste, and the required weapons were sought out, John Moser, who remaind behind, saw the room " filled with a dazzling glory, such as no tongue could describe," and wept for joy. The excitement had already mounted to visionary ecstasy. It was five o'clock when the weapons were brought upstairs. The holy Margaretta was then seated on her bed, wringing her hands, and crying to all to pray, " Help! help! all of you, that Christ may not be overcome in me. Strike, smite, cleave,—everywhere, on all sides—the floor, the walls! It is the will of God! smite on till I bid you stay. Smite and lose your lives if need be."

It was a wonder that lives were not lost in the extraordinary scene that ensued; the room was full of men and women; there were ten of them armed with hatchets, crowbars, clubs, pick-axes, raining blows on walls and floor, on chairs, tables, cupboards and chests. This lasted for three hours. Margaret remained on the bed, encouraging the party to continue; when any arm flagged she singled out the weary person, and exhorted him, as he loved his soul, to fight more valiantly and utterly defeat and destroy the devil. "Strike him! cut him down! the old adversary! the arch-fiend! whoso loseth his life shall find it. Fear nothing! smite till your blood runs down as sweat. There he is in yonder corner; now at him," and Elizabeth served as her echo, "Smite! strike on! He is a murderer, he is the young Napoleon, the coming anti-Christ, who entered into me and almost destroyed me."

This lasted, as already said, for three hours. The room was full of dust. The warriors steamed with their exertions, and the sweat rolled off them. Never had men and women fought with greater enthusiasm. The battle of Don Quixote against the wind-mills was nothing to this. What blows and wounds the devil and the young Duke of Reichstadt obtained is unrecorded, but walls and floor and furniture in the room were wrecked; indeed pitchfork and axe had broken down one wall of the house and exposed what went on inside to the eyes of a gaping crowd that had assembled without, amazed at the riot that went on in the house that was regarded as a very sanctuary of religion.

No sooner did the saint behold the faces of the

crowd outside than she shrieked forth, " Behold them !
the enemies of God ! the host of Satan, coming on !
But fear them not, we shall overcome."

At last the combatants were no longer able to raise
their arms or maintain themselves on their feet.
Then Margaret exclaimed, " The victory is won ! follow me ! " She led them downstairs into the common
sitting-room, where close-drawn curtains and fastened
shutters excluded the rude gaze of the profane. Here
a rushlight was kindled, and by its light the battle
continued with an alteration in the tactics.

In complete indifference to the mob that surrounded
the house and clamoured at the door for admission,
the saint ordered all to throw themselves on the
ground and thank heaven for the victory they had
won. Then after a pause of more than an hour the
same scene began again, and that it could recommence
is evidence how much man can do and endure, when
possessed by a holy craze.

It was afterwards supposed that the whole pious
community was drunk with schnaps ; but with injustice.
Their stomachs were empty ; it was their brains that
were drunk.

The holy Margaret, standing in the midst of the
prostrate worshippers, now ordered them to beat
themselves with their fists on their heads and breasts,
and they obeyed. Elizabeth yelled, " O, Margaret !
Do thou strike me ! Let me die for Christ."

Thereupon the holy one struck her sister repeatedly
with her fists, so that Elizabeth cried out with pain,
" Bear it ! " exclaimed Margaret ; " It is the wrath of
God ! "

The prima-donna of the whole comedy in the meanwhile looked well about her to see that none of the actors spared themselves. When she saw anyone slack in his self-chastisement, she called to him to re-double his blows. As the old man did not exhibit quite sufficient enthusiasm in self-torture, she cried, "Father, you do not beat yourself sufficiently!" and then began to batter him with her own fists. The ill-treated old man groaned under her blows, but she cheered him with, "I am only driving out the old Adam, father! It does not hurt you," and redoubled her pommelling of his head and back. Then out went the light.

All this while the crowd listened and passed re-marks outside. No one would interfere, as it was no one's duty to interfere. Tidings of what was going on did, however, reach the amtmann of the parish, but he was an underling, and did not care to meddle with-out higher authority, so sent word to the amtmann of the district. This latter called to him his secretary, his constable and a policeman, and reached the house of the Peter's family at ten o'clock. In his report to the police at Zürich he says : "On the 13th about 10 o'clock at night I reached Wildisbuch, and then heard that the noise in the house of the Peter's family had ceased, that all lights were out, and that no one was stirring. I thought it advisable not to disturb this tranquillity, so left orders that the house should be watched," and then he went into the house of a neigh-bour. At midnight, the policeman who had been left on guard came to announce that there was a renewal of disturbance in the house of the Peters. The amt-

mann went to the spot and heard muffled cries of
" Save us! have mercy on us! Strike away! he is a
murderer! spare him not!" and a trampling, and a
sound of blows, "as though falling on soft bodies."
The amtmann knocked at the window and ordered
those within to admit him.   As no attention was paid
to his commands, he bade the constable break open
the house door.   This was done, but the sitting-room
door was now found to be fast barred.   The constable
then ascended to the upper room and saw in what a
condition of wreckage it was.   He descended and informed the amtmann of what he had seen.   Again the
window was knocked at, and orders were repeated
that the door should be opened.   No notice was taken
of this ; whereupon the worthy magistrate broke in a
pane of glass, and thrust a candle through the window
into the room.

"I now went to the opened window, and observed
four or five men standing with their backs against the
door.   Another lay as dead on the floor.   At a little
distance was a coil of human beings, men and women,
lying in a heap on the floor, beside them a woman on
her knees beating the rest, and crying out at every
blow, ' Lord, have mercy!'   Finally, near the stove
was another similar group."

The amtmann now ordered the sitting-room door
to be broken open.   Conrad Moser, who had offered
to open to the magistrate, was rebuked by the saint,
who cried out to him: "What, will you give admission
to the devil?"

"The men," says the magistrate in his report,
" offered resistance, excited thereto by the women,

who continued screaming. The holy Margaret especially distinguished herself, and was on her knees vigorously beating another woman who lay flat on the floor on her face. A second group consisted of a coil of two men and two women lying on the floor, the head of one woman on the body of a man, and the head of a man on that of a girl. The rest staggered to their feet one after another. I tried remonstrances, but they were unavailing in the hubbub. Then I ordered the old Peter to be removed from the room. Thereupon men and women flung themselves upon him, in spite of all our assurances that no harm would be done him. With difficulty we got him out of the room, with all the rest hanging on to him, so that he was thrown on the floor, and the rest clinging to him tumbled over him in a heap. I repeated my remonstrances and insisted on silence, but without avail. When old Peter prepared to answer, the holy Margaret stayed him with, 'Father, make no reply. Pray!' All then recommenced the uproar. Margaret cried out: 'Let us all die! I will die for Christ!' Others called out, 'Lord save us!' and others, 'Have mercy on us!'"

The amtmann gave orders that the police were to divide the party and keep guard over some in the kitchen, and the rest in the sitting-room, through the night, and not to allow them to speak to each other. The latter order was, however, more than the police could execute. In spite of all their efforts, Margaretta and the others continued to exhort and comfort one another through the night.

Next morning each was brought before the magistrate and subjected to examination. All were sullen, resolute and convinced that they were doing God's will. As the holy Margaretta was led away from examination, she said to Ursula and the servant Heinrich, "The world opposes, but can not frustrate my work."

Her words came true, the world was too slow in its movements. The amtmann did not send in his report to the authorities of Zürich till the 16th, whereupon it was taken into consideration, and orders were transmitted to him that Margaret and Elizabeth were to be sent to an asylum. It was then too late.

After the investigation, the amtmann required the cobbler, John Morf, to march home to Illnau, John and Conrad Moser to return to their home, and Ursula Kündig to be sent back to her father. This command was not properly executed. Ursula remained, and though John Moser obeyed, he was prepared to return to the holy Margaret directly he was summoned.

As soon as the high priestess had come out of the room where she had been examined by the amtmann, she went to her own bed-chamber, where boards had been laid over the gaps between the rafters broken by the axes and picks, during the night. Elizabeth, Susanna, Ursula, and the maid sat or stood round her and prayed.

At eight o'clock, the father and his son, Caspar, rejoined her, also her eldest sister, Barbara, arrived from Trüllikon. The servant, Heinrich, formed one more in the re-assembled community, and the ensuing night was passed in prayer and spiritual exercises. These were not conducted in quiet. To the exhortations of Margaret, both Elizabeth and the house-maid entreated that the devil might be beaten out of them. But now Ursula interfered, as the poor girl Elizabeth had been badly bruised in her bosom by the blows she had received on the preceding night. When the Saturday morning dawned, Margaret stood up on her bed and said, "I see the many souls seeking salvation through me. They must be assisted; would that a sword were in my hand that I might fight for them." A little later she said, with a sigh of relief, " The Lamb has conquered. Go to your work."

Tranquillity lasted for but a few hours. Magdalena, Moser's wife, had arrived, together with her husband and Conrad. The only one missing was the dearly beloved Jacob, who was far on his way homeward to Illnau and his hardly used wife, Regula.

At ten o'clock, the old father, his five daughters, his son, the two brothers, John and Conrad Moser, Ursula Kündig, the maid Jäggli, and the man Heinrich Ernst, twelve in all, were assembled in the upper room.

Margaret and Elizabeth sat side by side on the bed, the latter half stupified, looking fixedly before her, Margaret, however, in a condition of violent nervous surrexitation. Many of the weapons used in wreck-ing the furniture lay about; among these were the large hammer, and an iron wedge used for splitting wood. All there assembled felt that something extra-ordinary was about to happen. They had everyone passed the line that divides healthy common-sense from mania.

Margaretta now solemnly announced, " I have given a pledge for many souls that Satan may not have them.

Among these is the soul of my brother Caspar. But I cannot conquer in the strife for him without the shedding of blood." Thereupon she bade all present recommence beating themselves with their fists, so as to expel the devil, and they executed her orders with wildest fanaticism.

The holy maid now laid hold of the iron wedge, drew her brother Caspar to her, and said, " Behold, the Evil One is striving to possess thy soul ! " and thereupon she began to strike him on head and breast with the wedge. Caspar staggered back; she pursued him striking him, and cutting his head open, so that he was covered with blood. As he afterwards declared, he had not the smallest thought of resistance ; the power to oppose her seemed to be taken from him. At length, half stunned, he fell to the ground, and was carried to his bed by his father and the maid Jäggli. The old man no more returned upstairs, consequently he was not present at the terrible scene that ensued. But he took no steps to prevent it. Not only so, but he warded off all interruption from without. Whilst he was below, someone knocked at the door. At that moment Susanna was in the room with him, and he bade her inquire who was without. The man gave his name as Elias Vogel, a mason, and asked leave to come in. Old Peter refused, as he said the surgeon was within. Elias endeavoured to push his way in but was resisted, and the door barred against him. Vogel went away, and meeting a policeman told him what had taken place, and added that he had noticed blood-stains on the sleeves of both old Peter and Susanna. The policeman, thinking that

Peter's lie was truth, and that the surgeon was really in the house, and had been bleeding the half crazy people there, took no further notice of what he had heard, and went his way.

Meanwhile, in the upper room the comedy had been changed into a ghastly tragedy. As soon as the wounded Caspar had been removed, the three sisters, Barbara, Magdalena, and Susanna left the room, the two latter, however, only for a short while. Then the holy Margaret said to those who remained with her, "To-day is a day of great events. The contest has been long and must now be decided. Blood must flow. I see the spirit of my mother calling to me to offer up my life." After a pause she said, "And you—all—are you ready to give your lives?" They all responded eagerly that they were. Then said Margaret, "No, no; I see you will not readily die. But I—I must die."

Thereupon Elizabeth exclaimed, " I will gladly die for the saving of the souls of my brother and father. Strike me dead, strike me dead ! " Then she threw herself on the bed and began to batter her head with a wooden mallet.

" It has been revealed to me," said Margaret, "that Elizabeth will sacrifice herself." Then taking up the iron hammer, she struck her sister on the head. At once a spiritual fury seized on all the elect souls, and seizing weapons they began to beat the poor girl to death. Margaret in her mania struck at random about her, and wounded both John Moser and Ursula Kündig. Then she suddenly caught the latter by the wrist and bade her kill Elizabeth with the iron wedge. Ursula shrank back, "I cannot! I love her too dearly!" "You must," screamed the saint; "it is ordained." "I am ready to die," moaned Elizabeth. "I cannot! I cannot!" cried Ursula. "You must," shouted Margaret. "I will raise my sister again, and I also will rise again after three days. May God strengthen your arm."

As though a demoniacal influence flowed out of the holy maid, and maddened those about her, all were again seized with frenzy. John Moser snatched the hammer out of her hand, and smote the prostrate girl with it again, and yet again, on head and bosom and shoulders. Susanna brought down a crow-bar across her body, the servant-man Heinrich belaboured her with a fragment of the floor planking, and Ursula, swept away by the current, beat in her skull with the wedge. Throughout the turmoil, the holy maid yelled: "God strengthen your arms! Ursula, strike home! Die for Christ, Elizabeth!" The last words heard from the martyred girl were an exclamation of resignation to the will of God, as expressed by her sister.

One would have supposed that when the life was thus battered out of the unfortunate victim, the murderers would have come to their senses and been filled with terror and remorse. But it was not so. Margaret sat beside the body of her murdered· sister, the blaze of spiritual ecstasy in her eyes, the blood-stained hammer in her right hand, terrible in her inflexible determination, and in the demoniacal energy which was to possess her to the last breath she drew. Her bosom heaved, her body quivered, but her voice was firm and her tone authoritative, as she said, "More blood must flow. I have pledged myself for the saving of many souls. I must die now. You must crucify me." John Moser and Ursula, shivering with horror, entreated, "O do not demand that of us." She replied, "It is better that I should die than that thousands of souls should perish."

So saying she struck herself with the hammer on the left temple. Then she held out the weapon to John Moser, and ordered him and Ursula to batter her with it. Both hesitated for a moment.

"What!" cried Margaret turning to her favourite disciple, "will you not do this? Strike, and may God brace your arm!" Moser and Ursula now struck her with the hammer, but not so as to stun her.

"And now," said she with raised voice, "crucify me! You, Ursula, must do the deed."

"I cannot! I cannot!" sobbed the wretched girl.

"What! will you withdraw your hand from the work of God, now the hour approaches? You will be responsible for all the souls that will be lost, unless you fulfil what I have appointed you to do."

"But O! not I—!" pleaded Ursula.

"Yes—you. If the police authorities had executed me, it would not have fallen to you to do this, but now it is for you to accomplish the work. Go, Susan, and fetch nails, and the rest of you make ready the cross."

In the meantime, Heinrich, the man-servant, frightened at what had taken place, and not wishing to have anything more to do with the horrible scene in the upper chamber, had gone quietly down into

c

the wood-house, and was making stakes for the vines. There Susanna found him, and asked him for nails, telling him for what they were designed. He composedly picked her out nails of suitable length, and then resumed his work of making vine stakes. Susanna re-ascended to the upper room, and found Margaret extended on the bed beside the body of Elizabeth, with the arms, breast, and feet resting on blocks of wood, arranged, whilst Susanna was absent, by John Moser and Ursula, under her in the fashion of a cross.

Then began the horrible act of crucifixion, which is only conceivable as an outburst of religious mania, depriving all who took part in it of every feeling of humanity, and degrading them to the level of beasts of prey. At the subsequent trial, both Ursula and John Moser described their condition as one of spiritual intoxication.

The hands and feet of the victim were nailed to the blocks of wood. Then Ursula's head swam, and she drew back. Again Margaret called her to continue her horrible work. "Go on! go on! God strengthen your arm. I will raise Elizabeth from the dead, and rise myself in three days." Nails were driven through both elbows and also through the breasts of Margaret; not for one moment did the victim express pain, nor did her courage fail her. No Indian at the stake endured the cruel ingenuity of his tormentors with more stoicism than did this young woman bear the martyrdom she had invoked for herself. She impressed her murderers with the idea that she was endowed with supernatural strength. It could not be otherwise, for what she endured was beyond the measure of human strength. That in the place of human endurance she was ˙possessed with the Berserker strength of the *furor religiosus*, was what these ignorant peasants could not possibly know. Conrad Moser could barely support himself from fainting, sick and horror-struck at the scene. He exclaimed, " Is not this enough ? " His brother, John, standing at the foot of the bed, looked into space with glassy eyes. Ursula, bathed in tears, was bowed over the victim. Magdalena Moser had taken no active part in the crucifixion; she remained the whole time, weeping, leaning against a chest.

The dying woman smiled. " I feel no pain. Be yourselves strong," she whispered. " Now, drive a nail or a knife through my heart."

Ursula endeavoured to do as bidden, but her hand shook and the knife was bent. " Beat in my skull ! " this was the last word spoken by Margaret. In their madness Conrad Moser and Ursula Kündig obeyed, one with the crowbar, the other with the hammer.

It was noon when the sacrifice was accomplished,— dinner-time. Accordingly, all descended to the sitting-room, where the meal that Margaret Jäggli had been in the meantime preparing was served and eaten.

They had scarce finished before a policeman entered with a paper for old Peter to sign, in which he made himself answerable to produce his daughters before the magistrates when and where required. He signed it with composure, " I declare that I will cause my daughters, if in good health, to appear before the Upper Amtsmann in Andelfingen when so required." Then the policeman departed without a suspicion that the two girls were lying dead in the room above. On Sunday the 16th, the servant Heinrich was sent on horseback to Illnau to summon Jacob Morf to come to Wildisbuch and witness a great miracle. Jacob came there with Heinrich, but was not told the circumstances of the crucifixion till he reached the house. When he heard what had happened, he was frightened almost out of his few wits, and when taken upstairs to see the bodies, he fainted away. Nothing—no representations would induce him to remain for the miraculous resurrection, and he hastened back to Illnau, where he took to his bed. In his alarm and horror he sent for the pastor, and told him what he had seen.

But the rest of the holy community remained stead-fast in their faith. On the night of Sunday before Monday morning broke, Ursula Kündig and the servant man Heinrich went upstairs with pincers and drew out the nails that transfixed Margaretta. When asked their reason for so doing, at the subsequent trial, they said that they supposed this would facilitate Margaretta's resurrection. *Sanctus furor* had made way for *sancta simplicitas.*

The night of Monday to Tuesday was spent in prayer and Scripture-reading in the upper chamber, and eager expectation of the promised miracle, which never took place. The catastrophe could no longer be concealed. Something must be done. On Tuesday, old John Peter pulled on his jacket and walked to Trüllikon to inform the pastor that his daughter Elizabeth had died on the Saturday at 10 a.m., and his daughter Margaretta at noon of the same day.

We need say little more. On Dec. 3rd, 1823, the trial of all incriminated in this frightful tragedy took place at Zürich and sentence was pronounced on the following day. Ursula Kündig was sentenced to sixteen years' imprisonment, Conrad Moser and John Peter to eight years, Susanna Peter and John Moser to six years, Heinrich Ernst to four years, Jacob Morf to three, Margaret Jäggli to two years, Barbara Baumann and Casper Peter to one year, and Magdalena Moser to six months with hard labour. The house at Wildisbuch was ordered to be levelled with the dust, the plough drawn over the foundation, and that no house should again be erected on the spot.

Before the destruction, however, a pilgrimage of Pietists and believers in Margaret Peter had visited the scene of her death, and many had been the exclamations of admiration at her conduct. "Oh, that it had been I who had died!" "Oh, how many souls must she have delivered!" and the like. *Magna est stultitia et prævalebit.*

At a time like the present, when there is a wave of warm, mystic fever sweeping over the country, and carrying away with it thousands of ignorant and impetuous souls, it is well that the story—repulsive though it be—should be brought into notice, as a warning of what this spiritual excitement may lead to —not, indeed, again, maybe, into bloodshed. It is far more likely to lead to, as it has persistently, in every similar outbreak, into moral disorders, the record of which, in the case of Margaretta Peter, we have passed over almost without a word.

Authority : Die Gekreuzigte von Wildisbuch, von J. Scherr, 2nd Edit., St. Gall. 1867.   Sherr visited the spot, collected information from eye-witnesses, and made copious extracts from the records of the trial in the Zürich archives, where they are contained in Vol. 166, folio 1044, under the heading : "Akten betreffened die Gräuel—Scenen in Wildisbuch."

A Northern Raphael.

HERE and there in the galleries of North Germany and Russia may be seen paintings of delicacy and purity, delicacy of colour and purity of design, the author of which was Gerhard von Kügelgen. The majority of his paintings are in private hands ; but an Apollo, holding the dying Hyacinthus in his arms, is in the possession of the German Emperor; Moses on Horeb is in the gallery of the Academy of Fine Arts at Dresden ; a St. Cæcilia and an Adonis, painted in 1794 and 1795, were purchased by the Earl of Bristol; a Holy Family is in the Gallery at Cassel ; and some of the sacred subjects have found their way into churches.

In 1772, the wife of Franz Kügelgen, a merchant of Bacharach on the Rhine, presented her husband with twin sons, the elder of whom by fifteen minutes is the subject of this notice. His brother was named Karl. Their resemblance was so great that even their mother found a difficulty in their early childhood in distinguishing one from the other.

Bacharach was in the Electorate of Co'ogne, and when the Archbishop-Elector, Maximilian Franz, learned that the twins were fond of art, in 1791, he very liberally gave them a handsome sum of money to enable them to visit Rome and there prosecute their studies.

Gerhard was at once fascinated by the statuary in the Vatican, and by the pictures of Raphael. The ambition of his life thenceforward was to combine the beauty of modelling of the human form that he saw in the Græco-Roman statues with the beauty of colour that he recognised in Raphael's canvases. Karl, on the other hand, devoted himself to landscapes.

In 1795 the brothers separated, Gerhard that he might visit Munich. Thence, in the autumn, he went to Riga with a friend, and there he remained rather over two years, and painted and disposed of some fifty-four pictures. Then he painted in St. Petersburg and Reval, and finally settled into married life and regular work at Dresden in 1806. There he became a general favourite, not only on account of his artistic genius, but also because of the fascination of his modest and genial manner. He was honoured by the Court, and respected by everyone for his virtues. Orders flowed in on him, and his paintings commanded good prices. The king of Saxony ennobled him, that is to say, raised him out of the bürger-stand, by giving him the privilege of writing a *Von* before his patronymic.

Having received an order from Riga for a large altar picture, he bought a vineyard on the banks of the Elbe, commanding a charming prospect of the river and the distant blue Bohemian mountains. Here he resolved to erect a country house for the summer, with a large studio lighted from the north. The construction of this residence was to him a great pleasure and occupation. In November, 1819, he wrote to his brother, " My house shall be to us a veritable fairy palace, in which to dwell till the time comes, when through a little, narrow and dark door we pass through into that great habitation of the Heavenly Father in which are many mansions, and where our whole family will be re-united. Should it please God to call me away, then Lily (his wife) will find this an agreeable dower-house, in which she can supervise the education of the children, as the distance from the town is only an hour's walk."

The words were written, perhaps, without much thought, but they foreshadowed a terrible catastrophe. Kügelgen would pass, before his fairy palace was ready to receive him, through that little, narrow door into the heavenly mansions.

The Holy Week of 1820 found him in a condition of singularly deep religious emotion. He was a Catholic, but had, nevertheless, allowed his son to be confirmed by a Protestant pastor. The ceremony had greatly affected him, and he said to a friend, who was struck at the intensity of his feeling, " I know I shall never be as happy again till I reach Heaven."

On March 27th, on the very day of the confirmation, he went in the afternoon a walk by himself to his vineyard, to look at his buildings. He invited one of his pupils to accompany him, but the young man had some engagement and declined.

At 5 p.m. he was at the new house, where he paid the workmen, gave some instructions, and pointed out where he would do some planting, so as to enhance the picturesqueness of the spot. At some time between six and seven he left, to walk back to Dresden, along the road from Bautzen.

Every one who has been at the Saxon capital knows that road. The right bank of the Elbe above Dresden rises in picturesque heights covered with gardens and vineyards, from the river, and about a mile from the bridge is the Linkes Bad, with its pleasant gardens, theatre, music and baths. That road is one of the most charming, and, therefore, the most frequented outside the capital. On the evening in question the Easter moon was shining.

Kügelgen did not return home. His wife sent his son, the just confirmed boy, aged 17 years, to the new house, to inquire for her husband. The boy learned there that he had left some hours before. He returned home, and found that still his father had not come in. The police were communicated with, and the night was spent in inquiries and search, but all in vain. On the following morning, at 9 a.m., as the boy was traversing the same road, along with a gensdarme, he deemed it well to explore a footpath beside the river, which was overflowed by the Elbe, and there, finally, amongst some reeds they discovered the dead body of the artist, stripped of his clothes to his shirt and drawers, lying on his face.

Gerhard von Kügelgen had been murdered. His features were cut and bruised, his left temple and jaw were broken. Footsteps, as of two persons, were traceable through the river mud and across a field to the highway. Apparently the artist had been murdered on the road, then carried or dragged to the path, stripped there, and then cast among the rushes

About twenty-four paces from where he lay, between him and the highway, his cap was found.

The excitement, the alarm, aroused in Dresden was immense. Not only was Kügelgen universally respected, but everyone was in dismay at the thought that his own safety was jeopardised, if a murder such as this could be perpetrated on the open road, within a few paces of the gates. Indeed, the place where the crime was committed was but a hundred strides from the Linkes Bad, one of the most popular resorts of the Dresdeners.

It was now remembered that only a few months before, near the same spot, another murder had been committed, that had remained undiscovered. In that case the victim had been a poor carpenter's apprentice.

On the same day as the body of Kügelgen was found, the Government offered a sum equal to £150 for the discovery of the murderer. A little later, some children found among the rubbish, outside the Black Gate of the Dresdener Vorstadt, a blue cloth cloak, folded up and buried under some stones. It was recognised as having belonged to Kügelgen. Moreover, in the pocket was the little "Thomas-à-Kempis" he always carried about with him.

It was concluded that the murderer had not ventured to bring all the clothing of Kügelgen into the town, through the gate, and had, therefore, hidden portions in places whence he could remove them one by one, unobserved. The murderer was, undoubtedly, an inhabitant of the city.

From March 29th to April 4th the police remained

without any clue, although a description of the garments worn by the murdered man, and of his watch,
was posted up at every corner, and sent round to the
nearest towns and villages.

The workmen who had been engaged on Kügelgen's
house were brought before the police. They had left
after his departure, and had received money from
him ; but they were discharged, as there was no evidence against them.

As no light seemed to fall on this mysterious case,
the police looked up the circumstances of the previous
murder. On December 29th, 1819, a carrier on the
highroad had found a body on the way. It was
ascertained to be that of a carpenter's apprentice,
named Winter. His skull had been broken in. Not
a trace of the murderer was found ; not even footprints had been obsesved. However, it was learned
that the wife of a labourer had been attacked almost
at the same spot, on the 28th December, by a man
wearing a military cap and cloak ; and she had only
escaped him by the approach of a carriage, the sound
of the wheels having alarmed him, and induced him
to fly. He had fled in the direction of the Black
Gate and the barracks.

The anxiety of the Dresdeners seemed justified.
There was some murderous ruffian inhabiting the Vorstadt, who hovered about the gates, waylaying, not
wealthy men only, but poor charwomen and apprentices.

The military cloak and cap, the direction taken by
the assailant in his flight, gave a sort of clue—and the
police suspected that the murderer must be sought
among the soldiers.

On April 4th two Jewish pawnbrokers appeared before the police, and handed over a silver watch which had been left with them at 9 a.m. on the 20th March—that is to say on the morning after the murder of Kügelgen—and which agreed with the advertised description of the artist's lost watch. It was identified at once. The man who had pawned it, the Jews said, wore the uniform of an artillery soldier.

At the request of the civil authorities, the military officers held an inquisition in the barracks. All the artillery soldiers were made to pass before the Jew brokers, but they were unable to identify the man who had deposited the watch with them. Somewhat later in the day one of these Jews, as he was going through the street, saw a man in civil dress, whom he thought he recognised as the fellow who had given him the watch. He went up to him at once and spoke about the watch. The man at first acknowledged that he had pawned one, then denied, and threatened the Jew when he persevered in clinging to him. A gensdarme came up, and hearing what the controversy was about arrested the man, who gave his name as Fischer, a gunner.

Fischer was at once examined, and he doggedly refused to allow that he had given up a watch to the Jew.

Suspicion against him was deepened by his declaring that he had heard nothing of the murder—a matter of general talk in Dresden—and that he had not seen the notices with the offer of reward for the discovery of the murderer. On the following day, April 5th, however, he admitted having pawned the watch, which he pretended to have found outside the Black Gate. A few hours later he withdrew this confession, saying that he was so bewildered with the questions put to him, and so alarmed at his arrest, that he did not well know what he said. It was observed that Fischer was a man of very low intellectual power.

The same day he was invested in his uniform, and presented before the pawnbrokers. Both unanimously declared that he was *not* the man who had entered their shop and deposited the watch with them. They both declared that though Fischer had the same height and general build as the man in question, and the same fair hair, yet that the face was different.

With this, the case against Fischer broke down; nevertheless, though he had been handed over by the military authorities to the civil power, he remained under arrest. The public was convinced of his guilt, and the police hoped by keeping him in prison to draw from him later some information which might prove serviceable.

And, in fact, after he had been a fortnight under arrest, he volunteered a statement. He was conducted at once before the magistrate, and confessed that he had murdered Von Kügelgen. He, however, stoutly denied having laid hands on the carpenter Winter. Nevertheless, on the way back to his cell he told his gaoler that he had committed this murder as well. Next day he was again brought before the magistrate, and confessed to both murders. He was taken to the spots where the two corpses had been found, and there he renewed his confession, though without entering into any details.

But on the next morning, April 21, he begged to be again heard, and he then asserted that his former confessions were false. He had confessed merely because he was weary of his imprisonment and the poor food he was given, and decided to die. When spoken to· by the magistrate seriously, and remonstrated with for his contradictions, he cried out that he was innocent. Let them torture him as much as they pleased, he wished to die.

But hardly was he back in his prison than he told the gaoler that it was true that he was the murderer of both Kügelgen and Winter. Again he confessed before the magistrate, and again, on the 27th, withdrew his confession and protested his innocence.

· On the 21st April a new element in the case came to light that perplexed the question not a little.

A Jewish pawnbroker, Löbel Graff, announced that on February 3, 1820, he had received from the gunner Kaltofen a green coat, and on the 4th April a dark-blue cloth coat, stained with spots of oil, also a pair of cloth trousers. As both coats seemed to him suspicious, and to resemble those described in the advertisements, he had questioned Kaltofen about them, but had received equivocal answers, and Kaltofen at last admitted that he had bought them from the gunner Fischer.

John Gottfried Kaltofen was a young man of 24 years, servant to one of the officers, and therefore did not live in the barracks. He was now taken up. His manner and appearance were in his favour. He was frank, and at once admitted that he had disposed of the two coats to Graff, and that he had bought them of Fischer. On confrontation with the latter he repeated what he had said. Fischer fell into confusion, denied all knowledge of Kaltofen, protested his innocence, and denied the sale of the coats, one of which had in the meantime been identified as having belonged to Winter, and the other to Kügelgen.

On April 27th a search was made in the lodgings of Kaltofen, and three keys were found there, hidden away, and these proved to have belonged to Kügelgen. At first Kaltofen declared that he knew nothing of these keys, but afterwards said that he remembered on consideration that he had found them in the pocket of the blue coat he had purchased from Fischer, and had put them away before disposing of the coat, and had given them no further thought. Not many minutes after Fischer had been sent back to prison, he begged to be brought before the magistrate again, and now admitted that it was quite true that he had sold both coats to Kaltofen.

Whilst this confession was being taken down, however, he again hesitated, broke down, and denied having sold them to Kaltofen, or any one else. "I can't say anything more," he cried out; "my head is dazed."

By this statement he remained, protesting his innocence, and he declared that he had only confessed his guilt because he was afraid of ill-treatment in the prison if he continued to assert his innocence. It must he remembered that the gaolers were as convinced of his guilt as were the public of Dresden; and it is noticeable that under pressure from them Fischer always acknowledged his guilt; whereas, when before

the magistrates he was ready to proclaim that he was
innocent. At this time it was part of the duty of a
gaoler, or was supposed to be such, to use every
possible effort to bring a prisoner to confession. And
now, on April 27th, a third gunner appeared on the
scene. His name was Kiessling, and he asked the
magistrate to take down his statement, which was to
the effect that Kaltofen, who had been discharged,
had admitted to him that he had murdered Kügelgen
with a cudgel, and that he had still got some of his
garments hidden in his lodgings. But—so said
Kiessling—Kaltofen had jauntily said he would lay
it all on Fischer. Kiessling, moreover, produced a
pair of boots, that he said Kaltofen had left with him
to be re-soled, as he was regimental shoemaker. And
these boots were at once recognised as having been
those worn by Kügelgen when he was murdered.

Kaltofen was at once re-arrested, and brought into
confrontation with Kiessling. He retained his composure, and said that it was quite true that he had given
a pair of boots to Kiessling to re-sole, but they were a
pair that he had bought in the market. But, in the
meantime, another investigation of his lodgings had
been made, and a number of articles found that had
certainly belonged to the murdered men, Winter and
Kügelgen. They were ranged on the table, together
with the pair of boots confided to Kiessling, and
Kaltofen was shown them. Hitherto, the young man
had displayed phlegmatic composure, and an openness of manner that had impressed all who saw him
in his favour. His intelligence, had, moreover, contrasted favourably with that of Fischer. But the

D

sight of all these articles, produced before him, staggered Kaltofen, and, losing his presence of mind, he turned in a fury upon his comrade, the shoemaker, and swore at him for having betrayed his confidence. Only after he had poured forth a torrent of abuse, could the magistrate bring him to say anything about the charge, and then—still hot and panting from his onslaught on Kiessling—he admitted that he, not Fischer, was the murderer in both cases. Fischer, he said, was wholly innocent, not only of participation in, but of knowledge of the crimes. The summary of his confession, oft repeated and never withdrawn, was as follows :—Being in need of money, he had gone out-side the town thrice in one week, at the end of December, 1819, with the intent of murdering and robbing the first person he could attack with security. For this purpose, he had provided himself with a cudgel under his cloak. On the 29th December he selected Winter as his first victim. He allowed him to pass, then stole after him, and suddenly dealt him a blow on the back of his head, before the young man turned to see who was following him. Winter dropped, whereupon he, Kaltofen, had struck him twice again on the head. Then he divested his victim of collar, coat, hat, kerchief, watch, and a little money—not more than four shillings in English coins, and a few tools. He was engaged on pulling off his boots and trousers, when he was alarmed by hearing the tramp of horses and the sound of wheels, and he ran off across the fields with his spoil. He got Kiessling to dispose of the hat for him, the other articles he himself sold to Jews. Whether it was he

also who assaulted the poor woman we are not informed. In like manner Kaltofen proceeded with
Kügelgen. He was again in want of money. He
had been gambling, and had lost what little he had
On the Monday in Holy Week, 1820, he took his
cudgel again and went out along the Bautzen Road.
The moon shone brightly, and he met a gentleman
walking slowly towards Dresden, in a blue cloak. He
allowed him to pass, then followed him. As a woman
was walking in the same direction, but at a quicker rate,
he delayed his purpose till she had disappeared behind the first houses of the suburb. Then he hastened
on, walking lightly, and springing up behind Kügelgen,
struck him on the right temple with his cudgel from
behind. Kügelgen fell without uttering a cry,
Kaltofen at once seized him by the collar and dragged
him across a field to the edge of the river. There he
dealt him several additional blows, and then proceeded to strip him. Whilst thus engaged, he
remembered that the dead man had dropped his
walking-stick on the high road when first struck.
Kaltofen at once desisted from what he was about, to
return to the road and recover the walking-stick. On
coming back to his victim, he thought there was still
life in him; Kügelgen was moving and endeavouring
to rise. Whereupon, with his cudgel, Kaltofen repeatedly struck him, till all signs of life disappeared.
He now completed his work of spoliation, pulled off
the boots, untied the neckerchief, and ransacked the
pockets. He found in addition to the watch the sum
of about half-a-guinea. He then stole away among
the rushes till he reached the Linkes Bad, where he

returned to the main road. He concealed the cloak at the Black Gate, but carried the rest of his plunder to his lodgings.

His confession was confirmed by several circumstances. Kiessling was again required to repeat what he had heard from Kaltofen, and the story as told by him agreed exactly with that now confessed by the murderer. Kiessling added that Kaltofen had told him he was puzzled to account for Fischer's self-examination, as he knew that the man had nothing to do with the murder. A third examination of Kaltofen's lodgings resulted in the discovery of all the rest of the murdered man's effects. Moreover, when Kaltofen was confronted with the two Jews who had taken the silver watch on the 24th, they immediately recognised him as the man who had disposed of it to them.

Finally, he confessed to having been associated with Kiessling in two robberies, one of which was a burglarious attack on his own master.

The case was made out clearly enough against Kaltofen, and it seemed equally clear that Fischer was innocent. Moreover, from the 24th April onwards, Fischer never swerved from his protestation of complete innocence. When questioned why he had confessed himself guilty, he said that he had been pressed to do so by the gaoler, who had several times fastened him for a whole night into the stocks, and had threatened him with severer measures unless he admitted his guilt. The gaoler admitted having so treated Fischer once, but Fischer insisted that he had been thus tortured on two consecutive nights.

It was ascertained that Fischer had not only known about the murder of Kügelgen, but had attended his funeral, and yet he had pretended entire, or almost entire, ignorance when first arrested. When asked to explain this, he replied that he was so frightened that he took refuge in lies. That he was a dull-minded, extremely ignorant man, was obvious to the judges and to all who had to do with him; he was aged thirty, and had spent thirteen years in the army, had conducted himself well, but had never been trusted with any important duties on account of his stupidity. He had a dull eye, and a heavy countenance. Kaltofen, on the other hand, was a good-looking, well-built young fellow, of twenty-four, with a bright, intelligent face; his education was above what was ordinary in his class. It was precisely this that had excited in him vanity, and craving for pleasures and amusements which he could not afford. His obliging manners, his trimness, and cheerfulness, had made him a favourite with the officers.

As already intimated, he was fond of play, and it was this that had induced him to commit his murders. He admitted that he had felt little or no compunction, and he said frankly that it was as well for society that he was taken, otherwise the death of Kügelgen would have been followed by others. He spoke of the crimes he had committed with openness and indifference, and maintained this condition of callousness to the end. It seems to have been customary on several occasions for the Lutheran pastors who attended the last hours of criminals to publish their opinions as to the manner in which they prepared for death, and their ideas as to the motives for the crimes committed, an eminently indecent proceeding to our notions. In this case, the chaplain who attended on Kaltofen rushed into the priest after the execution. He said, " Play may have occasioned that want of feeling which will commit the most atrocious crime, without compunction, for the gratification of a temporary requirement. Kaltofen, without being rude and rough towards his fellows, but on the contrary obliging and courteous, came to regard them with brutal indifference." Only twice did he feel any twinge of conscience, he said, once before his first murder, and again at the funeral of his second victim, which he attended. The criminal was now known, had confessed, and had confessed that he had no accomplice. Moreover, he declared that Fischer was wholly innocent. Not a single particle of evidence was forthcoming to incriminate Fischer, apart from his own retracted confessions. Nevertheless he was not liberated.

The police could not believe that Kaltofen had been without an accomplice. There were stabs in the face and body of Kügelgen, and Kaltofen had professed to have used no other weapon than a cudgel. The murderer said that he had dragged the body over the field to the rushes, and it was agreed that there must have been evidence of this dragging. Some witnesses had, indeed, said they had seen such, but others protested that there were footprints as of two men. This, however, could be explained by Kaltofen's admission that he had gone back to the road for the walking-stick.

Then, again, Fischer, when interrogated, had given particulars which agreed with the circumstances in a remarkable manner. He was asked to explain this. "Well," said he, "he had heard a good deal of talk about the murders, and he was miserable at the thought of spending long years in prison, and so had confessed." When asked how he knew the particulars of the murder of Winter, he said that he had been helped to it by the gaoler. He had said first, "I went to his left side"—whereupon the gaoler had said, "Surely you are wrong, it was on the right," thereat Fischer had corrected himself and said, "Yes, of course—on the right."

The case was now ready for final sentence, and for this purpose all the depositions were forwarded on September 12th to the Judicial Court at Leipzig. But, before judgment was pronounced, the depositions were hastily sent for back to Dresden—for, in the meantime, the case had passed into a new phase. On October 5th, the gaoler—the same man who had brought about the confession of Fischer—announced that Kaltofen had confided to him that Fischer really had been his accomplice in both the murders. Kaltofen at once was summoned before the magistrate, and he calmly, and with emphasis, declared that Fischer had assisted him on both occasions, and that he had not allowed this before, because he and Fischer had sworn that neither would betray the other. Fischer had never mentioned his name, and he had accordingly done his utmost to exculpate Fischer.

According to his account, he and Fischer had been

walking together on the morning of March 26th, between 9 and 10, when they planned a murder together for the following day. However, there was rebutting evidence to the effect that on the morning in question Fischer had been on guard, at the hour named, before the powder magazine; he had not been released till noon. Other statements of Kaltofen proved to be equally untrue.

What could have induced Kaltofen to deliberately charge a comrade in arms with participation in the crime, if he were guiltless? There was no apparent motive. He could gain no reprieve by it. It did not greatly diminish his own guilt.

It was necessary to enter into as close investigation as was possible into the whereabouts of Fischer at the time of the two murders. It was not found possible to determine where he was at the time when Winter was killed, but some of his comrades swore that on March 27th he had been present at the roll-call at 6 p.m., and had come into barrack before the second roll-call at half-past eight. The murder of Kügelgen had taken place at eight o'clock, and the distance between the barrack and the spot where it had been committed was 3487 paces, which would take a man about 25 minutes to traverse. If, as his comrades asserted, Fischer had come in shortly after eight, then it was quite impossible that he could have been present when Kügelgen was murdered; but not great reliance can be placed on the testimony of soldiers as to the hour at which a comrade came into barrack just seven months before on a given day.

The case was perplexing. The counsel for Fischer

—his name was Eisenstück—took a bold line of defence. He charged the gaolor with having manipulated Kaltofen, as he had Fischer. This gaoler's self-esteem was wounded by the discovery that Kaltofen and not Fischer was the murderer, and his credit was damaged by the proceedings which showed that he had goaded an unhappy man, confided to his care, into charging himself with a crime he had never committed. Eisenstück asserted that this new charge was fabricated in the prison by the gaoler in concert with Kaltofen for his own justification. But, whatever may be thought of the character and conduct of this turnkey, it is difficult to understand how he could prevail on a cool-headed man like Kaltofen thus to take on himself the additional guilt of perjury, and such perjury as risked the life of an innocent man. Kaltofen never withdrew this assertion that Fischer was an accomplice. He persisted in it to his last breath.

The depositions were again sent to the faculty at Leipzig, on Dec. 18th, to give judgment on the following points.

1. The examination of the body of Kügelgen had revealed stabs made with a sharp, two-edged instrument, as well as blows dealt by a blunt weapon. Kaltofen would admit that he had used no other instrument than a cudgel.

2. It would have been a difficult matter for one man to drag a dead body from the road to the bed of rushes, without leaving unmistakable traces on the field traversed ; and such were not, for certain, found. It was therefore more probable

that the dead man had been carried by two persons to the place where found.

It must be observed that crowds poured out of
Dresden to see the place where the body lay as soon
as it was known that Kügelgen had been discovered,
and consequently no accurate and early examination
of tracks across the field had been made.

3. That it would have been difficult for Kaltofen
   alone to strip the body. This may be doubted;
   it would be difficult possibly, but not impossible,
   whilst the body was flexible.

4. A witness had said that she had met two men outside the Black Gate on the evening of the 27th
   March, of whom one was wrapped in a cloak and
   seemed to be carrying something under it. We
   should much like to know when the woman gave
   this evidence. Unfortunately, that is what is not
   told us.

5. Kaltofen, in a letter to his parents, had stated that
   he had an accomplice, but had not named him.

These were the points that made it appear that
Kaltofen had an accomplice. An accomplice in some
of his crimes he had—Kiessling.

There were other points that made it appear that
Fischer had assisted him in the murders.

6. Fischer's denial that he knew anything about the
   murder of Kügelgen when he was arrested,
   whereas it was established that he had attended
   the funeral of the murdered man.

7. His repeated confessions that he had assisted at
   the murders, and his acquaintance with the particulars and with the localties.

8. Kaltofen's asservations that Fischer was his associate in the murders.

In favour of Fischer it may be said that his conduct in the army had for thirteen years been uniformly good, and there was no evidence that he had been in any way guilty of dishonesty. Nor was he a man of extravagant habits like Kaltofen, needing money for his pleasures. He was a simple, inoffensive, and very stupid man. His confessions lose all their effect when we consider how they were extorted from him by undue influence.

Against Kaltofen's later accusation must he set his repeated declaration, during six months, that Fischer was innocent. Not only this, but his assertion in confidence to Kiessling that he was puzzled what could have induced Fischer to avow himself guilty of a crime, of which he—Kaltofen—knew him to be innocent. When Kiessling gave this evidence on April 24th, Kaltofen did not deny that he had said this, but flew into a paroxysm of fury with his comrade for betraying their private conversation.

Again, not a single article appertaining to either of the murdered men was found with Fischer. All had been traced, without exception, to Kaltofen. It was the latter who had concealed Kügelgen's coat, and had given his watch to the Jews. It was he who had got Kiessling to dispose of Winter's hat for him, and had given the boots of the last victim to Kiessling to be repaired.

On January 4th, 1821, the Court at Leipzig issued its judgment; that Kaltofen, on account of two murders committed and confessed, was to be put to death on the wheel; "but that John George Fischer be discharged on account of lack of evidence of complicity in the murders." The gaoler was discharged his office.

Kaltofen appealed against the sentence, but in vain. The sentence was confirmed. The ground of his appeal was, that he was not alone guilty. The King commuted the penalty of the wheel into execution by the sword.

The sentence of the court produced the liveliest commotion in Dresden. The feeling against Fischer was strong and general; the gaoler had but represented the universal opinion. Fischer—who had confessed to the murder—Fischer, whom Kaltofen protested was as deeply stained in crime as himself, was to go scot free. The police authorities did not carry out the sentence of discharge in its integrity; they indeed released him from prison, but placed him under police supervision, and he was discharged from the Artillery on the plea that he had forsworn himself. The pastor Jaspis was entrusted with the preparation of Kaltofen for death; and we know pretty well what passed between him and the condemned man, as he had the indecency to publish it to the world. Jaspis had, indeed, visited him in prison when he was first arrested, and then Kaltofen had asserted that he had committed the murders entirely unassisted. On Jaspis remarking to him in April, 1820, that there were circumstances that rendered this eminently improbable, Kaltofen cut him short with the answer, "I was by myself." Afterwards, when he had changed his note, Jaspis reminded him of his previous declaration, but

Kaltofen pretended not to remember ever having made it.

Towards the end of his days, Kaltofen was profoundly agitated, and was very restless. When Jaspis gave him a book of prayers and meditations for such as were in trouble, he put it from him, and said the book was unsuitable, and was adapted only to the innocent. He had visitors who combined piety with inquisitiveness, and came to discuss with him the state of his soul. Kaltofen's vanity was inflamed, and he was delighted to pose before these zealots. When he heard that Jaspis had preached about him in the Kreuz Kirche on the Sunday before his execution, he was greatly gratified, and said, " He would really like to hear what had been said about him."

Jaspis thereupon produced his sermon, and read it over to the wretched man,—but tells us that even the most touching portions of the address failed to awake any genuine compunction in his soul. Unless he could play the saint, before company, he was cold and indifferent. His great vanity, however, was hurt at the thought that his assertion was disbelieved, that Fischer was his associate in his crimes. He was always eager and inquisitive to know what rumours circulated in the town concerning him, and was gratified to think that he was the topic of the general conversation.

On the night before his execution he slept soundly for five hours, and then lit his pipe and smoked composedly. His condition was, however, not one of bluntness of sense, for he manifested considerable readiness and consciousness up to the last. He had drawn up a dying address which he handed to pastor Jaspis, and on which he evidently placed great importance, as when his first copy had caught fire when he was drying it, he set to work to compose a second. He knew his man—Jaspis—and was sure he would publish it after the execution. The paper was a rigmarole in which he posed to the world.

On reaching the market-place where the execution was to take place, he repeated his confession, but on this occasion without mention of a confederate. His composure gave way, and he began to sob. On reaching the scaffold, however, the sight of the vast crowd assembled to see him die restored to him some of his composure, as it pleased his vanity; but he again broke down, as he made his last confession to the Lutheran pastor. His voice trembled, and the sweat broke out on his brow. Then he sprang up and shouted, so that all could hear—"Gentlemen, Fischer deserved the same punishment as myself." In another moment his head fell from his body.

The words had been audible throughout the market-place by everyone. Who could doubt that his last words were true?

Fischer happened that very day (July 12th) to be in Dresden. He had been seen, and had been recognised.

He had come to Dresden to see his counsel, and ask him to use his influence to obtain his complete discharge from police supervision, and restoration to his rights as an honest man and a soldier, with a claim to a pension.

A vast crowd of people rolled from the place of

execution to the house of Eisenstück, shouting, and threatening to tear Fischer to pieces.

But Eisenstück was not the man to be terrified. He summoned a carriage, entered it along with Fischer, and drove slowly, with the utmost composure, through the angry crowd.

On August 26th, 1822, by command of the king, Fischer's name was replaced in the army list, and he received his complete discharge from all the consequences of the accusations made against him. He was guaranteed his pension for his "faithful services through 16 years, and in the campaigns of 1813, 1814, and 1815, in which he had conducted himself to the approval of all his officers."

How are we to explain the conduct of Kaltofen? The simplest way is to admit that he spoke the truth; but against this is to be opposed his denial that Fischer was guilty during the first six months that he was under arrest. And it is impossible to believe that Fischer was guilty, on the sole testimony of Kaltofen, without any confirmatory evidence.

It is rather to be supposed that the inordinate vanity of the young culprit induced him to persist in denouncing his innocent brother gunner, so as to throw off his own shoulders some of the burden of that crime, which, he felt, made him hateful in the eyes of his fellow-citizens, and perhaps to induce them to regard him as misled by an older man, more hardened and experienced in crime, thus arousing their pity and sympathy in place of their disgust.

Jaspis, the pastor, did not himself believe in the criminality of Fischer, and proposes a solution which

he gives conjecturally only. He suggests that Kaltofen was misled by the confession of Fischer into the
belief that he really had committed a murder or two,
though not those of Winter and Kügelgen, and that
when he declared on the scaffold that "Fischer deserved to die as much as himself," he spoke under this
conviction. This explanation is untenable, for the
miserable man had repeatedly charged Fischer with
assisting him in committing these two particular
crimes. The explanation must be found in his self-
conceit and eagerness to present himself in the best
and most affecting light before the public. And he
gained his point to some extent. The mob believed
him, pitied him, became sentimental over him, wept
tears at his death, and cursed the unfortunate Fischer.
The apparent piety, the mock heroics, the graceful
attitudes, and the good looks of the murderer had won
their sympathies, and the general opinion of the vulgar was that they had assisted at the sublimation of
a saint to the seventh heaven, and not at the well-de-
served execution of a peculiarly heartless and brutal
murderer.

A month had hardly passed since Kaltofen's execu-
cution before Dresden was shocked to hear of another
murder—on this occasion by a young woman. On
August 12th, 1821, this person, who had been in a state
of excitement ever since the edifying death of Kaltofen, invited to her house a young girl, just engaged to
be married, and deliberately murdered her; then
marched off to the police and confessed her crime—
the nature of which she did not disguise. She desired
to make the same affecting and edifying end as Kalto-

jen. Above all, she wanted to get herself talked about
by all the mouths in Dresden. The police on visiting
her house found the murdered girl lying on the bed.
On the door in large letters the murderer had inscribed the date of Kaltofen's martyrdom, July 12th,
and she had committed her crime on the same day
one month after, desirous to share his glory.

Such was one consequence of this execution. A
small farce also succeeded it. Influenced by the
general excitement provoked by the murder of
Kügelgen, the Jews had assembled and agreed, should
any of them be able to discover the murderer, that
they would decline the £150 offered by Government
for information that might lead to the apprehension
of the guilty. But Hirschel Mendel, the Jew who
had produced the watch, put in his claim; whereupon
Löbel Graff, who had produced the coat, put in a
counter claim. This occasioned a lawsuit between
the two Jews for the money. A compromise was
finally patched up, by which each received half.

Gerhard von Kügelgen had been buried in the
Catholic cemetery at Dresden on Maundy Thursday
evening by moonlight. A great procession of art
students attended the funeral cortège with lighted
torches, and an oration was pronounced over his grave
by his friend Councillor Böttiger.

His tomb may still be seen in the cemetery; on it
is inscribed :—

FRANZ GERHARD VON KÜGELGEN.
Born, 6 Feb, 1772.
Died 27 March, 1820.

On the other side is the text, S. John, xiv. 27.

E

Kügelgen left behind him two sons and a daughter. The eldest son, Wilhelm, pursued his father's profession as an artist, and the Emperor of Russia sent an annual grant of money to assist him in his studies. There is a pleasant book, published anonymously by him, "An Old Man's Youthful Reminiscences," the first edition of which was issued in 1870, and which had reached its eighth edition in 1876.

Kügelgen's twin brother Karl Ferdinand, after spending some years in St. Petersburg and in Livonia, settled at Reval, and died in 1832. He was the author of a "Picturesque Journey in the Crimea," published in 1823.

Authority :—F. Ch. A. Hasse : Das Leben Gerhards von Kügelgen. Leipzig, 1824. He gives in the Supplement an excerpt from the records of the trial. As frontispiece is a portrait of the artist by himself, very Raphaelesque.

The Poisoned Parsnips.

AT the time when the banished Bourbons were wandering about Europe seeking temporary asylums, during the period of Napoleon's supremacy, a story circulated in 1804 relative to an attempt made in Warsaw, which then belonged to Prussia, upon the life of the Royal Family then residing there. It was said that a plot had been formed, that was well nigh successful, to kill Louis XVIII., his wife, the Duke and Duchess of Angoulême, and such of the Court as sat at the Royal table, with a dish of poisoned parsnips. It was, moreover, whispered that at the bottom of the plot was no other than Napoleon himself, who sought to remove out of his way the legitimate claimants to the Gallic throne.

The article in which the account of the attempt was made public was in the *London Courier* for August 20th, 1804, from which we will now take the leading facts.

The Royal Family was living in Warsaw. Napoleon Bonaparte employed an agent of the name of Galon Boyer at Warsaw to keep an eye on them, and this man it was reported had engaged assassins at the instigation of Napoleon to poison Louis XVIII. and the rest of the Foyal Family. The *Courier* of August 21st, 1804, says: "Some of the daily papers, which were not over anxious to discredit the conspiracy im-

67

puted to Mr. Drake [1] affect to throw some doubt upon the account of the attempt upon the lives of the Royal Family at Warsaw. They seem to think that had Bonaparte desired such a plan, he could have executed it with more secrecy and effect. Undoubtedly his plans of assassination have hitherto been more successful, because his hapless victims were within his power—his wounded soldiers at Jaffa, Toussaint L'Ouverture, Pichegru, and the Duke D'Enghien. He could send his bloodhounds into Germany to seize his prey; but Warsaw was too remote for him; he was under the necessity of having recourse to less open means of sending his assassins to act secretly. But it is deemed extraordinary that the diabolical attempt should have failed. Why is it extraordinary that a beneficent Providence should interpose to save the life of a just prince? Have we not had signal instances of that interposition in this country? For the accuracy of the account we published yesterday, we pledge ourselves [2] that the fullest details authenticated by all Louis the XVIII.'s

---

[1] Drake was envoy of the British Government at Munich; he and Spencer Smith, Chargé d'Affaires at Würtemberg, were accused by Napoleon of being at the bottom of a counter revolution, and an attempt to obtain his assassination. It was true that Drake and Smith were in correspondence with parties in France with the object of securing Hagenau and Strassburg and throwing discord among the troops of the Republic, but they never for a moment thought of obtaining the assassination of the First Consul, as far as we can judge from their correspondence that fell into the hands of the French police.

[2] Unfortunately the British Museum file is imperfect, and does not contain the Number for August 20th.

Ministers—by the venerable Archbishop of Rheims—by the Abbé Edgeworth, who administered the last consolation of religion to Louis the XVI., have been received in this country. All those persons were present when the poisoned preparation was analysed by very eminent physicians, *who are the subjects of the King of Prussia.*

"The two wretches who attempted to corrupt the poor Frenchman were openly protected by the French Consul or Commercial Agent.

"The Prussian Governor would not suffer them to be arrested in order that their guilt or innocence might be legally investigated. Is it to be believed that had there been no foundation for the charge against them, the French agent would have afforded them less open protection, and thereby strengthened the charge brought against them? If they were protected and paid by the French agent, is it probable that he paid them out of his own pocket, employed them in such a plot of his own accord, and without order and instructions from his own Government, from Bonaparte? Besides, did not the President Hoym acknowledge his fears that some attempt would be made upon the life of Louis the XVIII.?

"The accounts transmitted to this country were sent from Warsaw one hour after the king had set out for Grodno."

The *Courier* for August 24th, 1804, has the following note :—"We have another strong fact which is no slight evidence in our minds of Bonaparte's guilt. The plot against Louis the XVIII. was to be executed at the end of July—it would be known about the beginning of August. At that very period Bonaparte prohibits the importation of all foreign journals without exception—that is, of all the means by which the people could be informed of the diabolical deed. Why does he issue this prohibition at the present moment, or why does he issue it at all? Fouché says in his justification of it that it is to prevent our knowing when the expedition sails. Have we ever received any news about the expedition from the French papers? No, no! the prohibition was with a view to the bloody scene to be acted at Warsaw."

The *Courier* of August 22nd contained full particulars. We will now tell the whole story, from beginning to end, first of all as dressed out by the fancy of Legitimists, and then according to the real facts of the case as far as known.

Napoleon, it will be remembered, had been appointed First Consul for life on August 2nd, 1802, but the Republic came to an end, and the French Empire was established by the Senate on May 18th, 1804.

It was supposed—and we can excuse the excitement and intoxication of wrath in the minds of all adherents of the Bourbons which could suppose it— that Napoleon, who was thus refounding the Empire of Charlemagne, desired to secure the stability of this new throne by sweeping out of his way the legitimate claimants to that of France. The whole legend of the attempt to assassinate Louis XVIII. by means of a dish of poisoned parsnips is given us in complete form by the author of a life of that prince, twenty years after the event.[1]   It is to this effect :

[1] A. de Beauchamp, Vie de Louis XVIII.   Paris, 1824.

When the King (Louis XVIII.) was preparing for his journey from Warsaw to Grodno an atrocious attempt to assassinate him was brought to light, which leaves no manner of doubt that it was the purpose of those who were the secret movers in the plot to remove by poison both the King and Queen and also the Duke of Angoulême and his wife. Two delegates of Napoleon had been in Warsaw seeking for a man who could execute the plan. A certain Coulon appeared most adapted to their purpose, a man indigent and eager for money. He had previously been in the service of one of the emigré nobles, and had access to the kitchen of the Royal Family.

The agents of Napoleon gave Coulon drink, and as he became friendly and lively under the influence of punch, they communicated to him their scheme, and promised him money, the payment of his debts, and to effect his escape if he would be their faithful servant in the intrigue. Coulon pretended to yield to their solicitations, and a rendezvous was appointed where the plans were to be matured. But no sooner was Coulon at liberty than he went to his former master, the Baron de Milleville, master of horse to the Queen, and told him all. The Baron sought the Duc de Pienne, first gentleman of the Royal household, and he on receiving the information communicated it to the Count d'Avaray, Minister of Louis XVIII. Coulon received orders to pretend to be ready to carry on the plot. He did this with reluctance, but he did it. He told the agents of Napoleon that he was in their hands and would blindly execute their orders. They treated him now to champagne, and revealed to him

the details of the attempt. He was to get into the
kitchen of the Royal household, and was to pour the
contents of a packet they gave him, into one of the
pots in which the dinner for the Royal table was being
cooked, Coulon then demanded an instalment of his
pay, and asked to be given 400 louis d'or. One of the
agents then turned to the other and asked if he thought
Boyer would be disposed to advance so much—this
was Galon Boyer, the head agent sent purposely to
Warsaw as spy on the Royal Family, and the principal mover in the attempt.

The other agent replied that Boyer was not at the
moment in Warsaw, but he would be back in a couple
of days. Coulon stuck to his point, like a clever rascal, and refused to do anything till he felt gold in his
palm, and he was bidden wait till Boyer had been
communicated with. He was appointed another
meeting on the moors at Novawies outside the city.

As, next evening, Coulon was on his way to the place
named, he observed that he was followed by a man.
Suddenly out of the corn growing beside the road
started a second. They were the agents. They
paid him a few dollars, promised to provide hand-
somely for him in France, by giving him 400 louis d'or
and a situation under Government ; and handed him
a bottle of liquor that was to stimulate his courage at
the crucial moment, and also a paper packet that contained three parsnips, that had been scooped out and
filled with poison. These he was to insinuate into one
of the pots cooking for dinner, and induce the cook to
overlook what he had done, and serve them up to the
Royal Family.

The King then lived in a chateau at Lazienki, about a mile out of Warsaw. Thither hastened Coulon as fast as his legs could carry him, and he committed the parsnips to the Baron de Milleville. The Count d'Avaray and the Archbishop of Rheims put their seals on the parcel; after that the parsnips had first been shown to the Prussian authorities, and they had been asked in all form to attest the production of the poisoned roots, and to order the arrest of the two agents of Napoleon, and to confront them with Coulon,—and had declined. Louis, when informed of the attempt, showed his wonted composure. He wrote immediately to the Prussian President, Von Hoym, and requested him to visit him at Lazienki, and consult what was to be done.

Herr Von Hoym did not answer; nor did he go to the King, but communicated with his superiors. Finally there arrived a diplomatic reply declining to interfere in the matter, as it was the concern of the police to investigate it, and it should be taken up in the ordinary way.

Thereupon the King requested that Coulon and his wife should be secured, and that specialists should be appointed who, along with the Royal physician, might examine the parsnips alleged to be poisoned.

But the Prussian courts declined again to take any steps. The policy of the Prussian Cabinet under Count Haugwitz was favourable to a French alliance, and the King of Prussia was among the first of the greater Powers which had formally recognised the French Emperor. On condition that the French troops occupying Hanover should not be augmented and that war, if it broke out with Russia, should be so carried on as not to inconvenience and sweep over Prussian territory, Prussia had undertaken to observe a strict neutrality. In return for these concessions, which were of great moment to Napoleon, he openly proclaimed his intention to augment the strength of Prussia, and it was hoped at Berlin that the price paid would be the incorporation of Hanover with Prussia.

At this moment, consequently, the Prussian Government was most unwilling to meddle in an investigation which threatened to lead to revelations most compromising to the character of Napoleon, and most inconvenient for itself.

As the Prussian courts would not take up the matter of the parsnips, a private investigation was made by the Count d'Avaray, with the Royal physician, Dr. Lefèvre, and the Warsaw physican, Dr. Gagatkiewicz, together with the Apothecary Guidel and a certain Dr. Bergonzoni. The seals were broken in their presence, and the three roots were examined. It was ascertained that they were stuffed with a mixture of white, yellow, and red arsensic. This having been ascertained, and a statement of the fact duly drawn up and signed, the president of the police, Herr von Tilly, was communicated with. He, however, declined to interfere, as had the President von Hoym. "Thus," says M. Beauchamp, "one court shuffled the matter off on another, backwards and forwards, so as not to have to decide on the matter—a specimen of the results of the system adopted at this time by the Prussian Cabinet."

No other means of investigation remained but for

Count d'Avaray to have the matter gone into by the
court of the exiled King. They examined Coulon,
who held firmly to his story as told to the Baron de
Milleville, and all present were convinced that he
spoke the truth.

As the King could obtain no justice from the hands
of Prussia, he suffered the story to be made public in
order that the opinion of all honourable men in
Europe might be expressed on the conduct of both
Napoleon and of the Prussian Ministry. "The impression made," says M. Beauchamp, "especially in
England, was deep. Men recalled Bonaparte's former
crimes that had been proved,—the poisoning at Jaffa,
the—at the time—very fresh indignation provoked by
the murder of the Count de Frotté, of Pichegru, of
Captain Wright, of the Duke d'Enghien, of Toussaint
l'Ouverture ; they recalled the lack of success he had
experienced in demanding of Louis XVIII. a formal
renunciation of his claims, and weighed well the determination of his character. Even the refusal of the
Prussian courts to go into the charge (for if it had
been investigated they must needs have pronounced
judgment on it)—encouraged suspicion. Hardly an
English newspaper did not condemn Napoleon as the
instigator of an attempt that providentially failed."

Such is the legend as formulated by M. de Beauchamp. Fortunately there exists documentary evidence in the archives of the courts at Berlin that gives
an altogether different complexion to the story, and
entirely clears the name of Napoleon from stain of
complicity in this matter. It throws, moreover, a
light, by no means favourable, on those of the

Legitimist party clustered about the fallen mon-
arch.

Louis XVIII., obliged to fly from one land to
another before the forces of Napoleon, was staying
for a while at Warsaw, in the year 1804, under the
incognito of the Count de l'Isle. His misfortunes
had not broken his spirit or diminished his pretensions. He was surrounded by a little court in spite
of his incognito ; and as this little court had no
affairs of State to transact, it played a niggling game
at petty intrigue. This court consisted of the Count
d'Avaray, the Archbishop of Rheims, the Duke de
Pienne, the Marquis de Bonney, the Duke d'Avré de
Croy, the Count de la Chapelle, the Counts Damas
Crux and Stephen de Damas, and the Abbés Edgeworth and Frimont. Louis had assured Napoleon he
would rather eat black bread than resign his pretensions. At Warsaw he maintained his pretensions to
the full, but did not eat black bread ; he kept a very
respectable kitchen. The close alliance between
Prussia and France forced him to leave Warsaw and
migrate into Russia.

At this time there lived in Warsaw a certain Jean
Coulon, son of a small shopkeeper at Lyons, who had
led an adventurous life. At the age of nine he had
run away from home and attached himself to a
wandering dramatic company ; then had gone into
service to a wigmaker, and had lived for three years
at Barcelona at his handicraft. But wigs were going
out of fashion, and he threw up an unprofitable trade,
and enlisted in a legion of emigrés, but in consequence of some quarrel with a Spaniard was handed

over to the Spanish authorities. He purchased his pardon by enlisting in the Spanish army, but deserted and joined the French Republican troops, was in the battle of Novi, ran away, and joined the corps raised at Naples by Cardinal Ruffo. When this corps was dispersed, he went back to Spain, again enlisted, and was shipped for St. Lucia. The vessel in which he was, was captured by an English cruiser, and he was taken into Plymouth and sent up to Dartmoor as prisoner of war. After two years he was exchanged, and was shipped to Cuxhaven. Thence he went to Altona, where he asked the intervention of the Duke d'Avré in his favour. The Duke recommended him to the Countess de l'Isle, and he was taken into the service of her master of horse, the Baron de Milleville, and came to Warsaw in September, 1803. There he married, left his service and set up a café and billiard room that was frequented by the retainers and servants of the emigré nobility that hovered about the King and Queen. He was then aged 32, could speak Italian and Spanish as well as French, and was a thorough soldier of fortune, impecunious, loving pleasure, and wholly without principles, political or religious.

The French Chargé d'Affaires at Warsaw was Galon Boyer; he does not appear in the documents relative to the *Affaire Coulon*, not because the Prussian Government shirked its duty, but because he was in no way mixed up with the matter of the parsnips. It is quite true that, as M. de Beauchamp asserts, the Court of Louis XVIII. did endeavour to involve the Prussian authorities in the investigation, but it was in such a manner that it was not possible for them to act. On July 23rd, when the Count de l'Isle was determined to leave Warsaw, Count d'Avaray called on the President von Hoym, and told him in mysterious language that he was aware of a conspiracy in which were involved several Frenchmen and as many as a dozen Poles that sought the life of his august master. Herr von Hoym doubted. He asked for the grounds of this assertion, and was promised full particulars that same evening at eight o'clock. At the hour appointed, the Count appeared breathless before him, and declared that now he was prepared with a complete disclosure. However, he told nothing, and postponed the revelation to 10 o'clock. Then Avaray informed him that the keeper of the Café Coulon had been hired by some strangers to meet him that same night on the road to Novawies, to plan with him the murder, by poison, of the Count de l'Isle. The whole story seemed suspicious to von Hoym. It was now too late for him to send police to watch the spot where the meeting was to take place, which he might have done had d'Avaray condescended to tell him in time, two hours earlier. He asked d'Avaray where Coulon lived, that he might send for him, and the Count professed he did not know the address.

Next day Count d'Avaray read to the President von Hoym a document, which he said had been drawn up by members of the court of the Count de l'Isle, showed him a paper that contained twelve small parsnips, and requested him to subscribe the document and seal the parcel of parsnips. Naturally, the President declined to do this. He had not seen Coulon he did not know from whom Coulon had received the parcel, and he mistrusted the whole story. However, he requested that he might be furnished with an exact description of the two mysterious strangers, and when he had received it, communicated with the police, and had inquiry made for them in and about Warsaw. No one had seen or heard of any persons answering to the description.

Presently the Marquis de Bonney arrived to request the President, in the name of the Count de l'Isle, to have the parsnips examined by specialists. He declined to do so.

On July 26th, the Count d'Avaray appeared before the head of the Police, the President von Tilly, and showed him an attestation made by several doctors that they had examined three parsnips that had been shown them, and they had found in them a paste composed of arsenic and orpiment. Von Tilly thought the whole story so questionable that he refused to meddle with it. Moreover, a notary of Warsaw, who had been requested to take down Coulon's statement, had declined to testify to the genuineness of the confession, probably because, as Coulon afterwards insinuated, he had been helped to make it consistent by those who questioned him.

Louis XVIII. left Warsaw on July 30, and as the rumour spread that Coulon's wife had bought some arsenic a week before at an apothecary's shop in the place, the police inspector ordered her arrest. She was questioned and declared that she had, indeed, bought some rat poison, without the knowledge of her husband. Coulon was now taken up and questioned, and he pretended that he had given his wife orders to buy the rat poison, because he was plagued with vermin in the house.

Then the authorities in Warsaw sent all the documents relating to this matter, including the *procès verbal* drawn up by the courtiers of Louis XVIII., to Berlin, and asked for further instructions.

According to this *procès verbal* Coulon had confessed as follows: On the 20th July two strangers had entered his billiard room, and had assured him that, if he were disposed to make his fortune, they could help him to it. They made him promise silence, and threatened him with death if he disclosed what they said. After he had sworn fidelity and secrecy, they told him that he was required to throw something into the pot in which the soup was being prepared for the King's table. For so doing they would pay him 400 louis d'or. Coulon considered a moment; then the strangers promised they would provide a situation for his wife in France. After that one of them said to his fellow in Italian, " We must be off. We have no time to lose." Next day, in the evening, a third stranger appeared at his door, called him forth into the street, walked about with him through the streets of old and new Warsaw, till he was thoroughly bewildered, and did not know where he was, and, finally, entered with him a house, where he saw the two strangers who had been with him previously. Champagne was brought on table, and they all drank, and one of the strangers became tipsy. When Coulon promised to do what was required of him, he was told to secure some of the mutton-chops that were being prepared for the Royal table, and to manipulate them with the powder that was to be given him. That the cook might not notice what he was about, he was to treat him to large draughts of brandy. Coulon agreed, but asked first to touch the 400 louis d'or. Then the tipsy man shouted out, " That is all right, but will Boyer consent to it ? " The other stranger tried to check him, and said, " What are you saying ? Boyer is not here, he has gone out of town and will not be back for a couple of days." After Coulon had insisted on prepayment, he had been put off till the next evening, when he was to meet the strangers at 11 o'clock on the road to Novawies. There he was to receive money, and the powder for the King. He was then given one ducat, and led home at one o'clock in the morning. On the following night, at 11 o'clock, he went on the way to Novawies, and then followed what we have already given from the story of the man, as recorded by M. de Beauchamp. He received from the men a packet containing the parsnips, and some money—only six dollars. They put a kerchief under the earth beneath a tree, and bade him, if he had accomplished his task, come to the tree and remove the kerchief, as a token to them ; if, however, he failed, the kerchief was to be left undisturbed. The tree he had marked well, it was the forty-fifth along the road to Novawies. A small end of the kerchief peeped out from under the soil. The strangers had then given him a bottle of liqueur to stimulate his courage for the undertaking.

After that Coulon was left alone, he said that he

F

staggered homewards, but felt so faint that he would have fallen to the ground had not a Prussian officer, who came by, noticed his condition and helped him home. At the conclusion of the *procès verbal* came an exact description of the conspirators. Such was the document produced originally by the Count d'Avaray, and we can hardly wonder that, on hearing it, the Prussian civil and police authorities had hesitated about taking action. The so-called confession of Coulon seemed to them to be a rhodomontade got up for the purpose of obtaining money out of the ex-King and his Court.

From Berlin orders were sent to Warsaw to have the matter thoroughly sifted. Coulon and his wife were now again subjected to examination. He adhered at first to his story, but when he endeavoured to explain the purchase of the arsenic, and to fit it into his previous tale, he involved himself in contradictions.

The President at this point addressed him gravely, and warned him of the consequences. His story compromised the French chargé d'affaires, M. Galon Boyer, and this could not be allowed to be passed over without a very searching examination, that must inevitably reveal the truth. Coulon was staggered, and hastily asked how matters would stand with him if he told the truth. Then, after a little hesitation, he admitted that "he thought before the departure of the Count de l'Isle he would obtain for himself a sum of money, with which to escape out of his difficulties. He had reckoned on making 100 ducats out of this affair." He now told quite a different tale. With the departure of the court of the emigrés, he would lose his clientelle, and he was concerned because he owed money for the café and billiard table. He had therefore invented the whole story in hopes of imposing on the court and getting from them a little subvention. But, he said he had been dragged on further than he intended by the Count d'Avaray, who had swallowed his lie with avidity, and had urged him to go on with the intrigue so as to produce evidence against the conspirators.

That was why he had made up the figment of the meeting with the strangers on the road and their gift to him of the parsnips, which he admitted that he had himself scooped out and filled with the rat poison paste he had bought at the apothecary's.

So far so good. What he now said was precisely what the cool heads of the Prussian authorities had believed from the first. But Coulon did not adhere to this second confession. After a few days in prison he professed his desire to make another. He was brought before the magistrate, and now he said that the whole story was got up by the Count d'Avaray, M. de Milleville, and others of the surroundings of the exiled King, for the purpose of creating an outbreak of disgust in Europe against Napoleon, and of bringing about a revolt in France. He declared that he had been promised a pension of six ducats monthly, that when he gave his evidence M. de Milleville had paid him 35 ducats, and that he had been taken into the service, along with his wife, of the ex-Queen, as reward for what he had done.

There were several particulars which gave colour to this last version of Coulon's story. It was true that he had been given some money by Milleville, it was perhaps true that in their eagerness to prove a case of attempted assassination, some of those who conducted the inquiry had helped him to correct certain discrepancies in his narrative. Then, again, it was remarkable that, although the Count d'Avaray knew about the projected murder, he would not tell the Prussian President the facts till 10 o'clock at night, when it was too late to send the police to observe the pretended meeting on the Novawies road, and when Herr von Hoym asked for directions as to where Coulon lived that the police might be sent to arrest him on his return, and during his absence to search the house, the Count had pretended to be unable to say where Coulon lived. It was also true that de Milleville had repeatedly visited Coulon's house during the course of the intrigue, and that it was immediately after Coulon had been at Milleville's house that his wife was sent to buy the rat poison.

Coulon pretended to have heard M. de Milleville say that "This affair might cause a complete change in the situation in France, when tidings of what had been done were published." Moreover, he said that he had been despatched to the Archbishop of Rheim's with the message "Le coup est manqué."

But it is impossible to believe that the emigré court can have fabricated such a plot by which to cast on the name of Napoleon the stain of attempted assassination. The whole story reads like the clumsy invention of a vulgar adventurer. Coulon's second confession is obviously that of his true motives. He was in debt, he was losing his clientelle by the departure of the

Count, and it is precisely what such a scoundrel would do, to invent a lie whereby to enlist their sympathies for himself, and obtain from them some pecuniary acknowledgment for services he pretended to have rendered. The little court was to blame in its gullibility. Its blind hatred of Napoleon led it to believe such a gross and palpable lie, and, if doubts arose in any of their minds as to the verity of the tale told them, they suppressed them.

Coulon was found guilty by the court and was sentenced to five years' imprisonment. The judgment of the court was that he had acted in concert with certain members of the retinue of the Count de l'Isle, but it refrained from naming them.

The Murder of Father Thomas in Damascus.

THE remarkable case we are about to relate awoke great interest and excitement throughout three quarters of the world, and stirred up that hatred of the Jews which had been laid asleep after the persecutions of the Middle Ages, just at the time when in all European lands the emancipation of the Jew was being recognised as an act of justice. At the time the circumstances were imperfectly known, or were laid before the public in such a partial light that it was difficult to form a correct judgment upon them. Since then, a good deal of light has been thrown on the incident, and it is possible to arrive at a conclusion concerning the murder with more unbiased mind and with fuller information than was possible at the time.

The Latin convents of Syria stand under the immediate jurisdiction of the Pope, and are, for the most part, supplied with recruits from Italy. They are very serviceable to travellers, whom they receive with genial hospitality, and without distinction of creed. They are nurseries of culture and of industry. Every monk and friar is required to exercise a profession or trade, and the old charge against monks of being drones is in no way applicable to the busy members of the religious orders in Palestine.

In the Capuchin Convent at Damascus dwelt, in 1840, a friar named Father Thomas, a Sardinian by birth. For thirty-three years he had lived there, and had acted as physician and surgeon, attending to whoever called for his services, Mussulman or Christian, Turk, Jew or Frank alike. He set limbs, dosed with quinine for fever, and vaccinated against small-pox. Being well known and trusted, he was in constant practice, and his practice brought him, or, at all events, his order, a handsome annual income. His manners were, unfortunately, not amiable. He was curt, even rude, and somewhat dictatorial; his manners impressed as authoritative in the sickroom, but were resented in the market-place as insolent.

On February 5th, 1840, Father Thomas disappeared, together with his servant, a lay brother who always attended him. This disappearance caused great commotion in Damascus.

France has been considered in the East as the protector of Christians of the Latin confession. The French Consul, the Count Ratti-Menton, considered it his duty to investigate the matter.

Father Thomas had been seen to enter the Jews' quarter. Several Israelites admitted having seen him there. No one saw him leave it: consequently, it was concluded he had disappeared, been made away with, there. As none but Jews occupied the Ghetto, it was argued that Father Thomas had been murdered by Israelites. That was settled as a preliminary. But in the meantime the Austrian Consul had been making investigation as well as the Count Ratti-Menton, and he had obtained information that Father

Thomas and his servant had been noticed engaged in a violent quarrel and contest of words with some Mohammedans of the lowest class, in the market-place. No weight was attached to this, and the French Consul pursued his investigations in the Jews' quarter, and in that quarter alone.

Sheriff Pacha was Governor of Syria, and Count Ratti-Menton required him to allow of his using every means at his disposal for the discovery of the criminal. He also requested the Austrian Consul to allow a domiciliary visitation of all the Jews' houses, the Austrian Government being regarded as the protector of the Hebrews. In both cases consent was given, and the search was begun with zeal.

Then a Turk, named Mohammed-el-Telli, who was in prison for non-payment of taxes, sent word to the French Consul that, if he would obtain his release, he would give such information as would lead to the discovery of the murderer or murderers. He received his freedom, and denounced, in return, several Jews' houses as suspicious. Count Ratti-Menton at the head of a troop of soldiers and workmen, and a rabble assembled in the street, invaded all these houses, and explored them from attic to cellar.

One of the first names given by Mohammed-el-Telli was that of a Jewish barber, Negrin. He gave a confused and contradictory account of himself, but absolutely denied having any knowledge of the murder. In vain were every means used during three days at the French Consulate to bring him to a confession; after that he was handed over to the Turkish authorities. They had him bastinadoed, then tortured. During his torture, Mohammed-el-Telli was at his side urging him to make a clean breast. Unable to endure his sufferings longer, the barber declared his readiness to tell all. Whether what he said was based on reports circulating in the town, or was put into his mouth by his tormentors, we cannot tell. According to his story, on the evening of February the 5th a servant of David Arari summoned him into his house. He found the master of the house along with six other Israelitish rabbis and merchants, to wit, Aaron and Isaac Arari, Mussa Abul Afia, Moses Salonichi, and Joseph Laniado. In a corner of the room lay or leaned against the wall the Father Thomas, gagged and bound hand and foot. The merchants urged Negrin to murder the Capuchin in their presence, but he stedfastly refused to do so. Finally, finding him inflexible, they bought his silence with 600 piastres, (hardly £6) and dismissed him.

Thereupon, the governor ordered the arrest of David Arari and the other Jews named, all of whom were the richest merchants in the town—at all events the richest Jewish merchants. They, with one consent, solemnly protested their innocence. They, also, were subjected to the bastinado ; but as most of them were aged men, and it was feared that they might succumb under the blows, after a few lashes had been administered, they were raised from the ground and subjected to other tortures. For thirty-six hours the unhappy men were forced to stand upright, and were prevented from sleeping. They still persisted in denial, whereupon some of them were again beaten. At the twentieth blow they fainted. The French

Consul complained that the beating was inefficient—so the Austrian Consul reported, and at his instigation they were again bastinadoed, but again without bringing them to confession.

In the meantime, David Arari's servant, Murad-el-Fallat, was arrested, the man who was said to have been sent for the barber. He was dealt with more sharply than the others. He was beaten most cruelly, and to heighten his pain cold water was poured over his bruised and mangled flesh. Under the anguish he confessed that he had indeed been sent for the barber.

That was an insufficient confession. He was threatened with the bastinado again, and promised his release if he would reveal all he knew. Thereupon he repeated the story of the barber, with additions of his own. He and Negrin, said he, had by command of the seven rich merchants put the Father to death, and had then cut up the body and hidden the remains in a remote water conduit.

The barber, threatened with fresh tortures, confessed to the murder.

Count Ratti-Menton explored the conduit where the two men pretended the mutilated body was concealed, in the presence of the servant and barber, both of whom were in such a condition through the barbarous treatment to which they had been subjected, that they could not walk, and had to be carried to the spot. And actually there some bones were found, together with a cap. A surgeon pronounced that these were human bones. It was at once concluded that these were the remains of Father Thomas, and

as such were solemnly buried in the cemetery of the
Capuchin Convent.

David Arari's servant, Murad-el-Fallat, had related
that the blood of Father Thomas had been collected
in a copper vessel and drawn off and distributed
among the Jews for religious purposes. It was an
old and favourite belief among the ignorant that the
Jews drank the blood of Christians at Easter, or
mingled it with the Paschal unleavened dough. At
the same time the rumour spread that the rich
Hebrew Picciotto, a young man, nephew of the
Austrian Consul at Aleppo, had sent his uncle a
bottle of blood.

The seven merchants were led before the bones
that had been discovered. They persisted in the
declaration of their innocence. From this time forward, all scruple as to their treatment vanished, and
they were tortured with diabolical barbarity. They
received the bastinado again, they were burned where
their flesh was tenderest with red hot pincers. Red
hot wires were passed through their flesh. A German
traveller, present at the time, declares that the first
to acknowledge the truth of the charge was brought
to do so by immersing him after all these torments
for several hours in ice cold water; after which the
other six were lashed with a scourge made of hippopotamus hide, till half unconscious, and streaming
with blood, they were ready to admit whatever their
tormentors strove to worry out of them.

The Protestant missionary, Wildon Pieritz, in his
account enumerates the sufferings to which these unhappy men were subjected.

They were, 1st., bastinadoed.

2nd. Plunged in large vessels of cold water.

3rd. Placed under pressure till their eyes started out of their sockets.

4th. Their flesh, where most sensitive, was twisted and nipped till they went almost mad with agony.

5th. They were forced to stand upright for three whole days, and not suffered even to lean against a wall. Those who fell with exhaustion were goaded to rise again by the bayonets of the guard.

6th. They were dragged about by their ears, so that they were torn and bled.

7th. Thorns were driven up the quick of their nails on fingers and toes.

8th. Their beards were singed off, so that the skin was scorched and blistered.

9th. Flames were put under their noses so as to burn their nostrils.

The French Consul—let his name go down to posterity steeped in ignominy -- Count Ratti-Menton, was not yet satisfied. He was bent on finding the vials filled with the blood. Each of the seven questioned said he had not got one, but had given his vial to another. The last, Mussa Abul Afia, unable to endure his torments any longer, gave way, and professed his willingness to turn Mussulman. Nevertheless, he was again subjected to the scourge, and whipped till he named another confederate,—the Chief Rabbi Jacob Antibi, as the man to whom the blood had been committed. Mussa's confession, committed to writing, was as follows :—" I am *commanded*

to say what I know relative to the murder of Father
Thomas, and why I have submitted to become a
Mussulman. It is, therefore, my duty to declare the
truth. Jacob Antibi, Chief Rabbi, about a fortnight
before the event, said to me—'You know that according to our religion we must have blood. I have already
arranged with David Arari, to obtain it in the house
of one of our people, and you must be present and bring
me the blood.' I replied that I had not the nerve to
see blood flow ; whereupon, the Chief Rabbi answered
that I could stand in the ante-chamber, and I would
find Moses Salonichi and Joseph Laniado there. I
then consented. On the 10th of the month, Achach,
about an hour and a half before sun-down, as I was on
my way to the synagogue, I met David Arari, who
said to me: 'Come along to my house, you are wanted
there.' I replied that I would come as soon as I
had ended my prayers. 'No, no—come immediately !'
he said. I obeyed. Then he told me that Father
Thomas was in his house, and that he was to be sacri-
ficed that evening. We went to his house. There
we entered a newly-furnished apartment. Father
Thomas lay bound in the midst of all there assembled.
After sunset we adjourned to an unfurnished chamber,
where David cut the throat of the monk. Aaron and
Isaac Arari finished him. The blood was caught in a
vat and then poured into a bottle, which was to be
taken to the Chief Rabbi Jacob. I took the bottle
and went to him. I found him in his court waiting
for me. When he saw me enter, he retreated to his
cabinet, and I follow him thither, saying, 'Here, I
bring you what you desired.' He took the bottle and

put it behind a book-case. Then I went home. I have forgotten to say that, when I left Arari's house, the body was undisturbed. I heard David and his brother say that they had made a bad choice of a victim, as Father Thomas was a priest, and a well-known individual, and would therefore be sought for, high and low. They answered that there was no fear, no one would betray what had taken place. The clothing would be now burnt, the body cut to pieces, and conveyed by the servants to the conduit, and what remained would be concealed under some secret stairs. I knew nothing about the servant of Father Thomas. The Wednesday following, I met David, Isaac, and Joseph Arari, near the shop of Bahal. Isaac asked David how all had gone on. David replied that all was done that was necessary, and that there was no cause for fear. As they began to talk together privately, I withdrew, as I was not one who associated with the wealthiest of the Jews, and the Arari were of that class. The blood is required by the Jews for the preparation of the Paschal bread. They have been often accused of the same, and been condemned on that account. They have a book called Serir Hadurut (no such a book really exists) which concerns this matter; now that the light of Islam has shone on me, I place myself under the protection of those who hold the power in their hands."

Such was his confession. The French Consul, unable to find the blood, was bent on discovering more criminals; and the servant of David Arari, after further pressure, was ready to give further particulars. He said that, after the Father had been murdered, he was

sent to a rich Israelite, Marad Farhi, to invite him to
slaughter the servant of the Capuchin friar in the
same way as his master had been slaughtered. When
he took the message, he found the young merchant,
Isaac Picciotto, present, and delivered his message
before him. Next day this Picciotto and four other
Jews, Marad Farhi, Meir, and Assan Farhi, and
Aaron Stamboli, all men of wealth, came to his
master's house, and informed David Arari that they
had together murdered the Capuchin's serving-man
in the house of Meir Farhi. On another occasion
this same witness, Murad-el-Fallat, said that the
murder of the servant took place in the house of
David Arari ; but no importance was attached in this
remarkable case to contradictions in the evidence.

Picciotto, as son of a former Austrian Consul, a
nephew of the Consul at Aleppo, was able to take
refuge under the protection of Merlato, the Austrian
Consul at Damascus. On the demand of Count
Ratti-Menton, he was placed on his trial, but proved
an *alibi ;* on the evening in question, he and his wife
had been visiting an English gentleman, Mr. George
Macson.

Arari's servant now extended his revelations. He
said that he had been present at the murder of the
attendant on the Capuchin. This man had been
bound and put to death by seven Jews, namely, by
the four already mentioned, young Picciotto, Jacob
Abul Afia, and Joseph Menachem Farhi.

The French Consul was dissatisfied that Picciotto
should escape. He demanded of the Austrian Consul
that he should be delivered over to the Mussulman

Court to be tortured like the rest into confession. The Austrian Consul was in a difficult position. He stood alone over against a fanatical Christian and an embittered Mohammedan mob, and in resistance to the Egyptian Government and the representative of France. But he did not hesitate, he absolutely refused to surrender Picciotto. The general excitement was now directed against the Consul; he was subjected to suspicion as a favourer of the murderers, as even incriminated in the murder. His house was surrounded by spies, and every one who entered or left it was an object of mistrust.

All Damascus was in agitation; everyone sought to bring some evidence forward to help on the case against the Jews. According to one account, thirty-three—according to the report of the Austrian Consul, sixty-three Jewish children, of from four to ten years old, were seized, thrown into prison and tortured, to extract information from them as to the whereabouts of their parents and relations—those charged with the murder of the servant, and who had fled and concealed themselves. Those witnesses who had appeared before the court to testify to the innocence of the accused, were arrested, and treated with Oriental barbarity. Because Farach Katasch and Isaac Javoh had declared that they had seen Father Thomas on the day of the murder in another quarter of the town than the Ghetto, they were put to the torture. Isaac Javoh said he had seen Father Thomas on the road to Salachia, two miles from the Jews' quarter, and had there spoken to him. He was racked, and died on the rack.

A boy admitted that he had noticed Father Thomas and his servant in another part of the town. For so saying, he was beaten with such barbarity that he died twenty-four hours after. A Jewish account from Beyrut says: "A Jew dedicated himself to martyrdom for the sanctity of the ever-blessed Name. He went before the Governor, and said to him, 'Is this justice you do? It is a slander that we employ blood for our Paschal bread; and that it is so is known to all civilized governments. You say that the barber, who is a Jew, confessed it. I reply that he did so only under the stress of torture. Very likely the Father was murdered by Christians or by Turks.' The Governor, and the dragoman of the French Consul, Baudin by name, retorted, 'What! you dare to charge the murder on Turks or Christians?' and he was ordered to be beaten and tortured to death. He was barbarously scourged and hideously tormented, and urged all the while to confess the truth. But he cried ever, 'Hear, O Israel! The Lord thy God is one Lord!' and so crying he died."

As the second murder, according to one account, was committed in the house of Meir Farhi, Count Ratti-Menton had the water conduits and drains torn up all round it, and in the drain near them was found a heap of bones, a bit of flesh, and a fragment of leather—according to one account a portion of a shoe, according to that of the Austrian Consul, a portion of a girdle. It had—supposing it to have belonged to the murdered man—been soaking for a month in the drain, nevertheless, the brother of the servant who had disappeared identified it as having belonged to

G

the murdered man! Dr. Massari, Italian physician to Sheriff Pacha, and Dr. Rinaldo, a doctor practising in Damascus, declared that the bones were human remains, but they were examined by Dr. Yograssi, who proved them to be—sheep bones. One may judge from this what reliance can be placed on the assumption that the first collection of bones that were given Christian burial were those of a man, and of Father Thomas. As for the bit of flesh, it was thought to be a piece of liver, but whether of a human being or of a beast was uncertain or unascertained. The Jews' houses were now subjected to search. Count Ratti-Menton swept through the streets at the head of twenty sbirri, entering and ransacking houses at his own caprice, the Jews houses first of all, and then such houses of Christians as were supposed to be open as a harbour of shelter to the persecuted Israelites. Thus one night he rushed not only into the house of, but even the women's bedrooms of a merchant, Aiub, who stood under Austrian protection, hunting after secreted Jews, an outrage, in popular opinion, even in the East.

The Jews charged with the murder of the servant had not been secured. The greater number of the well-to-do Hebrews had fled the town. A hue-and-cry was set up, and the country round was searched. Their families were taken up and tortured into confessing where they were. A German traveller then in Damascus says that the prisons were crowded with unfortunates, and that the pen refuses to detail the torments to which they were subjected to wring from them the information required. The wife of Meir

Farhi and their child were imprisoned, and the child bastinadoed before its mother's eyes. At the three hundredth blow the mother's heart gave way, and she betrayed the hiding-place of her husband. He was seized. The hippopotamus scourge was flourished over his head, and knowing what his fellows had suffered, he confessed himself guilty. Assan Farhi, who was caught in his hiding-place, was imprisoned for a week in the French Consulate, and then delivered over to Turkish justice. Bastinado and the rack convinced him of his guilt, but he found means to despatch from his dungeon a letter to Ibrahim Pacha protesting his innocence.

It is as impossible as it is unnecessary to follow the story of the persecution in all its details. The circumstances have been given by various hands, and as names are not always recorded, it is not always possible to distinguish whether single cases are recorded by different writers with slight variations, or whether they are reporting different incidents in the long story.

The porter of the Jews' quarters, a man of sixty, died under bastinado, to which he was subjected for no other crime than not confessing that he had seen the murdered men enter the Ghetto.

In the meantime, whilst this chase after those accused of the second murder was going on, the seven merchants who had confessed to the murder of the Father had been lying in prison recovering from their wounds and bruises. As they recovered, the sense of their innocence became stronger in them than fear for the future and consideration of the past. They

withdrew their confessions.   Again were they beaten
and tormented.   Thenceforth they remained stedfast.
Two of the seven, David Arari, aged eighty, and
Joseph Laniado, not much younger, died of their
sufferings.   Laniado had protested that he could bring
evidence—the unimpeachable evidence of Christian
merchants at Khasbin—that he had been with them
at the time when it was pretended he had been engaged on the murder.   But he died before these
witnesses reached Damascus.   Then Count Ratti-
Menton pressed for the execution of the rest.

So stood matters when Herr von Hailbronner,
whose report on the whole case is both fullest and
most reliable, for the sequence of events, arrived in
Damascus.   He took pains to collect all the most
authentic information he could on every particular.

Damascus was in the wildest commotion. All classes
of the people were in a condition of fanatic excitement.   The suffering caused by the pressure of the
Egyptian government of Mohamed Ali, the threat
of an Oriental war, the plague which had broken out
in Syria, the quarantine, impeding all trade, were
matters that were thrust into the background by the
all-engrossing story of the murder and the persecution
of the Jews.

The condition of the Hebrews in Damascus became
daily more precarious.   The old antagonism, jealousy
of their riches, hatred caused by extortionate usury,
were roused and armed for revenge.   The barber,
though he had confessed that he was guilty of the
murder, was allowed to go scot-free, because he had
betrayed his confederates.   What an encouragement

was offered to the rabble to indulge in false witness against rich Jews, whose wealth was coveted!

Mohamed Ali's government desired nothing better than the confiscation of their goods. A pack of ruffians sought occasion to extract money out of this persecution by bribes, or to purchase pardon for past offences by denouncing the innocent.

It is well at this point to look a little closer at the French Consul, the Count Ratti-Menton. On him rests the guilt of this iniquitous proceeding, rather than on the Mussulman judges. He had been twice bankrupt when French Consul in Sicily. Then he had been sent as Consul to Tiflis, where his conduct had been so disreputable, that on the representation of the Russian Government he had been recalled. He had then been appointed Consul at Damascus. In spite of all this, and the discredit with which his conduct with regard to the Jews, on account of the murder of Father Thomas, had covered him, his part was warmly taken up by the Ultramontane Press, and the French Government did its utmost to shield him. M. Thiers even warmly defended him. The credit of France was thought to be at stake, and it was deemed advisable to stand by the agent of France, and make out a case for him as best might be.

It is quite possible, it is probable, that he was thoroughly convinced that the Jews were guilty, but that does not justify his mode of procedure. It is possible also that bribes may—as was said—have been offered him by the Jews if he would desist from his persecution, but that he refused these bribes shows that he was either not an unredeemed rascal, or that he conceived he had gone too far to withdraw.

The Turkish and Egyptian authorities acted as always has been and will be their manner, after their nature, and in their own interest. We expect of them nothing else, but that the representative of one of the most enlightened nations of Europe, a man professing himself to be a Christian, and civilized, a member of a noble house, should hound on the ignorant and superstitious, and give rein to all the worst passions of an Oriental rabble, against a helpless and harmless race, that has been oppressed, and ill-treated, and slandered for centuries, is never to be looked over and forgiven. The name of Ratti-Menton must go down branded to posterity; and it is to be regretted that M. Thiers should have allowed his love of his country to so carry him away as to induce him to throw the shield over a man of whose guilt he must have been perfectly aware, having full information in his hands. This shows us to what an extent Gallic vanity will blind the Gallic eye to the plain principles of truth and right.

Ratti-Menton had his agents to assist him—Baudin, chief of his bureau at the Consulate; Francois Salins, a native of Aleppo, who acted as interpreter, spy, and guard to the Consulate; Father Tosti, a French Lazarist, who, according to the Austrian Consul, "seemed to find in this case an opportunity for avenging on the race the death of his Divine Master;" also a Christian Arab, Sehibli Ayub, a man of bad character, who was well received by Ratti-Menton, because of his keenness as spy and readiness as denunciator.

What followed now passes all belief. After that countless poor Jews had been accused, beaten, tortured, and killed, it occurred to the judges that it would be as well to ascertain the motive for the crime. It had been said by those who had confessed that the Pater and his servant had been put to death in order to obtain their blood to mingle with the dough for the Paschal wafer. The disappearance of the two men took place on February 5th. Easter fell that year on April 18th, so that the blood would have to be preserved two months and a half. That was an inconsequence which neither the French Consul nor the Egyptian authorities stooped to consider. Orders were issued that the Talmud and other sacred books of the Jews should be explored to see whether, or rather where in them, the order was given that human blood should be mingled with the Paschal dough. When no such commands could be discovered, it was concluded that the editions presented for examination were purposely falsified.

Now, there were distinct indications pointing in quite another direction, which, if followed, might have elucidated the case, and revealed the actual criminals. But these indications were in no case followed. Wildon Pieritz, an Evangelical Missionary, then in Damascus, as well as the Austrian Consul, agree in stating that three days before the disappearance of Father Thomas he was seen in violent altercation with a Turkish mule-driver, who was heard to swear he would be the death of the priest. The altercation was so violent that the servant of Father Thomas seized the mule-driver by the throat and maltreated

him so that blood flowed—probably from his nose.
Father Thomas lost his temper and cursed the mussulman and his religion. The scene created great
commotion, and a number of Turks were very angry,
amongst them was one, a merchant, Abu Yekhyeh,
who distinguished himself. Wildon Pieritz in a letter to the *Journal de Smyrne* on May 14th, 1840,
declares that when the news of the disappearance of
Father Thomas began to excite attention, this
merchant, Abu Yekhyeh, hanged himself.

We may well inquire how it was that none of these
facts came to be noticed. The answer is to hand.
Every witness that gave evidence which might exculpate the accused Jews, and turn attention in another
direction, was beaten and tortured, consequently, those
who could have revealed the truth were afraid to do so.

Even among the Mohammedans complaints arose
that the French Consul was acting in contravention
to their law, and a feeling gradually grew that a great
injustice was being committed—that the Jews were
innocent. Few dared allow this in the first fever of
popular excitement, but nevertheless it awoke and
spread.

At first the Austrian Consul had been subjected not
to annoyance only, but to danger of life, so violent
had been the popular feeling against him because of
the protection he accorded to one of the accused.
Fortunately Herr Merlato was a man of pluck. He
was an old soldier who had distinguished himself as a
marine officer. He not only resolutely protected young
Picciotto, but he did his utmost to hinder the proceedings of Ratti-Menton; he invoked the assist-

ance of the representatives of the other European Powers, and finally every Consul, except the French, agreed to unite with him in representations to their governments of the iniquitous proceedings of Ratti-Menton, and to use their influence with the Egyptian authorities to obtain the release of the unhappy accused.

The bastinadoes and tortures now ceased. Merlato obtained the release of several of those who were in confinement; and finally the only Jews who remained in prison were the brothers Arari, Mussa Salonichi, and the renegade Abul Afia. Of the supposed murderers of the servant only the brothers Farhi were still held in chains.

Matters were in this condition when the news of what had taken place at Damascus reached Europe and set all the Jews in commotion. Every effort was made by them, in Vienna, Leipzig, Paris and London, indeed in all the great cities of Europe, to convince the public of the absurdity of the charge, and to urge the governments to interfere in behalf of the sufferers.

Finally all the representatives of the European governments at Alexandria, with the exception of the French, remonstrated with Mohamed Ali. They demanded that the investigation should be begun *de novo;* the French Consul-General, M. Cochelet, alone objected. But the action of the Jews of Europe had more influence with Mohamed Pacha than the representations of the Consuls. The house of Rothschild had taken the matter up, and Sir Moses Montefiore started from London, and M. Cremieux from Paris as a diplomatic embassy to the Viceroy at Alexandria to convince him, by such means as is most efficacious to an Oriental despot, of the innocence of the accused at Damascus.

The arguments these delegates employed were so extremely satisfactory to the mind of Mohamed Pacha, that he quashed the charges against the Jews of Damascus, in spite of the vehement protest of M. Cochelet, the representative of France. When the Viceroy issued a firman ordering the incriminated Jews to be discharged as innocent and suffered to abide in peace, M. Cochelet strove in vain to have the firman qualified or altered into a pardon.

Thus ended one of the most scandalous cases of this century. Unfortunate, innocent men were tortured and put to death for a crime that had never been proved. That the two Europeans had been murdered was merely matter of conjecture. No bodies had been found. There was no evidence worth a rush against the accused, and no motive adduced deserving of grave consideration. "What inhumanities were committed during the eight months of this persecution," wrote Herr Von Hailbronner, "will never be wholly known. But it must call up a blush of shame in the face of an European to remember that Europeans provoked, favoured and stimulated it to the last."

Authorities : "Morgenland and Abendland," by Herr Von Hailbronner,—who, as already mentioned, was present in Damascus through part of the time. "Damascia," by C. H. Löwenstein, Rödelheim, 1840. Reports and debates in the English Parliament at the time. The recently published Diaries of Sir Moses Montefiore, 2 vols., 1890 ; his Centenal Biography, 1884, vol. I., p. 213-288 ; and the article summing up the whole case in "Der Neue Pitaval," by Dr. J. C. Hitzig and Dr. W. Häring, 1857, Vol. I.

Some Accusations against Jews.

THE story just given of the atrocious treatment of the Jews of Damascus on a false accusation naturally leads to a brief sketch of their treatment in the Middle Ages on similar charges. Not, indeed, that we can deal with all of the outrages committed on the sons of Abraham, Isaac, and Jacob—that would require volumes—but only notice some of those which they have had to suffer on the same or analogous false charges.

These false accusations range under three heads :—

1. They have been charged with poisoning the wells when there has been an outbreak of plague and malignant fever.

2. They have been charged with stealing the Host and with stabbing it.

3. Lastly, with having committed murders in order to possess themselves of Christian blood, to mingle with the dough wherewith to make their Paschal cakes.

We will leave the first case on one side altogether, and as we have already considered one instance—not by any means the last case of such an accusation levied against them in Europe—we will take it before we come to the instances of their being accused of stealing the Host.

But *why* should they be supposed to require

Christian blood? One theory was that by common participation in it, the Jewish community was closer bound together; another, that it had a salutary medicinal effect. That is to say, having made up their minds in the Middle Ages that Jews did sacrifice human beings and drink their blood, they beat about for the explanation, and caught at any wild theory that was proposed.[1]

John Dubravius in his Bohemian History, under the year 1305, relates: "On Good Friday the Jews committed an atrocious crime against a Christian man, for they stretched him naked to a cross in a concealed place, and then, standing round, spat on him, beat him, and did all they could to him which is recorded of their having done to Christ. This atrocious act was avenged by the people of Prague upon the Jews, with newly-invented punishments, and of their property that was confiscated, a monument was erected." But there were cases earlier than this. Perhaps the earliest is that of S. William of Norwich, in 1144; next, S. Richard of Paris, 1179; then S. Henry of Weissemburg, in Alsace, in 1220; then S. Hugh of Lincoln, in 1255, the case of which is recorded by Matthew Paris. A woman at Lincoln lost her son, a child eight years old. He was found in a well near a Jew's house. The Jew was arrested, and promised his life if he would accuse his brethren of the murder. He did so, but was hanged never-

---

[1] Antonius Bonfinius: Rer. Hungaricarum Dec., v. l., 3, gives *four* reasons. Thomas Cantipratensis, Lib. II., c. 29, gives another and preposterous one, not to be quoted even in Latin.

theless. On this accusation ninety-two of the richest
Jews in Lincoln were arrested, their goods seized to
replenish the exhausted Royal exchequer ; eighteen
were hung forthwith, the rest were reserved in the
Tower of London for a similar fate, but escaped
through . the intervention of the Franciscans, who,
says Matthew Paris, were bribed by the Jews of
England to obtain their release. On May 15th, 1256,
thirty-five of the wretched Jews were released. We
are not told what became of the remaining thirty-nine,
whether they had been discharged as innocent, or
died in prison. The story of little Hugh has been
charmingly told in Chaucer's Canterbury Tales.

A girl of seven years was found murdered at
Pforzheim, in 1271 ; the Jews were accused, mobbed,
maltreated, and executed. In 1286, a boy, name
unknown, disappeared in Munich, with the same
results to the Jews. In 1292, a boy of nine, at
Constance—same results. In 1303 "the perfidious
Jews, accustomed to the shedding of Christian
blood," says Siffrid, priest of Meisen, in 1307,
" cruelly murdered a certain scholar, named Conrad,
son of a knight of Weissensee, in Thuringia, after that
they had tortured him, cut all his sinews, and opened
his veins. This took place before Easter. The
Almighty, who is glorious in His Saints, however did
not suffer the murder of the innocent boy to remain
concealed, but destroyed the murderers, and adorned
the martyrdom of their innocent victim with miracles.
For when the said Jews had taken the body of the
lad to many places in Thuringia to bury it secretly,
by God's disposition they were always foiled in their

attempt to make away with it.   Wherefore, returning
to Weissensee, they hung it to a vine.   Then the
truth having been revealed, the soldiers rushed out of
the castle, and the citizens rose together with the
common people, headed by Frederick, son of Albert
Landgrave of Thuringia, and killed the Jews tumultuously."

The story of S. Werner, the boy murdered by the
Jews in 1287, at Wesel, on the Rhine, and buried at
Bacharach, is well known.   The lovely chapel erected
over his body is now a ruin.   But Werner was not
the only boy martyred by the Jews on the Rhine.
Another was S. Johanettus of Siegburg.

S. Andrew of Heiligenwasser, near Innsbrück, is
another case, in 1462; S. Ludwig of Ravensburg, in
1429, again another.   Six boys were said to have
been murdered by Jews at Ratisbon, in 1486; and
several cases come to us out of Spanish history.
In Poland, in 1598, in the village of Swinarzew, near
Lositz, lived a peasant, Matthias Petrenioff, with his
wife, Anna.   They had several children, among them
a boy named Adalbert.   One day in Holy Week the
boy was in the fields ploughing with his father.   In
the evening he was sent home, but instead of going
home directly, he turned aside to visit the village of
Woznik, in which lived a Jew, Mark, who owned a
pawnshop, and had some mills.   The son of Mark,
named Aaron, and the son-in-law, Isaac, overtook the
boy as they were returning to Woznik in their cart
and took him up into it.

As the child did not return home, his father went
in search of him, and hearing that he had been seen

in the cart between the two Jews, he went to the
house of Mark and inquired for him. Mark's wife
said she had not seen him. The peasant now became frightened. He remembered the stories that
floated about concerning the murder of Christian
children by Jews, and concluded that his boy had
been put to death by Mark and his co-religionists.
At length the body of the child was discovered in a
pond, probably gnawed by rats,—but the marks on
the body were at once supposed to be due to the
weapons of the Jews. Immense excitement reigned
in the district, and finally two servants of the Jews,
both Christians, one Athanasia, belonging to the
Greek Church, and another, Christina, a Latin, confessed that their masters had murdered the boy.
He had been concealed in a cellar till the eve of the
Passover, when the chief Jews of the district had been
assembled, and the boy had been bled to death in
their presence. The blood was put into small phials
and each Jew provided with one at least. This led to
a general arrest of the Jews, when the rack produced
the requisite confession. Isaac, son-in-law of Mark,
in whose house the butchery was said to have taken
place, declared under torture that the Jews partook of
the blood of Christians in bread, and also in wine, but
he professed to be unable to account for the custom.
Filled, however, with remorse for having thus falsely
accused his people and his relatives, he hung himself
in prison. Mark and Aaron were condemned to be
torn to pieces alive ; and, of course, the usual spoliation
ensued. We have the account of this atrocious
judicial murder from the pen of a Jesuit, Szembeck,

who extracted the particulars from the acts of the court of Lublin, in which the case was tried, and from those drawn up by order of the bishop of the diocese of Luz, in which the murder occurred, and who obtained or sanctioned a canonization of the boy-martyr.

Another still more famous case is that of S. Simeon, of Trent, in 1475, very full details of which are given in the Acta Sanctorum of the Bollandists, as the victim was formally canonized by Pope Benedict XIV., and the Roman Martyrology asserts the murder by the Jews in these terms :—

"At Trent (on March 24th) the martyrdom of S. Simeon, a little child, cruelly slain by the Jews, who was glorified afterwards by several miracles."

The story as told and approved at the canonization was as follows : On Tuesday, in Holy Week, 1475, the Jews met to prepare for the approaching Passover, in the house of one of their number, named Samuel ; and it was agreed between three of them, Samuel, Tobias, and Angelus, that a child should be crucified, as an act of revenge against the Christians who cruelly maltreated them. Their difficulty, however, was how to get one. Samuel sounded his servant Lazarus, and attempted to bribe him into procuring one, but the suggestion so scared the fellow that he ran away. On the Thursday, Tobias undertook to get the boy, and going out in the evening, whilst the people were in church, he prowled about till he found a child sitting on the threshold of his father's door, aged twenty-nine months, and named Simeon. The Jew began to coax the little fellow to follow him, and the boy, after being lured away, was led to the house of Samuel, whence during the night he was conveyed to the synagogue, where he was bled to death, and his body pierced with awls.

All Friday the parents sought their son, but found him not. The Jews, alarmed at the proceedings of the magistrates, who had taken the matter up, consulted together what was to be done. It was resolved to put the body back into its clothes and throw it into the stream that ran under Samuel's window, but which was there crossed by a grating. Tobias was to go to the bishop and magistrates and inform them that a child's body was entangled in the grate. This was done. Thereupon John de Salis, the bishop, and James de Sporo, the governor, went to see the spot, had the body removed, and conveyed to the cathedral. As, according to popular superstition, blood was supposed to flow from the wound when a murderer drew near, the officers of justice were cautioned to observe the crowds as they passed.

It was declared that blood exuded as Tobias approached. On the strength of this, the house of Samuel and the synagogue were examined, and it is asserted that blood and other traces of the butchery were found. The most eminent physicians were called to investigate the condition of the corpse, and they pronounced that the child had been strangled, and that the wounds were due to stabs. The popular voice now accusing the Jews, the magistrates seized on them and threw them into prison, and on the accusation of a renegade more than five of the Jews were sentenced to death. They were broken on the

H

wheel and then burnt. The body of the child is enshrined at Trent, and a basin of the blood preserved as a relic in the cathedral.

This must suffice for instances of accusations of murder for religious purposes brought against the Jews. In every case false. Another charge brought against them was Sacrilege. Fleury in his Ecclesiastical History gives one instance. " In the little town of Pulca, in Passau, a layman found a bloody Host before the house of a Jew, lying in the street upon some straw. The people thought that this Host was consecrated, and washed it and took it to the priest, that it might be taken to the church, where a crowd of devotees assembled, concluding that the blood had flowed miraculously from wounds dealt it by the Jews. On this supposition, and without any other examination, or any other judicial procedure, the Christians fell on the Jews, and killed several of them ; but wiser heads judged that this was rather for the sake of pillage than to avenge a sacrilege. This conjecture was justified by a similar event, that took place a little while before at Neuburg, in the same diocese, where a certain clerk placed an unconsecrated Host steeped in blood in a church, but confessed afterwards before the bishop that he had dipped this Host in blood for the purpose of raising hostility against the Jews." [1]

In 1290, a Jew named Jonathan was accused in Paris of having thrown a Host into the Seine. It floated. Then he stabbed it with his knife, and blood flowed. The Jew was burnt alive, and the

[1] Fleury, Hist. Eccl., vi. p. 110.

people clamored for a general persecution of the Hebrews.

In Bavaria, in 1337, at Dechendorf, some Hosts were discovered which the Jews had stabbed. The unhappy Hebrews were burnt alive.

In 1326, a Jew convert, a favourite of Count William the Good, of Flanders, was accused of having struck an image of the Madonna, which thereupon bled. The Jew was tortured, but denied the accusation. Then he was challenged to a duel by a fanatic. He, wholly unaccustomed to the use of weapons, succumbed. That sufficed to prove his guilt. He was burnt.

In 1351, a Jew convert was accused, at Brussels, of having pretended, on three occasions, to communicate, in order that he might send the Hosts to his brethren at Cologne, who stabbed them, and blood flowed.

The traveller who has been in Brussels must certainly have noticed the painted windows all down the nave of S. Gudule, in the side aisles, to left and right. They represent, in glowing colours, the story of the miraculous Hosts preserved in the chancel to the north of the choir, where seven red lamps burn perpetually before them.

The story is as follows: In 1370, a rich Jew of Enghien bribed a converted Hebrew, named John of Louvain, for 60 pieces of gold, to steal for him some Hosts from the Chapel of S. Catherine. Hardly, however, had the Jew, Jonathan, received the wafers, before he was attacked by robbers and murdered. His wife, alarmed, and thinking that his death was due to the sacrilege, resolved to get rid of the wafers. It may have been remarked in the stories of murders by Jews, that they were represented as finding great difficulty in getting rid of the dead bodies. In these stories of sacrilege, no less difficulty was encountered in causing the disappearance of the Hosts. Moreover, the Jews invariably proceeded in the most roundabout and clumsy way, inviting discovery. The widow of the murdered Jonathan conveyed the Hosts to the synagogue at Brussels. There, on Good Friday, the Jews took advantage of the Hosts to stab them with their knives, in mockery of Christ and the Christian religion. But blood squirted from the transfixed wafers. In terror, they also resolved to get rid of the miraculous Hosts, and found no better means of so doing than bribing a renegade Jewess, named Catharine, to carry them to Cologne. They promised her twenty pieces of gold for her pains. She took the Hosts, but, troubled in conscience, revealed what she had undertaken to her confessor. The ecclesiastical authorities were informed, Catherine was arrested, imprisoned, and confessed. All the Jews dwelling in Brussels were taken up and tortured; but in spite of all torture refused to acknowledge their guilt. However, a chaplain of the prince, a man named Jean Morelli, pretended to have overheard a converted Jew say, "Why do not these dogs make a clean breast? They know that they are guilty." This man was that John of Louvain who had procured the theft of the wafers. He was seized. He at once confessed his participation in the crime. That sufficed. All the accused, he himself included, were condemned to death. They were executed with hideous cruelty; after having had their flesh torn off by red-hot pinchers, they were attached to stakes and burnt alive, on the Vigil of the Ascension, 1370. Every year a solemn procession of the Saint Sacrement de Miracle commemorates this atrocity, or the miracle which led to it.

Unfortunately, there exists no doubt whatever as to the horrible execution of the Jews on the false charge of having stolen the Hosts, but there is very good reason for disbelieving altogether the story of the miracle of the bleeding Hosts.

Now, it is somewhat remarkable that not a word is said about this miracle before 1435, that is to say, for 65 years, by any writer of the period and of the country. The very first mention of it is found in a Papal bull of that date, addressed to the Dean and Chapter of S. Gudule, relative to a petition made by them that, as they wanted money for the erection of a chapel to contain these Hosts, indulgences might be granted to those who would contribute thereto. The Pope granted their request.

Now, it so happens that the official archives at Brussels contains two documents of the date, 1370, relative to this trial. The first of these is the register of the accounts of the receiver-general of the Duke of Brabant. In that are the items of expenditure for the burning of these Jews, a receipt, and the text is as follows: "Item, recepta de bonis dictorum judeorum, postquam combusti fuerant circa ascensionem Domini lxx, quæ defamata fuerant de sacramentis punicè et furtivè acceptis." That is to say, that a certain sum flowed into the Duke's exchequer from the goods of the Jews, burnt for having "guiltily and furtively obtained the Hosts." "Punice" is an odd word, but its signification is clear enough. Now, in 1581, on May 1st, the magistrates of Brussels forbade the exercise of the Catholic religion, in a proclamation in which, when mentioning certain frauds committed by the Roman Church, they speak of "The Sacrament of the Miracle, which," say they, "by documentary evidence can be proved never to have bled nor to have been stabbed." No question—they had seen this entry in which no mention is made of the stabbing—no allusion made to the bleeding. Moreover, in the same archives is the contemporary episcopal letter addressed to the Dean of S. Gudule on the subject of these Hosts. In this document there is no mention made by the bishop of the stabbing or of the miracle. It is stated that the Hosts were obtained by the Jews in order that they might insult and outrage them. It is curious that the letter should not specify their having done this, and done it effectually, with their knives and daggers. Most assuredly, also, had there been any suspicion of a miracle, the bishop would have referred to it in the letter relative to the custody of these very Hosts.

After the whole fable of the stabbing and bleeding had grown up, no doubt applied to these Hosts from a preceding case of accusation against Jews, that of 1351, less than thirty years before, it was thought advisable, if not necessary, to produce some evidence in favour of the story ; but as no such evidence was obtainable, it was manufactured in a very ingenious manner. The entry in the register of accounts was published by the Père Ydens, after a notary had been required to collate the text. This notary—his name was Van Asbroek—gave his testimony that he had made an exact and literal transcript of the entry. What he and the Père Ydens gave as their exact, literal transcript was "recepta de bonis dictorum Judœorum . . . . quæ defamata fuerant de sacramen*to puncto* et furtive accep*to*." Ingenious, but disingenuous. In the first place they altered "sacramentis" from plural into singular, and then, the adverb *punicè*, "guiltily," into *puncto*, stabbed.

Subsequently, Father Ydens and his notary have been quoted and requoted as authoritative witnesses. However, the document is now in the Archives at Brussels, and has been lithographed from a photograph for the examination of such as have not the means of obtaining access to the original.[1] The last jubilee of this apocryphal miracle was celebrated at Brussels in July, 1870.

Le Jubilé d'un faux Miracle (extrait de la Revue de Belgique), Bruxelles, 1870.

The Coburg Mausoleum.

AT the east end of the garden of the Ducal residence of Coburg is a small, tastefully constructed mausoleum, adorned with allegorical subjects, in which are laid the remains of the deceased dukes. Near the mausoleum rise a stately oak, a clump of rhododendron, a cluster of acacias, and a group of yews and weeping-willows.

The mausoleum is hidden from the palace by a plantation of young pines.

The Castle of Coburg is one of the most interesting and best preserved in Germany. It stands on a height above the little town, and contains much rich wood-carving of the 15th and 16th centuries. Below the height, but a little above the town, is the more modern residence of the Dukes Ehrenburg, erected in 1626 by the Italian architect Bonallisso, and finished in 1693. It has that character of perverse revolt against picturesqueness that marked all the edifices of the period. It has been restored, not in the best style, at the worst possible epoch, 1816. The south front remains least altered; it is adorned with a handsome gateway, over which is the inscription, " Fried ernährt, Unfried verzehrt "—not easily rendered in English :—

" Peace doth cherish—
Strife makes perish."

The princes of Coburg by their worth and kindly behaviour have for a century drawn to them the hearts of their subjects, and hardly a princely house in Germany is, and has been, more respected and loved.

Duke Franz died shortly after the battle of Jena. During his reign, by his thrift, geniality, and love of justice he had won to his person the affections of his people, though they resented the despotic character of his government under his Minister Kretschmann. He was twice married, but left issue only by the second wife, Augusta, a princess of Reuss, who inherited the piety and virtues which seem to be inrooted in that worthy house.

Only a few weeks after her return from Brussels, where she had seen her son, recently crowned King of the Belgians, did the Duchess Augusta of Sachsen-Coburg die in her seventy-sixth year, November 16th, 1831. The admiration and love this admirable princess had inspired drew crowds to visit the body, as it lay in state in the residence at Coburg, prior to the funeral, which took place on the 19th, before day-break, by the light of torches. The funeral was attended by men and women of all classes eager to express their attachment to the deceased, and respect for the family. A great deal was said, and fabled, concerning this funeral. It was told and believed that the Dowager Duchess had been laid in the family vault adorned with her diamond rings and richest necklaces. She was the mother of kings, and the vulgar believed that every royal and princely house with which she was allied had contributed some jewel towards the decoration of her body.

Her eldest son, Ernst I., succeeded his father in

1806 as Duke of Sachsen-Coburg-Saalfeld, and in 1826 became Duke of Sachsen-Coburg-Gotha. The second son, Ferdinand, married in 1816 the wealthiest heiress of Hungary, the Princess Rohary, and his son, Ferdinand, became in 1836 King of Portugal, and his grandson, Ferdinand, by his second son, is the present reigning Prince of Bulgaria.

The third son, Leopold, married Charlotte, only daughter of George IV. of England, and in 1831 became King of the Belgians. Of the five daughters, the eldest was married to the Grand-Duke Constantine of Russia, the second married the Duke of Kent, in 1818, and was the mother of our Queen, Victoria. The third married Duke Alexander of Würtemberg.

Among those who were present at the funeral of the Duchess Augusta was a Bavarian, named Andreas Stubenrauch, an artisan then at Coburg. He was the son of an armourer, followed his father's profession, and had settled at Coburg as locksmith. He was a peculiarly ugly man, with low but broad brow, dark-brown bristly hair, heavy eyebrows and small cunning grey eyes. His nose was a snub, very broad with huge nostrils, his complexion was pale ; he had a large mouth, and big drooping underlip. His short stature, his lack of proportion in build, and his uncomely features, gave him the appearance of a half-witted man. But though he was not clever he was by no means a fool. His character was in accordance with his apperance. He was a sullen, ill-conditioned, in-temperate man.

Stubenrauch had been one of the crowd that had passed by the bed on which the Duchess lay in state, and had cast covetous eyes at the jewellery with which the body was adorned. He had also attended the funeral, and had come to the conclusion that the Duchess was buried with all the precious articles he had noticed about her, as exposed to view before the burial, and with a great deal more, which popular gossip asserted to have been laid in the coffin with her.

The thought of all this waste of wealth clung to his mind, and Stubenrauch resolved to enter the mausoleum and rob the body. The position of the vault suited his plans, far removed and concealed from the palace, and he made little account of locks and bars, which were likely to prove small hindrances to an accomplished locksmith.

To carry his plan into execution, he resolved on choosing the night of August 18-19, 1832. On this evening he sat drinking in a low tavern till 10 o'clock, when he left, returned to his lodgings, where he collected the tools he believed he would require, a candle and flint and steel, and then betook himself to the mausoleum.

In the first place, he found it necessary to climb over a wall of boards that encircled the portion of the grounds where was the mausoleum, and then, when he stood before the building, he found that to effect an entrance would take him more time and give him more work than he had anticipated.

The mausoleum was closed by an iron gate formed of strong bars eight feet high, radiating from a centre in a sort of semicircle and armed with sharp spikes. He found it impossible to open the lock, and he was

therefore obliged to climb over the gate, regardless of
the danger of tearing himself on the barbs. There
was but a small space between the spikes and the
arch of the entrance, but through this he managed to
squeeze his way, and so reach the interior of the building, without doing himself any injury.

Here he found a double stout oaken door in the floor
that gave access to the vault. The two valves were
so closely dovetailed into one another and fitted so
exactly, that he found the utmost difficulty in getting
a tool between them. He tried his false keys in vain
on the lock, and for a long time his efforts to prise
the lock open with a lever were equally futile. At
length by means of a wedge he succeeded in breaking a
way through the junction of the doors, into which he
could insert a bar, and then he heaved at one valve
with all his might, throwing his weight on the lever.
It took him fully an hour before he could break open
the door. Midnight struck as the valve, grating on
its hinges, was thrown back. But now a new and unexpected difficulty presented itself. There was no
flight of steps descending into the vault, as he had
anticipated, and he did not know the depth of the
lower pavement from where he stooped, and he was
afraid to light a candle and let it down to explore
the distance.

But Stubenrauch was not a man to be dismayed by
difficulties. He climbed back over the iron-spiked
gates into the open air, and sought out a long and
stout pole, with which to sound the depth, so as to
know what measures he was to take to descend.
Going into the Ducal orchard, he pulled up a pole to

which a fruit tree was tied, and dragged it to the mausoleum, and with considerable difficulty got it through the gateway, which he again surmounted with caution and without injury to himself.

Then, leaning over the opening, holding the pole in both hands, he endeavoured to feel the depth of the vault. In so doing he lost his balance, and the weight of the pole dragged him down, and he fell between two coffins some twelve feet below the floor of the upper chamber. There he lay for some little while unconscious, stunned by his fall. When he came to himself, he sat up, felt about with his hands to ascertain where he was, and considered what next should be done.

Without a moment's thought as to how he was to escape from his position, about the possibility of which he was not in the smallest doubt, knowing as he did his own agility and readiness with expedients, he set to work to accomplish his undertaking. With composure Stubenrauch now struck a light and kindled the candle. When he had done this, he examined the interior of the vault, and the coffins he found there, so as to select the right one. Those of the Duchess Augusta and her husband the late Duke were very much alike, so much so that the ruffian had some difficulty in deciding which was the right one. He chose, however, correctly that which seemed freshest, and he tore off it the black cover. Under this he found the coffin very solid, fastened by two locks, which were so rusted that his tools would not turn in them. He had not his iron bar and other implements with him now; they were above on the floor of the upper chamber. With great difficulty he succeeded at length in breaking one of the hinges, and he was then able to snap the lower lock, whereas that at the top resisted all his efforts. However, the broken hinge and lock enabled him to lift the lid sufficiently for him to look inside. Now he hoped to be able to insert his hand, and remove all the jewellery he supposed was laid there with the dead lady. To his grievous disappointment he saw nothing save the fading remains of the Duchess, covered with a glimmering white mould, that seemed to him to be phosphorescent. The body was in black velvet, the white luminous hands crossed over the breast. Stubenrauch was not the man to feel either respect for the dead or fear of aught supernatural. With both hands he sustained the heavy lid of the coffin as he peered in, and the necessity for using both to support the weight prevented his profane hand from being laid on the remains of an august and pious princess. Stubenrauch did indeed try more than once to sustain the lid with one hand, that he might grope with the other for the treasures he fancied must be concealed there, but the moment he removed one hand the lid crashed down.

Disappointed in his expectations, Stubenrauch now replaced the cover, and began to consider how he might escape. But now—and now only—did he discover that it was not possible for him to get out of the vault into which he had fallen. The pole on which he had placed his confidence was too short to reach to the opening above. Every effort made by Stubenrauch to scramble out failed. He was caught in a trap—and what a trap! Nemesis had fallen on the ruffian at

once, on the scene of his crime, and condemned him
to betray himself.

Although now for the first time deadly fear came
over him, as he afterward asserted, it was fear because
he anticipated punishment from men, not any dread
of the wrath of the spirits of those into whose domain
he had entered. When he had convinced himself
that escape was quite impossible, he submitted to the
inevitable, lay down between the two coffins and tried
to go to sleep ; but, as he himself admitted, he was
not able to sleep soundly.

Morning broke—it was Sunday, and a special
festival at Coburg, for it was the twenty-fifth anniver-
sary of the accession of the Duke, so that the town
was in lively commotion, and park and palace were
also in a stir.

Stubenrauch sat up and waited in hopes of hearing
someone draw near who could release him. About
9 o'clock in the morning he heard steps on the gravel,
and at once began to shout for assistance.

The person who had approached ran away in
alarm, declaring that strange and unearthly noises
issued from the Ducal mausoleum. The guard was
apprised, but would not at first believe the report.
At length one of the sentinels was despatched to the
spot, and he returned speedily with the tidings that
there certainly was a man in the vault. He had
peered through the grating at the entrance and had
seen the door broken open and a crowbar and other
articles lying about.

The gate was now opened, and Stubenrauch removed in the midst of an assembled crowd of angry

and dismayed spectators. He was removed to prison, tried, and condemned to eighteen months with hard labour.

That is not the end of the story. After his discharge, Stubenrauch never settled into regular work. In 1836 he was taken up for theft, and again on the same charge in 1844. In the year 1854 he was discovered dead in a little wood near his home; between the fingers of his right hand was a pinch of snuff, and in his left hand a pistol with which he had blown out his own brains. In his pockets were found a purse and a brandy bottle, both empty.

Jean Aymon.

JEAN AYMON was born in Dauphiné, in 1661, of Catholic parents. He studied in the college of Grenoble. His family, loving him, neglected nothing which might contribute to the improvement of his mind, and the professors of Grenoble laboured to perfect their intelligent pupil in mathematics, languages, and history.

From Grenoble, Aymon betook himself to Turin, where he studied theology and philosophy. But there was one thing neither parents nor professors were able to implant in the young man—a conscience. He was thoroughly well versed in all the intricacies of moral theology and the subtleties of the school-men; he regarded crime and sin as something deadly indeed, but deadly only to other persons. Theft was a mortal sin to every one but himself. Truth was a virtue to be strictly inculcated, but not to be practised in his own case.

His parents, thinking he would grow out of this obliquity of moral vision, persisted in their scheme of education for the lad—probably the very worst which, with his peculiar bent of mind, they could have chosen for him. Having finished his studies at Turin, his evil star led him to Rome, where his talents soon drew attention to him, and Hercules de Berzet, Bishop of Saint Jean de Maurienne, in Savoy, named him chaplain, and had him ordained, by brief of Innocent XI., before the age fixed by the Council of Trent, "because of the probity of his life, his virtues and other merits ! "—such were the reasons.

Shortly after his installation as chaplain to the bishop, his patron entrusted him with a delicate case. De Berzet had lately been deep in an intrigue to obtain a cardinal's hat. He had been disappointed, and he was either bent on revenge, or, perhaps, hoped to frighten the Pope into giving him that which he had solicited in vain. He set to work, raking up all the scandal of the Papal household, and acting the spy upon all the movements of the familiars of the court. After a very little while, this worthy prelate had succeeded in gathering together enough material to make all the ears in Europe tingle, and this was put into the hands of the young priest to work into form for publication.

As Aymon looked through these scandalous memoirs, he made his own reflections. "The publication of this will raise a storm, undoubtedly ; but the first who will perish in it will be my patron, and all who sail in his boat." Aymon noticed that M. de Camus, Bishop of Grenoble, was most compromised by the papers in his hands, and would be most interested in their suppression. Aymon, without hesitation, tied up the bundle, put it in his pocket, and presented himself before the bishop, ready to make them over to him for a consideration. He was well received, as may be supposed, and in return for the papers was given a living in the diocese. But this did not satisfy the restless spirit of Aymon ; he had

imbibed a taste for intrigue, and there was no place
like the Eternal City for indulging this taste. He
was, moreover, dissatisfied with his benefice, and
expected greater rewards for the service he had done
to the Church. Innocent XI. received him well, and
in 1687 appointed him his protonotary. Further he
did not advance. At the Papal Court he made his
observations, and whether it was that he was felt to
be somewhat of a spy, or through some intrigue, his
star began to set, when Aymon, too well aware that
a falling man may sink very low, suddenly fled from
Rome, crossed the border into Switzerland, and in a
few days was a convert to the straitest sect of the
Calvinists. But the Swiss are poor, and their ministers are in comfortable, though not lucrative positions.
Holland was the paradise of Calvinism, and to Holland Aymon repaired. Here he obtained a cure of
importance, and married a lady of rank.

But even now, Aymon was not satisfied. Among
the Protestants of the Low Countries there are no
bishops, and no man can soar higher than the pulpit
of a parish church. Aymon was convinced that he
had climbed as high as he could in the Church of
Calvin, and that he had a soul for something higher
still. His next step was extraordinary enough. He
wrote in December, 1705, to M. Clement, of the
Bibliothèque du Roi, at Paris, stating that he had in
his possession the " Herbal " of the celebrated Paul
Hermann, in forty folio volumes, and that he offered
it to the King for 3200 livres, a trifle over what it had
cost him. He added that he was a renegade priest, who
had sought rest in Protestantism, but had found none

—nay! he had discovered it to be a hot-bed of every
kind of vice, and that he yearned for the Church of
his baptism.   He hinted that he had made some discoveries of the utmost political importance, and that
he would communicate them to the King if he could
be provided with a passport.

Clement made inquiries of the superintendent of
the Jardin-Royal as to the expediency of purchasing
the " Herbal," and received a reply in the negative.

Aymon wrote again, saying little more of the
" Herbal," and developing his schemes.   He said that
he had State secrets to confide to the Ministers of the
Crown, besides which, he volunteered to compose a
large and important work on the state of Protestantism, " full of proofs so authentic, and so numerous,
that, if given to the light of day, as I purpose, it
would probably not only restrain all those who meditate seceding from the Roman Church, but also would
persuade all those, who are not blinded by their
passions, to return to the Catholic faith."

Clement, uncertain what to answer, showed these
letters to some clergy of his acquaintance, and, acting
on their advice, he presented them to M. de Pontchartrain, who communicated the proposal of Aymon
to the King.

A passport was immediately granted, and Aymon
left Holland, assuring his congregation that he was
going for a little while to Constantinople on important
matters of religion.

On his arrival in Paris, he presented himself before
M. Clement, to assure him of the fervour of his zeal
and the earnestness of his conversion.   Clement

received him cordially, and took him to Versailles to
see M. de Pontchartrain. In this interview Aymon
made great promises of being serviceable to the
Church and to the State, by the revelations he was
about to make ; but M. de Pontchartrain treated his
protestations very lightly, and handed him over to
the Cardinal de Noailles, Archbishop of Paris.

The conference with the cardinal was long. The
archbishop addressed a homily to the repentant
sinner, who listened with hands crossed on his breast,
his eyes bent to earth, and his cheeks suffused with
tears. Aymon sighed forth that he had quitted the
camp of the Amalekites for ever, and that he was
determined to turn against them their own weapons.
Clement, who was present, now stepped forward and
reminded the prelate that Aymon had abandoned a
lucrative situation, at the dictates of conscience, and
that though he might, of course, expect to be re-
warded hereafter, still that remuneration in this life
would not interfere with these future prospects.
The cardinal quite approved of this sentiment, and
promised to see what he could do for the convert.
In the meantime, he wished Aymon to spend a
retreat in some religious house, where he could
meditate on the error of his past life, and expiate, as
far as in him lay, his late delinquencies by rigorous
penances. Aymon thanked the cardinal for thus,
unasked, granting him the request which was upper-
most in his thoughts, and then begged to be allowed
the use of the Royal Library, in which to pursue his
theological researches, and to examine the documents
which were necessary for the execution of his design

of writing a triumphant vindication of the Catholic
faith, and a complete exposure of the abominations
of Protestantism. M. Clement readily accorded this,
at the request of the archbishop, and Jean Aymon
was sent to the seminary of the Missions Etrangères.

Aymon now appeared as a model penitent. He
spent a considerable part of the night in prayer
before the altar, he was punctual in his attendance on
all the public exercises of religion, and his conversation, morning, noon, and night, was on the errors and
disorders of the Calvinist Church. When not engaged in devotions, he was at the library, where he
was indefatigable in his research among manuscripts
which could throw light on the subject upon which
he was engaged. Indeed, his enthusiasm and his
zeal for discoveries wearied the assistants. Clement
himself was occupied upon the catalogues, and was
unable to dance attendance on Aymon; and the
assistants soon learned to regard him as a bookworm
who would keep them on the run, supplying him with
fresh materials, if they did not leave him to do pretty
much what he liked.

Time passed, and Aymon heard no more of the
reward promised by the cardinal. He began to
murmur, and to pour his complaints into the reluctant
ear of Clement, who soon became so tired of hearing
them, that the appearance of Aymon's discontented
face in the library was a signal for him to plead
business and hurry into another apartment. Aymon
declared that he should most positively publish nothing till the king or the cardinal made up to him the

losses he had endured by resigning his post in Holland.

All of a sudden, to Clement's great relief, Aymon disappeared from the library. At first he was satisfied to be freed from him, and made no inquiries; but after a while, hearing that he had also left the Missions Etrangères, he made search for the missing man. He was nowhere to be found.

About this time Aymon's congregation at the Hague were gratified by the return of their pastor, not much bronzed by exposure to the sun of Constantinople, certainly, but with his trunks well-stocked with valuable MSS.

A little while after, M. Clement received the following note from a French agent resident at the Hague :—

"Information is required relative to a certain Aymon, who says that he was chaplain to M. le Cardinal de Camus, and apostolic protonotary. After having lived some while at the Hague, whither he had come from Switzerland, where he had embraced the so-called Reformed religion, he disappeared, and it was ascertained that he was at Paris, whither he had taken an Arabic Koran in MS., which he had stolen from a bookseller at the Hague. He has only lately returned, laden with spoils—thefts, one would rather say, which he must have made at Paris, where he has been spending five or six months in some publicity. . . . He has with him the Acts of the last Council of Jerusalem held by the Greeks on the subject of Transubstantiation, and some other documents supposed to be stolen from the Bibliothèque du Roi. The man has powerful supporters in this country.—March 10, 1707."

The "Council of Jerusalem" was one of the most valuable MSS. of the library—and it was in the hands of Aymon! Clement flew to the cabinet where this inestimable treasure was preserved under lock and key. The cabinet was safely enough locked— but alas! the MS. was no longer there.

A few days after, Clement heard that Aymon had crossed the frontier with several heavy boxes, which, on inquiry, proved to be full of books. What volumes were they? The collections in the Royal Library consisted of 12,500 MSS. The whole had to be gone through. It was soon ascertained that another missing book was the original Italian despatches and letters of Carlo Visconti, Apostolic Nuncio at the Council of Trent.

There was no time to be lost. Clement wrote to the Hague to claim the stolen volumes, and to institute legal proceedings for their recovery, before the collection could be dispersed, and he appointed, with full powers, William de Voys, bookseller at the Hague, to seize the two volumes said to be in the possession of Aymon.

A little while after some more MSS. volumes were missed; they were "The Italian Letters of Prospero S. Croce, Nuncio of Pius IV.," "The Embassy of the Bishop of Angoulême to Rome in 1560-4," "Le Registre des taxes de la Chancellerie Romaine," "Dialogo politico sopra i tumulti di Francia," nine Chinese MSS., a copy of the Gospels of high antiquity in uncial characters, another copy of the Gospels, no less valuable, and the Epistles of S. Paul, also very ancient.

Shortly after this, two Swiss, passing through the Hague, were shown by Aymon some MSS. which agreed with those mentioned as lost from the Royal Library; but besides these, they saw numerous loose sheets, inscribed with letters of gold, and apparently belonging to a MS. of the Bible. Clement had now to go through each MS. in the library and find what had been subtracted from them. Fourteen sheets were gone from the celebrated Bible of S. Denys. From the Pauline Epistles and Apocalypse, a MS. of the seventh century, and one of the most valuable treasures of the library, thirty-five sheets had been cut. There were other losses of less importance.

Whilst Clement was making these discoveries, De Voys brought an action against Aymon for the recovery of the "Council of Jerusalem" and the "Letters of Visconti."

Jean Aymon was not, however, a man to be despoiled of what he had once got. He knew his position perfectly, and he knew the temper of those around him. He was well aware that in order to gain his cause he had only to excite popular passion. His judges were enemies to both France and Catholicism, he had but to make them believe that a plot was formed against him by French Papists for obtaining possession of certain MSS. which he had, and which contained a harvest of scandals and revelations overwhelming to Catholics, and he knew that his cause was safe.

He accordingly published a defence, bearing the

following title :—"Letter of the Sieur Aymon,
Minister of the Holy Gospel, to M. N., Professor of
Theology, to inform people of honour and savants of
the extraordinary frauds of certain Papistical doctors,
and of the vast efforts they are now making, along
with some perverted Protestants, who are striving
together to ruin, by their impostures, the Sieur
Aymon, and to deprive him of several MSS., &c."—
La Haye, dated 1707. Aymon in his pamphlet took
high moral ground. He was not pleading his own
cause. Persecuted, hunted down by Papists, by
enemies of the Republic and of the religion of
Christ, he scorned their calumnies and despised their
rage. He would bow under the storm, he would endure
the persecution cheerfully—for "Blessed are those that
are persecuted for righteousness' sake ;" but higher
interests were at stake than his own fair fame. For
himself he cared little ; for the Protestant faith he
cared everything. If the Papists obtained their suit,
they would wrest from his grasp documents most
compromising to themselves. They would leave no
stone unturned to secure them—they *dare not* leave
them in the hands of a Protestant pastor. Their
story of the " Acts of the Council of Jerusalem " was
false. They said that it had been obtained by Olier
de Nanteuil, Ambassador of France at Constantinople,
in 1672, and had been transmitted to Paris, where
Arnauld had seen and made use of it in preparing his
great work on the " Perpetuity of the Faith." They
further said that the Bibliothèque du Roi had obtained
it in 1696. On the other hand, Aymon asserted that
Arnauld had falsified the text in his treatise on the

"Perpetuity of the Faith," and that, not daring to let his fraud appear, he had never given the MS. to the Royal Library, but had committed it to a Benedictine monk of S. Maur, who had assisted him in falsifying it and making an incorrect translation. This monk would never have surrendered the MS. but that conscience had given him no rest till he had transmitted it to one who would know how to use it aright. He, Aymon, had solemnly promised never to divulge the name of this monk, and even though he and the Protestant cause were to suffer for it, that promise should be held sacred. He challenged the library of the King to prove its claim to the "Council of Jerusalem!" All books in the Bibliothèque du Roi have the seal of the library on them. This volume had three seals—that of the Sultan, that of the Patriarch of Jerusalem, and that of Olier de Nanteuil; but he defied any one to see the library mark on its cover, or on any of its sheets. Aymon wound up his audacious pamphlet by prophesying that the Papists of France would not be satisfied with this claim, but would advance many others, for they knew that in his hands were documents of the utmost importance to them to conceal. Aymon was too clever for Clement: he had mixed up truth with fiction in such a way that the points which Clement had to admit tended to make even those who were not bigoted hesitate about condemning Aymon.

Clement replied to this letter by stating the whole story of Aymon's deception of the Cardinal de Noailles and others. With regard to the "Council of Jerusalem," it was false that it had ever been in a Benedictine monastery. "It is true," he said, "that in the Monastery of S. Germain-des-Prés there are documents relating to the controversies between the Catholics and Greek schismatics, but they are all in French." He produced an attestation, signed by the prior, to the effect that the MS. in question had never been within the walls of his monastery. Clement was obliged to allow that a Benedictine monk had been employed by Arnauld to translate the text of the Council; he even found him out, his name was Michel Foucquère; he was still alive, and the librarian made him affirm in writing that he had restored the volume, on the completion of his translation, to Dom Luc d'Achery. Clement sent a copy of the register in the library, which related how and when the volume had come into the possession of the King. It was true that it bore no library seal, but that was through an oversight.

Aymon wrote a second pamphlet, exposing Clement more completely, pointing out the concessions he was obliged to make, and finally, in indignant terms, hurling back on him the base assertion made to injure him in the eyes of an enlightened Protestant public, that he had ever treated with the government or clergy of Paris relative to a secession to the ranks of Popery. But that he had been to Paris; that he had met the Cardinal Archbishop, he admitted; but on what ground? He had met him and twenty-four prelates besides, gathered in solemn conclave, and had lifted up his voice in testimony against them; had disputed with them, and, with the Word of God in his mouth, had put them all to silence! No idea of his ever leaving the reformed faith had ever entered his head. No! he had been on a mission to the Papists of France, to open their eyes and to convert them.

The news of the robbery had, however, reached the ears of the King, Louis XIV., and he instructed M. de Torcy to demand on the part of Government the restitution of the stolen MSS. M. de Torcy first wrote to a M. Hennequin at Rotterdam, who replied that Aymon had justified himself before the Council of State from the imputations cast upon him. He had been interrogated, not upon the theft committed in Paris, but on his journey to France. Aymon had proved that this expedition had been undertaken with excellent intentions, and had been attended with supreme success, since he had returned laden with manuscripts the publication of which would cause the greatest confusion in the Catholic camp. Hennequin added, that after having been deprived of his stipend, as suspected, on it having been ascertained that he had visited Paris instead of Constantinople, Aymon, having cleared his character, had recovered it. Such was the first result of the intervention of Louis XIV. in this affair.

"The stamp of the Royal Library is on all the MSS., except the 'Council of Jerusalem,'" said Clement. "Let the judges insist on examining the books in the possession of Aymon, and all doubt as to the theft will be removed."

But this the judges refused to do.

It was pretended that Aymon was persecuted; it was the duty of the Netherland Government to protect a subject from persecution. He had made dis-

coveries, and the Catholics dreaded the publication
of his discoveries, therefore a deep plot had been laid
to ruin him.

Aymon had now formed around him a powerful
party, and the Calvinist preachers took his side
unanimously. It was enough to read the titles of the
books stolen to be certain that they contained curious
details on the affairs which agitated Catholics and
Protestants from the sixteenth century.

All that the Dutch authorities cared for now was
to find some excuse for retaining these important
papers, and the inquiry was mainly directed to the
proceedings of Aymon in France. If, as it was
said, he had gone thither to abjure Calvinism and
betray his brethren, he deserved reprimand, but if,
on the other hand, he had penetrated the camp of the
enemy to defy it, and to witness a good confession in
the heart of the foe, he deserved a crown. Clement,
to display Aymon in his true colours, acting on the
advice of the Minister, sent copies of Aymon's letters.
It was not thought that the good faith of the French
administration would be doubted. Aymon swore
that the letters were not his own, but that they had
been fabricated by the Government; and he offered
to stake his head on the truth of what he said. At
the same time he dared De Torcy to produce the
originals.

He had guessed aright: he knew exactly how far
he could go. The Dutch court actually questioned
the good faith of these copies, and demanded the
originals. This, as Aymon had expected, was taken
by De Torcy as an insult, and all further communi-

cation on the subject was abruptly stopped. It was a clever move of Aymon. He inverted by one bold stroke the relative positions of himself and his accuser : the judges at the Hague required M. de Torcy to re-establish his own honour before proceeding with the question of Aymon's culpability. In short, they supposed that one of the Ministers of the Crown, for the sake of ruining a Protestant refugee, had deliberately committed forgery.

The matter was dropped. After a while Aymon published translations of some of the MSS. in his possession, and those who had expected great results were disappointed. In the meantime poor Clement died, heart-broken at the losses of the library committed to his care.

At last the Dutch Government, after the publication of Aymon's book, and after renewed negotiation, restored the "Council of Jerusalem" to the Bibliothèque du Roi. It still bears traces of the mutilations and additions of Aymon.

In 1710, the imposter published the letters of Prospero S. Croce, which he said he had copied in the Vatican, but which he had in fact stolen from the Royal Library. In 1716 he published other stolen papers. Clement was succeeded by the Abbé de Targny, who made vain attempts to recover the lost treasures. The Abbé Bignon succeeded De Targny, and he discovered fresh losses. Aymon had stolen Arabic books as well as Greek and Italian MSS. There was no chance of recovering the lost works through the courts of law, and Bignon contented himself with writing to Holland, England, and Germany to inquire whether any of the MSS. had been bought there.

The Baron von Stocks wrote to say that he had purchased some leaves of the Epistles of S. Paul, some pages of the S. Denis Bible, and an Arabic volume from Aymon for a hundred florins, and that he would return them to the library for that sum. They were recovered in March, 1720.

About the same time Mr. Bentley, librarian to the King of England, announced that some more of the pages from the Epistles of S. Paul were in Lord Harley's library; and that the Duke of Sunderland had purchased various MSS. at the Hague from Aymon. In giving this information to the Abbé Bignon, Mr. Bentley entreated him not to mention the source of his information. M. de Bozé thereupon resolved to visit England and endeavour to recover the MSS. But he was detained by various causes.

In 1729, Earl Middleton offered, on the part of Lord Harley, to return the thirty-four leaves of the Epistles in his possession, asking only in return an acknowledgment sealed with the grand seal. Cardinal Fleury, finding that the Royal signature could hardly be employed for such a purpose, wrote in the King's name a letter to the Earl of Oxford of a flattering nature, and the lost MSS. were restored in September, 1729.

Those in the Sunderland collection have not, I believe, been returned.

And what became of Aymon? In 1718 he inhabited the Chateau of Riswyck. Thence he sent to the brothers Wetstein, publishers at Amsterdam, the proofs of his edition of the letters of Visconti. It appeared in 1719 in two 12mo volumes, under the title " Lettres, Anecdotes, et Mémoires historiques du nonce Visconti, Cardinel Préconisé et Ministre Secret de Pie IV. et de ses créatures." The date of his death is not known.

Authority: Hauréau, J. Singularités Historiques et Litéraires. Paris, 1881.

The Patarines of Milan.

I.

IN the eleventh century, nearly all the clergy in the north of Italy were married.[1] It was the same in Sicily, and it had been the same in Rome,[2] but there the authority and presence of the Popes had sufficed to convert open marriage into secret concubinage.

But concubinage did not in those times mean exactly what it means now. A *concubina* was an *uxor* in an inferior degree; the woman was married in both cases with the ring and religious rite, but the children of the concubine could not inherit legally the possessions of their father. When priests were without wives, concubines were tolerated wives without the legal status of wives, lest on the death of the priest his children should claim and alienate to their own use property belonging to the Church. In noble and royal families it was sometimes the same, lest estates should be dismembered. On the death of a wife, her

[1] " Cuncti fere cum publicis uxoribus . . . . ducebant vitam." " Et ipsi, ut ccrnitur, sicut laici, palam uxores ducunt."—*Andr. Strum.* "*Vit. Arialdi.*" " Quis clericorum non esset uxoratus vel concubinarius ?—*Andr. Strum.* " *Vit. S. Joan. Gualberti.*"

[2] " Cœperunt ipsi presbyteri et diacones laicorum more uxores ducere suscepsosque filios hæredes relinquere. Nonnulli etiam episcoporum verecundâ omni contemptâ, cum uxoribus domo simul in unâ habitare."--*Victor Papa* " *in Dialog.*"

place was occupied by a concubine, and the sons of the latter could not dispute inheritance with the sons of the former. Nor did the Church look sternly on the concubine. In the first Toledian Council a canon was passed with regard to communicating those who had one wife or one concubine ;—such were not to be excluded from the Lord's Table,[1] so long only as each man had but one wife or concubine, and the union was perpetual.

But, though concubinage was universal among the clergy in Italy, at Milan the priests openly, boldly claimed for their wives a position as honourable as could be accorded them ; and they asserted without fear of contradiction that their privilege had received the sanction of the great Ambrose himself. Married bishops had been common, and saintly married prelates not unknown. St. Severus of Ravenna had a wife and daughter, and though the late biographer asserts that he lived with his wife as with a sister after he became a bishop, this statement is probably made to get over an awkward fact.[2] When he was about to

---

[1] "Qui unius mulieris, aut uxoris, aut concubinæ (ut ei placuerit) sit conjunctione contentus."—1st Conc. of Toledo, can. 17. "Hæ quippe, licet nec uxoribus, nec Reginarum decore et privilegiis gaudebant, erant tamen veræ uxores," say the Bollandist Fathers, and add, that it is a vulgar error " Concubinæ appellationem solis iis tribuere, quæ corporis sui usum uni viro commodant, nullo interim legitimo nexu devinctæ."—Acta SS., Jun. T. L. p. 178.

[2] It is the same with St. Gregory, Nyssen, Baronius, Alban, Butler, and other modern Hagiographers make this assertion boldly, but there is not a shadow of evidence, in any ancient authorities for his life, that this was the case.

die, he went to the tomb where his wife and daughter
lay, and had the stone removed.   Then he addressed
them thus—"My dear ones, with whom I lived so
long in love, make room for me, for this is my grave,
and in death we shall not be divided."   Thereupon
he descended into the grave, laid himself between his
wife and daughter, and died.   St. Heribert, Archbishop of Milan, had been a married man with a wife
esteemed for her virtues.[1]

By all accounts, friendly and hostile, the Lombard
priests were married openly, legally, with religious
rite, exchange of ring, and notarial deed.   There was
no shame felt, no supposition entertained that such
was an offence.[2]

How was this inveterate custom to be broken
through?   How the open, honest marriage to be perverted into clandestine union?   For to abolish it
wholly was beyond the power of the Popes and
Councils.   It was in vain to appeal to the bishops,
they sympathised with their clergy.   It was in vain
to invoke the secular arm ; the emperors, the
podestas, supported the parish-priests in their contumacious adherence to immemorial privilege.

[1] "Hic Archiepiscopus habuit uxorem nobilem mulierem ;
quæ donavit dotem suam monasterii S. Dionysii, quæ usque
hodie Uxoria dicitur."—*Calvaneus Fiamma, sub ann.* 1040.

[2] "Nec vos terreat," writes St. Peter Damianl to the wives of
the clergy "quod forte, non dicam fidei, sed perfidiæ vos
annulus subarrhavit ; quod rata et monimenta dotalia notarius
quasi matrimonii jure conscripserit : quod juramentum ad
confirmandam quodammodo conjugii copulam utrinque processit.
Ignorantes quia pro uniuscujusque fugaci voluptate concubitus
mlle annorum negotiantur incendium.'

To carry through the reform on which they were bent, to utterly abolish the marriage of the clergy, the appeal must be made to the people.

In Milan this was practicable, for the laity, at least the lower rabble, were deeply tinged with Patarinism, and bore a grudge against the clergy, who had been foremost in bringing the luckless heretics to the rack and the flames; and one of the most cherished doctrines of the Patarines was the unlawfulness of marriage. What if this anti-connubial prejudice could be enlisted by the strict reformers of the Church, and turned to expend its fury on the clergy who refused to listen to the expostulations of the Holy Father?

The Patarines, whom the Popes were about to enlist in their cause against the Ambrosian clergy, already swarmed in Italy. Of their origin and tenets we must say a word.

It is a curious fact that, instead of Paganism affecting Christianity in the earliest ages of the Church, it was Christianity which affected Paganism, and that not the Greek and Roman idolatry, which was rotten through and through, but the far subtler and more mystical heathenism of Syria, Egypt, Persia, and Mesopotamia. The numerous Gnostic sects, so called from their claim to be the possessors of the true *gnosis*, or knowledge of wisdom, were not, save in the rarest cases, of Christian origin. They were Pagan philosophical schools which had adopted and incorporated various Christian ideas. They worked up Biblical names and notions into the strange new creeds they devised, and, according as they blended more or less of Christian teaching with their own, they drew to themselves disciples of various tempers. Manes, who flourished in the middle of the third century, a temporary and nominal convert to the Gospel, blended some of these elder Gnostic systems with the Persian doctrines of Zoroaster, added to a somewhat larger element of Christianity than his predecessors had chosen to adopt. His doctrines spread and gained an extensive and lasting hold on the minds of men, suppressed repeatedly, but never disappearing wholly, adopting fresh names, emerging in new countries, exhibiting an irrepressible vitality, which confounded the Popes and Churchmen from the third to the tenth centuries.

The tradition of Western Manicheism breaks off about the sixth century; but in the East, under the name of Paulicians, the adherents of Manichean doctrines endured savage persecutions during two whole centuries, and spread, as they fled from the sword and stake in the East, over Europe, entering it in two streams—one by Bulgaria, Servia, and Croatia, to break out in the wild fanaticism of the Taborites under Zisca of the Flail; the other, by way of the sea, inundating northern Italy and Provence. In Piedmont it obtained the name of Patarinism; in Provence, of Albigensianism.

With Oriental Manicheism, the Patarines and Albigenses of the West held that there were two co-equal conflicting principles of good and evil; that matter was eternal, and waged everlasting war against spirit. Their moral life was strict and severe. They fasted, dressed in coarse clothing, and hardly, reluctantly suffered marriage to the weaker, inferior disciples. It was absolutely forbidden to those who were, or esteemed themselves to be, perfect.

Already, in Milan, St. Heribert, the married archbishop, had kindled fires, and cast these denouncers of wedlock into them. In 1031 the heretics held the castle of Montforte, in the diocese of Asti. They were questioned : they declared themselves ready to witness to their faith by their blood. They esteemed virginity, and lived in chastity with their wives, never touched meat, and prayed incessantly. They had their goods in common. Their castle stood a siege. It was at length captured by the Archbishop. In the marketplace were raised a cross on one side, a blazing pyre on the other. The Patarines were brought forth, commanded to cast themselves before the cross, confess themselves to be heretics, or plunge into the flames. A few knelt to the cross ; the greater number covered their faces, rushed into the fire, and were consumed.[1]

St. Augustine, in his book on Heresies, had already described these heretics. He, who had been involved in the fascinating wiles of Manicheism, could not be ignorant of them. He calls them Paternians, or Venustians, and says that they regarded the flesh as the work of the devil—that is, of the evil principle, because made of matter.

In the eleventh century, in Lombardy, they are called Patarines, Patrins, or Cathari. Muratori says that they derived their name from the part of the town of Milan in which they swarmed, near the Con-

[1] Landulf Sen. ii. c. 27.

trada di Patari; but it is more probable that the quarter was called after them.

In 1074 Gregory VII. in solemn conclave will bless them altogether, by name, as the champions of the Holy See, and of the Truth; in 1179 Alexander III. will anathematise them altogether, as heretics meet to be burned. Frederick II., when seeking reconciliation with Honorius III. and Gregory IX., will be never weary of offering hecatombs of Patarines, in token of his orthodoxy.

Ariald, a native of Cuzago, a village near Milan, of ignoble birth, in deacon's orders, was chosen for the dangerous expedient of enlisting the Patarine heretics against the orthodox but relaxed clergy of that city. Milan, said a proverb, was famous for it clergy; Ravenna for its churches. In morals, in learning, in exact observance of their religious duties, the clergy of Milan were prominent among the priests of Lombardy. But they were all married. The Popes could expect no support from the Archbishop, Guido Vavasour; none from the Emperor Henry IV., then a child. Ariald was a woman-hater from infancy, deeply tinged with Patarinism. We are told that even as a little boy the sight of his sisters was odious to him.[1] He began to preach in Milan in 1057, and

---

[1] For authorities we have Andrew of Vallombrosa, *d.* A.D. 1170, a disciple of Ariald. He was a native of Parma. He afterwards went to Florence, where he was mixed up with the riots occasioned by St. John Gualberto in 1063. He joined the Order of Vallombrosa, and became Abbot of Strumi. At least, I judge, and so do the Bollandists, that Andrew of Vallombrosa and Andrew of Strumi are the same.

the populace was at once set on fire [1] by his sermons.
They applauded vociferously his declaration that the
married clergy were no longer to be treated as priests,
but as " the enemies of God, and the deceivers of
souls."

Then up rose from among the mob a clerk named
Landulf, a man of loud voice and vehement gesture,
and offered to join Ariald in his crusade.   The crowd,
or, at least, a part of it, enthusiastically cheered ;
another part of the audience, disapproving, deeming
it an explosion of long-suppressed Manicheism, which
would meet with stern repression, thought it prudent
to withdraw.

A layman of fortune, named Nazarius, offered his
substance to advance the cause, and his house as a
harbour for its apostles.

The sermon was followed by a tumult.   The whole
city was in an uproar, and the married clergy were
threatened or maltreated by the mob.   Guido Vavasour de Velati, the Archbishop, was obliged to interfere.   He summoned Ariald and Landulf before him,
and remonstrated.   " It is unseemly for a priest to
denounce priests.   It is impolitic for him to stir up
tumult against his brethren.   Let not brothers condemn brothers, for whose salvation Christ died."
Then turning to Landulf, " Why do not you return to
your own wife and children whom you have deserted,
and live with them as heretofore, and set an example
of peace and order ?   Cast the beam out of thine
own eye, before thou pluckest motes out of the eyes
of thy brethren.   If they have done wrong, reprove

[1] " Plebs fere universa sic est accensa."

them privately, but do not storm against them before all the people." He concluded by affirming the lawfulness of priests marrying, and insisted on the cessation of the contest.[1] Ariald obstinately refused to desist. "Private expostulation is in vain. As for obstinate disorders you apply fire and steel, so for this abuse we must have recourse to desperate remedies."

He left the Archbishop to renew his appeals to the people. But dreading lest Guido should use force to restrain him, Ariald invoked the support of Anselm de Badagio, Bishop of Lucca, and received promise of his countenance and advocacy at Rome.

Guido Vavasour had succeeded the married Archbishop Heribert in 1040. His election had not satisfied the people, who had chosen, and proposed for consecration, four priests, one of whom the nobles were expected to select. But the nobles rejected the popular candidates, and set up in their place Guido Vavasour, and his nomination was ratified by the Emperor and by the Pope. He was afterwards, as we shall see, charged with having bribed Henry III. to give him the See, but was acquitted of the charge, which was denounced as unfounded by Leo IX. in 1059. The people, in token of their resentment, refused to be present at the first mass he sang. "He is a country bumpkin," said they. "Faugh! he smells of the cow-house."[2] Consequently there was

---

[1] "Hæc cum Guido placide dixisset; eo finem orationis dixerit, ut sacerdotibus fas esset dicere uxores ducere."—*Alicatus,* "*Vit. Arialdi.*"

[2] Arnulf., Gesta Archiepisc. Mediol. ap. Pertz, x. p. 17.

simmering discontent against the Archbishop for Ariald to work upon; he could unite the lower people, whose wishes had been disregarded by the nobles, with the Patarines, who had been haled before ecclesiastical courts for their heresy, in one common insurrection against the clergy and the pontiff.

According to Landulf the elder, a strong partisan of the Archbishop, another element of discontent was united to those above enumerated. The clergy of Milan had oppressed the country people. The Church had estates outside of Milan, vine and olive yards and corn-fields. The clergy had been harsh in exacting feudal rights and legal dues.

Ariald, as a native of a country village, knew the temper of the peasants, and their readiness to resent these extortions. Ariald worked upon the country-folk; Landulf, rich and noble, and eloquent in speech, on the town rabble; and the two mobs united against the common enemy.

Anselm de Badagio, priest and popular preacher at Milan, had been mixed up with Landulf and Ariald in the controversy relative to clerical marriage; but to stop his mouth the Archbishop had given him the bishopric of Lucca, in 1057, and had supplied his place as preacher at Milan by seven deacons. Landulf the elder relates that these deacons preached with such success that Anselm, in a fit of jealousy, returned to Milan to listen to their sermons, and scornfully exclaimed, "They may become preachers, but they must first put away their wives."

According to the same authority, Ariald bore a grudge against the Archbishop for having had occasion to rebuke him on account of some irregularity of which he had been guilty. But Landulf the elder is not to be trusted implicitly; he is as bigoted on one side as is Andrew of Strumi on the other.

In the meantime the priests and their wives were exposed to every sort of violence, and "a great horror fell on the Ambrosian clergy." The poor women were torn from their husbands, and driven from the city; the priests who refused to be separated from their companions were interdicted from the altar.[1]

Landulf was sent to Rome to report progress, and obtain confirmation of the proceedings of the party from the Pope. He reached Piacenza, but was unable to proceed farther; he was knocked down, and finding the way barred by the enemies of his party, returned to Milan. Ariald then started, and eluding his adversaries, arrived safely at Rome. He presented himself before Pope Stephen X., who was under the influence of Hildebrand, and, therefore, disposed to receive him with favour. Stephen bade him return to Milan, prosecute the holy war, and, if need be, shed his blood in the sacred cause.

The appeal to Rome was necessary, as the Archbishop and a large party of the citizens, together with all the clergy, had denounced Ariald and Landulf as Patarines. The fact was notorious that the secret and suspected Manichees in Milan were now holding up their heads and defying those who had hitherto controlled them. The Manichees suddenly found that

---

[1] "Sic ab eodem populo sunt persecuta et deleta (clericorum connubia) ut nullus existeret quin aut cogeretur tantum nefas dimittere, vel ad altare non accedere."—*Andr. Strum.*

from proscribed heretics they had been exalted into champions of orthodoxy. It was a satisfactory change for those who had been persecuted to become persecutors, and turn their former tyrants into victims. But now, to the confusion and dismay of the clergy, they found themselves betrayed by the Pope, and at the mercy of those who had old wrongs to resent. Fortified with the blessing of the Pope on his work, his orthodoxy triumphantly established by the supreme authority, Ariald rushed back to Milan, accompanied by papal legates to protect him, and proclaim his mission as divine. He was unmeasured in his denunciations. Dissension fast ripened into civil war. Ariald, at the head of a roaring mob, swept the clergy together into a church, and producing a paper which bound all of them by oath to put away their wives, endeavoured to enforce their subscription.

A priest, maddened to resentment, struck the demagogue in the mouth. This was the signal for a general tumult. The adherents of Ariald rushed through the streets, the alarm bells pealed, the populace gathered from all quarters, and a general hunting down of the married clergy ensued.

"How can the blind lead the blind?" preached Landulf Cotta. "Let these Simoniacs, these Nicolaitans be despised. You who wish to have salvation from the Lord, drive them from their functions; esteem their sacrifices as dogs' dung (*canina stercora*)! Confiscate their goods, and every one of you take what he likes!"[1] We can imagine the results of such

---

[1] Arnulf., *Gesta Ep. Mediol.* ap. Pertz, x. p. 18. It is necessary not to confound Landulf Cotta, the demagogue, with Lan-

license given to the lowest rabble. The nobles, over-awed, dared not interfere.

Nor were the clergy of the city alone exposed to this popular persecution. The preachers roved round the country, creating riots everywhere. This led to retaliation, but retaliation of a feeble, harmless sort. A chapel built by Ariald on his paternal estate was pulled down; and the married clergy resentfully talked of barking his chestnut trees and breaking down his vines, but thought better of it, and refrained.

A more serious attempt at revenge was the act of a private individual. Landulf Cotta was praying in a church, when a priest aimed at him with a sword, but without seriously hurting him. A cripple at the church door caught the flying would-be assassin; a crowd assembled, and Landulf with difficulty extricated the priest alive from their hands.

Ariald and Cotta now began to denounce those who had bought their cures of souls, or had paid fees on their institution to them. They stimulated the people to put down simony, as they had put down concubinage. "Cursed is he that withholdeth his hand from blood!" was the fiery peroration of a sermon on this subject by Ariald.

"Landulf Cotta," says Arnulf, "being master of the lay folk, made them swear to combat both simony and concubinage. Presently he forced this oath on the clergy. From this time forward he was constantly followed by a crowd of men and women, who watched around him night and day. He despised the churches,

dulf the elder, the historian, and Landulf the younger, the disciple and biographer of Ariald.

and rejected priests as well as their functions, under pretext that they were defiled with simony. They were called Patari, that is to say, beggars, because the greater part of them belonged to the lowest orders."[1]

"What shall we do?" asked a large party at Milan. "This Ariald tells us that if we receive the Holy Sacrament from married or simoniacal priests, we eat our own damnation. We cannot live without sacraments, and he has driven all the priests out of Milan."

The parties were so divided, that those who held with Ariald would not receive sacraments from the priests, the heavenly gift on their altars they esteemed as "dogs' dung;" they would not even join with them, or those who adhered to them, in prayer. "One house was all faithful," says Andrew of Strumi; "the next all unfaithful. In the third, the mother and one son were believing, but the father and the other son were unbelieving; so that the whole city was a scene of confusion and contention."

In 1058 Guido assembled a synod at Fontanetum near Novara, and summoned Ariald and Landulf Cotta to attend it. The synod awaited their arrival for three days, and as they did not come, excommunicated them as contumacious.

Landulf the younger, the biographer of Ariald, says that Pope Stephen X. reversed the sentence of the synod; but this account does not agree with what is related by Arnulf. Landulf the elder confounds the dates, and places the synod in the reign of Alexander II., and says that the Pope adopted a middle course, and

[1] Ap. Pertz, l.c., pp. 19, 20.

sent ambassadors to Milan to investigate the matter. Bonizo of Sutri says the same. All agree that Hildebrand was one of these commissioners. Hildebrand was therefore able to judge on the spot of the results of an appeal to the passions of the people. It is the severest condemnation to his conduct in 1073, to know for certain that he had seen the working of the power he afterwards called out. He then saw how great was that power; he must have been cruelly, recklessly, wickedly indifferent to the crimes which accompanied its invocation. Landulf the elder says that the second commissary was Anselm of Lucca, whilst Bonizo speaks indifferently of the "bishops *a latere*" as constituting the deputation. Guido was not in Milan when it arrived, he did not dare to venture his person in the midst of the people. The ambassadors were received with the utmost respect; they took on themselves to brand the Archbishop as a simoniac and a schismatic, and, according to Landulf, to do many other things which they were not authorised by the Pope to do; so that the dissension, so far from being allayed by their visit, only waxed more furious.

At the end of the year 1058, or the beginning of 1059, the Pope sent Peter Damiani, the harsh Bishop of Ostia, and Anselm, Bishop of Lucca, on a new embassy to Milan[1] They were received with respect by the Archbishop and clergy; but the pride of the

---

[1] We have a full account of this embassy in a letter of St. Peter Damiani to the Archdeacon Hildebrand (Petri Dam. *Opp.* iii ; *Opusc.* v. p. 37), besides the accounts by Bonizo, Arnulf, and Landulf the elder.

Milanese of all ranks was wounded by seeing the Bishop of Ostia enthroned in the middle, with Anselm of Lucca, the suffragan of Milan, upon his right, and their Archbishop degraded to the left of the Legate, and seated on a stool at his feet. Milan assembled at the ringing of the bells in all the churches, and the summons of an enormous brazen trumpet which shrieked through the streets. The fickle people asked if the Church of St. Ambrose was to be trodden under the foot of the Roman Pontiff. "I was threatened with death," wrote Peter Damiani to Hildebrand, "and many assured me that there were persons panting for my blood. It is not necessary for me to repeat all the remarks the people made on this occasion."

But Peter Damiani was not the man to be daunted at a popular outbreak. He placidly mounted the ambone, and asserted boldly the supreme jurisdiction of the chair of St. Peter. "The Roman Church is the mother, that of Ambrose is the daughter. St. Ambrose always recognised that mistress. Study the sacred books, and hold us as liars, if you do not find that it is as I have said."

Then the charges against the clergy were investigated by the legates, and not a single clerk in Milan was found who had not paid a fee on his ordination; "for that was the custom, and the charge was fixed," says the Bishop of Ostia. Here was a difficulty He could not deprive every priest and deacon in Milan, and leave the great city without pastors. He was therefore obliged to content his zeal with exacting from the bishops a promise that ordination in future

L

should be made gratuitously; and the Archbishop was constrained to deposit on the altar a paper in which he pronounced his own excommunication, in the event of his relaxing his rigour in suppressing the heresy of the Simoniacs and Nicolaitans, by which latter name those who insisted on the lawfulness of clerical marriage were described.

To make atonement for the past, the Archbishop was required to do penance for one hundred years, but to pay money into the papal treasury in acquittal of each year; which, to our simple understanding, looks almost as scandalous a traffic as imposing a fee on all clergy ordained. But then, in the one case the money went into the pocket of the bishops, and in the other into that of the Pope.

The clergy who had paid a certain sum were to be put to penance for five years; those who had paid more, for ten (also to be compensated by a payment to Rome!), and to make pilgrimages to Rome or Tours. After having accomplished this penance they were to receive again the insignia of their offices.

Then Peter Damiani re-imposed on the clergy the oaths forced on them by Ariald, and departed.

The Milanese contemporary historian, Arnulf, exclaims, "Who has bewitched you, ye foolish Milanese? Yesterday you made loud outcries for the priority of a see, and now you trouble the whole organisation of the Church. You are gnats swallowing camels. You say, perhaps, Rome must be honoured because of the Apostle. Well, but the memory of St. Ambrose should deliver Milan from such an affront as has been

inflicted on her.   In future it will be said that Milan
is subject to Rome." [1]

Guido attended a council held in Rome (April 1059),
shortly after this visitation.   Ariald also was present,
to accuse the Archbishop of favouring simony and
concubinage.   The legates had dealt too leniently
with the scandal.   Guido was defended by his suffragans of Asti, Novara, Turin, Vercelli, Alba, Lodi, and
Brescia.   "Mad bulls, they," says Bonizo; and Ariald
was forced to retire, covered with confusion.   The
Council pronounced a decree that no mercy should
be shown to the simoniacal and married clergy. [2]   An
encyclical was addressed by Nicholas II. to all Chris-
tendom, informing it that the Council had passed
thirteen canons, one of which prevented a layman
from assisting at a mass said by a priest who had a
concubine or a *subintroducta mulier.*   Priests, deacons,
and sub-deacons who should take "publicly" a concubine, or not send away those with whom they lived,
were to be inhibited from exercising all ministerial
acts and receiving ecclesiastical dues.

On the return of the bishops to their sees, one only
of them, Adelmann of Brescia, ventured to publish
these decrees.   He was nearly torn to pieces by his
clergy; an act of violence which greatly furthered the
cause of the Patarines. [3]

[1] Pertz, x. p. 21.

[2] "Nulla misericordia habenda est."

[3] Bonizo.   It is deserving of remark that Bonizo, an ardent
supporter of Hildebrand and the reforming party, calls that
Papal party by the name of *Patari*, thus showing that it was
really made up of the Manichean heretics.

In the same year Pope Nicholas sent legates into different countries to execute, or attempt to execute, the decrees passed against simony and concubinage— as clerical marriage was called. Peter Damiani travelled through several cities of Italy to exhort the clergy to celibacy, and especially to press this matter on the bishops. Peter Damiani was not satisfied with the conduct of the Pope in assuming a stern attitude towards the priests, but overlooking the fact that the bishops were themselves guilty of the same offence. A letter from him to the Pope exists, in which he exhorts him to be a second Phinehas (Numb. xxv. 7), and deal severely with the bishops, without which no real reform could be affected.[1]

Anselm de Badagio, Bishop of Lucca, the instigator of Landulf and Ariald, or at least their staunch supporter, was summoned on the death of Nicholas to occupy the throne of St. Peter, under the title of Alexander II. But his election was contested, and Cadalus, an anti-Pope, was chosen by a Council of German and Lombard prelates assembled at Basle. The contests which ensued between the rival Pontiffs and their adherents distracted attention from the question of clerical marriage, and the clergy recalled their wives.

In 1063, in Florence, similar troubles occurred. The instigator of these was St. John Gualberto, founder of the Vallombrosian Order. The offence there was rather simony than concubinage.

The custom of giving fees to those who appointed

---

[1] *Opp.* t. iii. ; *Opusc.* xiii. p. 188.

to benefices had become inveterate, and in many cases
had degenerated into the purchase of them. A Pope
could not assume the tiara without a lavish largess to
the Roman populace. A bishop could not grasp his
pastoral staff without paying heavy sums to the
Emperor and to the Pope. The former payment was
denounced as simony, the latter was exacted as an
obligation. But under some of the Emperors the
bishoprics were sold to the highest bidder. What
was customary on promotion to a bishopric became
customary on acceptance of lesser benefices, and no
priest could assume a spiritual charge without paying
a bounty to the episcopal treasury. When a bishop
had bought his throne, he was rarely indisposed to
sell the benefices in his gift, and to recoup a scandalous
outlay by an equally scandalous traffic. The Bishop
of Florence was thought by St. John Gualberto to have
bought the see. He was a Pavian, Peter Mediabardi.
His father came to Florence to visit his son. The
Florentines took advantage of the unguarded simplicity
of the old man to extract the desired secret from him.[1]

"Master Teulo," said they, "had you a large sum
to pay to the King for your son's elevation?"

"By the body of St. Syrus," answered the father,
"you cannot get a millstone out of the King's house
without paying for it."

"Then what did you pay?" asked the Florentines
greedily.[2]

[1] "Cui Florentini clam insidiantes tentando dicere cœperunt,"
&c. . . . . "ille utpote simplicissimus homo cœpit jurejurando
dicere," &c.—*Andrew of Genoa*, c. 62.

[2] "Alacres et avidi rem scisitari."

"By the body of St. Syrus!" replied the old man, "not less than three thousand pounds."

No sooner was the unguarded avowal made, than it was spread through the city by the enemies of the bishop.[1]

St. John Gualberto took up the quarrel. He appeared in Florence, where he had a monastery dedicated to St. Salvius, and began vehemently to denounce the prelate as a simoniac, and therefore a heretic. His monks, fired by his zeal, spread through the city, and exhorted the people to refuse to accept the sacramental acts of their bishop and resist his authority.

The people broke out into tumult. The bishop appealed to the secular arm to arrest the disorder, and officers were sent to coerce the monks of St. Salvius. They broke into the monastery at night, sought Gualberto, but, unable to find him, maltreated the monks. One received a blow on his forehead which laid bare the bone, and another had his nose and lips gashed with a sword. The monks were stripped, and the monastery fired. The abbot rolled himself in an old cloak extracted from under a bed, where it had been cast as ragged, and awaited day, when the wounds and tears of the fraternity might be exhibited to a sympathising and excitable people. Nor were they disappointed. At daybreak all the town was gathered around the dilapidated monastery, and people were eagerly mopping up the sacred blood

[1] For the account of what follows, in addition to the biography by Andrew of Strumi, we have the *Dialogues* of Desiderius of Monte Cassino, lib. iii.

that had been shed, with their napkins, thinking that they secured valuable relics. Sympathy with the injured was fanned into frenzied abhorrence of the persecutor.

St. John Gualberto appeared on the scene, blazing with the desire of martyrdom,[1] and congratulated the sufferers on having become confessors of Christ. "Now are ye true monks! But why did ye suffer without me?"

The secular clergy of Florence were, it is asserted, deeply tainted with the same vice as their bishop. They had all paid fees at their institution, or had bought their benefices. They lived in private houses, and were for the most part married. Some were even suspected to be of immoral life.[2]

But the preaching of the Saint, the wounds of the monks, converted some of the clergy. Those who were convinced by their appeals, and those who were wearied of their wives, threw themselves into the party of Gualberto, and clubbed together in common life.[3]

The Vallombrosian monks appealed to Pope Alexander II. against the bishop,[4] their thirst for

[1] "Martyrii flagrans amore."—*Andr. Strum.*

[2] "Quis clericorum propriis et paternis rebus solummodo non studebat? Qui potius inveniretur, proh dolor! qui non esset uxoratus vel concubinarius? De simoniâ quid dicam? Omnes pene ecclesiasticos ordines hæc mortifera bellua devoraverat, ut, qui ejus morsum evaserit, rarus inveniretur."—*Andr. Strum.*

[3] "Exemplo vero ipsius et admonitionibus delicati clerici, spretis connubiis, cœperunt simul in ecclesiis stare, et communem ducere vitam."—Atto Pistor., *Vit. S. Joan. Gualb.*

[4] For what follows, in addition to the above-quoted authorities, we have Berthold's *Chronicle* from 1054 to 1100; Pertz, *Mon. Sacr.* v. pp. 264-326.

martyrdom whetted not quenched.[1] If the Pope desired it, they would try the ordeal of fire to prove
their charge. Hildebrand, then only sub-deacon, but
a power in the councils of the Pope, urged on their
case, and demanded the deposition of the bishop.
But Alexander, himself among the most resolute opponents of simony, felt that there was no case. There
was no evidence, save the prattle of an old man over
his wine-cups. He refused the petition of the
monks, and was supported by the vast majority of the
bishops—there were over a hundred present.[2]

Even St. Peter Damiani, generally unmeasured in
his invectives against simony, wrote to moderate the
frantic zeal of the Vallombrosian monks, which
he denounced as unreasonable, intemperate, un-
just.

But the refusal of the Pope to gratify their resentment did not quell the vehemence of the monks and
the faction adverse to the bishop. The city was in a
condition of chronic insubordination and occasional
rioting. Godfrey Duke of Tuscany was obliged to interfere; and the monks were driven from their
monastery of St. Salvi, and compelled to retire to that
of St. Settimo outside of the gates.

Shortly after, Pope Alexander visited Florence.
The monks piled up a couple of bonfires, and offered
to pass between them in proof of the truth of their
allegation. He refused to permit the ordeal, and

---

[1] " Securiores de corona, quam jam gustaverant, martyrii."—
Andr. Strum.

[2] " Favebat enim maxima pars Episcoporum parti Petri, et
omnes pene erant monachis adversi."—*Andr. Strum.*

withdrew, leaving the bishop unconvicted, and therefore unrebuked.

The clergy of Florence now determined to demand
of the bishop that he should either go through the
ordeal himself, or suffer the monks to do so. As they
went to the palace, the people hooted them : " Go, ye
heretics, to a heretic ! You who have driven Christ
out of the city ! You who adore Simon Magus as
your God ! "

The bishop sullenly refused ; he would neither
establish his innocence in the fire, nor suffer the
monks to convict him by the ordeal.

The Podesta of Florence then, with a high hand, drove
from the town the clergy who had joined the monastic
faction. They went forth on the first Saturday in
Lent, 1067, amidst a sympathising crowd, composed
mostly of women,[1] who tore off their veils, and with
hair scattered wildly over their faces, threw themselves down in the road before the confessors, crying,
" Alas ! alas ! O Christ, Thou art expelled this city,
and how dost Thou leave us desolate ? Thou art not
tolerated here, and how can we live without Thee ?
Thou canst not dwell with Simon Magus. O holy
Peter, didst thou once overcome Simon ? and now
dost thou permit him to have the mastery ? We
deemed him bound and writhing in infernal flames,
and lo ! he is loose, and risen again to thy dishonour."

And the men said to one another, " Let us set fire
to this accursed city, which hates Christ."[2]

[1] " Maxime feminarum."

[2] " Et nos, viri fratres, civitatem hanc incendamus atque cum
parvulis et uxoribus nostris, quocumque Christus ierit, secum

The secular clergy were in dismay; denounced, deserted, threatened by the people, they sang no psalms, offered no masses. Unable to endure their position, they again visited the bishop, and entreated him to sanction the ordeal of fire. He refused, and requested the priests not to countenance such an unauthorised venture, should it be made. But the whole town was bent on seeing this ordeal tried, and on the Wednesday following the populace poured to the monastery of St. Settimo. Two piles of sticks were heaped near the monastery gate, measuring ten feet long by five wide, and four and a half feet high. Between them lay a path the length of an arm in width.

Litanies were chanted whilst the piles were reared, and then the monks proceeded to elect one who was to undergo the fire. The lot fell on a priest named Peter, and St. John Gualberto ordered him at once to the altar to say mass. All assisted with great devotion, the people crying with excitement. At the *Agnus Dei* four monks, one with the crucifix, another with holy water, the third with twelve lighted tapers, the fourth with a full censer, proceeded to the pyres, and set them both on fire.

This threw the people into an ecstasy of excitement, and the voice of the priests was drowned in the clamour of their tongues. The priest finished mass, and laid aside his chasuble. Holding the cross, in alb and stole and maniple, he came forth, followed by St.

eamus. Si Christiani sumus, Christum sequamur."—*Andr. Strum.*

John Gualberto and the monks, chanting. Suddenly
a silence fell on the tossing concourse, and a monk
appointed by the abbot stood forth, and in a clear
voice said to the people, "Men, brethren, and sisters !
we do this for the salvation of your souls, that henceforth ye may learn to avoid the leprosy of simony,
which has infected nearly the whole world ; for the
crime of simony is so great, that beside it every other
crime is as nothing."

The two piles were burning vigorously. The priest
Peter prayed, "Lord Christ, I beseech Thee, if Peter
of Pavia, called Bishop of Florence, has obtained the
episcopal throne by money, do Thou assist me in this
terrible ordeal, and deliver me from being burned, as
of old Thou didst deliver the three children in the
midst of the burning furnace." Then, giving the
brethren the kiss of peace, he stepped fearlessly between the burning pyres, and came forth on the farther side uninjured.

His linen alb, his silken stole and maniple, were un-
burnt. He would have again rushed through the
flames in the excess of his confidence, but was prevented by the pious vehemence of the people, who
surrounded him, kissed his feet, clung to his vest-
ments, and would have crushed him to death in
their eagerness to touch and see him, had he
not been rescued by the strong arms of burly
monks.

In after years he told, and talked himself into believing, that as he passed through the fire,
his maniple fell off. Discovering his loss ere
he emerged, he turned back, and deliberately

picked it up.   But of this nothing was said at the time.[1]

A letter was then drawn up, appealing to the Pope in the most vehement terms, to deliver the sheep of the Florentine flock from the ravening wolf who shepherded them, and urging him, not obscurely, to use force if need be, and compel by his troops the evacuation of the Florentine episcopal throne.   Peter of Pavia, the bishop, a man of gentle character, yielded to the storm.   He withdrew from Florence, and was succeeded by another Peter, whom the people called Peter the Catholic, to distinguish him from the Simoniac.   But Muratori adduces evidence that the former continued to be recognised by the Pope some time after his supposed degradation.   Thus ended the schism of Florence in the entire triumph of the Patarines.   Hildebrand was not unobservant; he proved afterwards not to be forgetful of the lesson taught by this schism,—the utilization of the rude mob as a powerful engine in the hands of the fanatical or designing.   It bore its fruit in the canons of 1074.

II.

Anselm de Badagio, Bishop of Lucca, had succeeded Nicholas II. to the Papal throne in 1061.   Cadalus of Parma had been chosen by the German and Lombard prelates on October 28th, and he assumed the name of Honorius II.   But no Roman Cardinal was

---

[1] It is not mentioned in the epistle of the Florentines to the Pope, narrating the ordeal and supposed miracle, which is given by Andrew of Strumi and Atto of Pistoja.

present to sanction this election. Cadalus was acknowledged by all the simoniacal and married clergy, when he entered Italy; but the Princess Beatrice and the Duke of Tuscany prevented him from advancing to Rome. From Parma Cadalus excommunicated Alexander, and from Rome, Alexander banned Honorius. The cause of Alexander was that of the Patarines, but the question of marriage and simony paled before the more glaring one, of which of the rival claimants was the actual Pope.

The voice of Landulf Cotta was silenced. A terrible cancer had consumed the tongue which had kept Milan for six years in a blaze of faction. But his room was speedily filled by a more implacable adversary of the married clergy—his brother, Herlembald, a stern, able soldier. An event in Herlembald's early life had embittered his heart against the less rigid clergy. His plighted bride had behaved lightly with a priest. He was just returned from a pilgrimage to Jerusalem, his zeal kindled to enthusiasm. He went to Rome, where he was well received by Alexander II. He came for authority to use his sword for the Patarines. The sectaries in Milan had said to him, "We desire to deliver the Church, besieged and degraded by the married priests; do thou deliver by the law of the sword, we will do so by the law of God." Alexander II., in a public consistory, created Herlembald "Defender of the Church," gave him the sacred banner of St. Peter, and bade him go back to Milan and shed blood—his, if necessary, those of the anti-Patarines certainly—in this miserable quarrel.

The result was that the Patarines were filled with

new zeal, and lost all compunction at shedding blood and pillaging houses. Herlembald established himself in a large mansion, which he fortified and filled with mercenaries; over it waved the consecrated banner of St. Peter. From this stronghold he issued forth to assail the obnoxious clergy. They were dragged from their altars and consigned to shame and insult. The services of the Church, the celebration of the sacraments, were suspended, or administered only by the one or two priests who adhered to the Patari. It is said that, in order to keep his rude soldiery in pay, Herlembald made every clerk take a solemn oath that he had ever kept innocence, and would wholly abstain from marriage or concubinage. Those who could not, or would not, take this oath were expelled the city, and their whole property eonfiscated to support the standing corps of hireling ruffians maintained by the Crusader. The lowest rabble, poor artisans and ass-drivers, furtively placed female ornaments in the chambers of the priests, and then, attacking their houses, dragged them out and plundered their property. By 1064, when a synod was held at Mantua by the Pope, Milan was purged of "Simoniacs and Nicolaitans," and the clergy who remained were gathered together into a house to live in common, under rule.

Guido of Milan and all the Lombard prelates attended that important synod, which saw the triumph of Alexander, his reconciliation with the Emperor, and the general abandonment of the anti-Pope, Cadalus.

In the following year, Henry IV. was under the tutelage of Adalbert of Bremen; he had escaped from

Anno, Archbishop of Cologne, who had favoured the strict faction and Alexander II. The situation in Lombardy changed simultaneously. Herlembald had assumed a power, an authority higher than that of the archbishop, whom he refused to recognise, and denounced as a heretic. Guido, weary of the nine years of strife he had endured, relieved from the fear of interference from Germany, resolved on an attempt to throw off the hateful yoke. The churches of Milan were for the most part without pastors. The married clergy had been expelled, and there were none to take their place. The Archbishop had been an obedient penitent for five years, compromising his one hundred years of penitence by payments into the Papal treasury; but as the cause of Alexander declined, his contrition languished, died out; and he resumed his demands for fees at ordinations and institutions, at least so clamoured Ariald and Herlembald in the ears of Rome.

A party in Milan had long resented the despotism of the " Law of God and the law of the sword " of Ariald and Herlembald, and an effort was made to break it, with the sanction, no doubt, of the Archbishop. A large body of the citizens rose, " headed," says Andrew of Strumi, " by the sons of the priests," and attacked the church and house of Ariald, but, unable to find him, contented themselves with wrecking the buildings. Thereupon Herlembald swept down at the head of his mercenaries, surrounded the crowd, and hewed them to pieces to the last man, " like the vilest cattle." [1]

[1] " Hæc ut nobilis Herembaldus ceterique Fideles audiere,

Guido, the Archbishop, now acted with resolution, and boldly took up the cause of the married clergy. Having heard that two priests of Monza, infected with Patarinism, had turned their wives out of their houses, he ordered the arrest of the priests, and punished them with imprisonment in the castle of Lecco. On hearing this, the Patarines flew to arms, and swarmed out of Milan after Ariald, who bore the banner of St. Peter, as Herlembald was absent at Rome. They met the mounted servants of the Archbishop near Monza, surprised them, and wrested from them a promise to surrender the priests. Three days after, the curates were delivered up. Ariald, at the head of the people, met them outside the gates, received them with enthusiasm, crying, " See, these are the brave martyrs of Christ!" and escorted them to a church, where they intoned a triumphant *Te Deum.*

Herlembald returned from Rome to Milan with a bull of excommunication fulminated by the Pope against the Archbishop. Guido summoned the Milanese to assemble in the cathedral church on the vigil of Pentecost.

In the meantime the Patarines were torn into factions on a subtle point mooted by Ariald. That demagogue had ventured to assail in a sermon the venerable custom of the Milanese, which required them to fast during the Rogation days. Was he greater than St. Ambrose? Did he despise the authority of the great doctor? On this awful subject

sumptis armis, in audacem plebem et temerariam irruere ; quos protinus exterminavere omnes, quasi essent vilissimæ pecudes." —*Andr. Strum.*

the Patarines divided, and with the division lost their strength.

Neither Herlembald nor Ariald seems to have been prepared for the bold action of the Archbishop. On the appointed day the cathedral was filled with substantial citizens and nobles. Herlembald missed the wolfish eyes, ragged hair, and hollow cheeks of his sectaries, and, fearing danger, leaped over the chancel rails, and took up his position near the altar. The Archbishop mounted the ambone with the bull of excommunication in his hand. "See!" he exclaimed, "this is the result of the turbulence of these demagogues, Ariald and Herlembald. This city, out of reverence to St. Ambrose, has never obeyed the Roman Church. Shall we be crushed? Take away out of the land of the living these disturbers of the public peace, who labour day and night to rob us of our ancient liberties."

He was interrupted by a shout of "Let them be killed!" Guido paused, and then cried out, "All who honour and cleave to St. Ambrose, leave the church, that we may know who are our adversaries." Instantly from the doors rolled out the dense crowd, seven hundred in number, according to the estimation of Andrew, the biographer of Ariald. Only twelve men were left within who stood firm to the Patarine cause. Ariald had, in the meantime, taken refuge in the choir beside Herlembald. The clergy selected Ariald, the laity Herlembald, for their victims. Ariald was dragged from the church, severely wounded. Herlembald escaped better; using his truncheon, he beat off his assailants till he had

M

climbed to a place of safety, whence he could not be easily dislodged.

As night fell, the Patarines gathered, stormed, and pillaged the palace of the Archbishop, and, bursting into the church, liberated Herlembald. Guido hardly escaped on horseback, sorely maltreated in the tumult. His adherents fled like smoke before the tempest. Ariald was found bleeding and faint, and was conveyed by the multitude in triumph to the church of St. Sepolcro. Then Herlembald called to the roaring mob to be still. "Let us ask Master Ariald whose house is to be first given up to sack."

But Ariald earnestly dissuaded from further violence, and entreated the vehement dictator to spare the lives and property of their enemies.

The surprise to the Archbishop's party was, however, temporary only. By morning they had rallied, and the city was again in their hands. Guido published an interdict against Milan, which was to remain in force as long as it harboured Ariald. No mass was said, no bells rang, the church doors were bolted and barred. Ariald was secretly removed by some of his friends to the village of St. Victor, where also Herlembald had been constrained to take refuge with a party of mercenaries. Thence they made their way to Pavia and to Padua, where they hoped to obtain a boat, and escape to Rome. But the whole country was up against them, and Herlembald was obliged to disband his soldiers, and attempt to escape in disguise. Ariald was left with a priest whose acquaintance Herlembald had made in Jerusalem. But a priest was the last person likely to secrete the

tyrant and persecutor of the clergy. He treacher-
ously sent word to the Archbishop, and Ariald was
taken by the servants of Olivia, the niece of Guido,
and conveyed to an island on the Lago Maggiore.
He was handed over to the cruel mercies of two
married priests, who directed his murder with cold-
blooded heartlessness, if we may trust the gossip
picked up later. His ears, nose and lips were cut
off. He was asked if he would acknowledge Guido
for Archbishop. "As long as my tongue can speak,"
he replied, "I will not." The servants of Olivia tore
out his tongue ; he was beaten by the two savage
priests, and when he fainted, was flung into the calm
waters of the lovely lake. Andrew of Vallombrosa,
or Strumi, followed in his trace, and hung about the
neighbourhood till he heard from a peasant the awful
story. He sought the mangled body.[1] It was found
and transported to Milan on the feast of the Ascension
following. For ten days it was exposed in the church
of St. Ambrose, that all might venerate it, and was
finally disposed in the convent of St. Celsus. In the
memory of man, never had such a crowd been seen.
The Archbishop deemed it prudent to retire, and
Herlembald profited by his absence to recover his
power, and make the people swear to avenge the
martyr, and unite to the death for the "good cause."
The events in Milan had their counterpart in the
other cities of Lombardy, especially at Cremona,

[1] Ariald was murdered on June 27, 1065. Andrew of Strumi
says 1066 ; but he followed the Florentine computation—he had
been a priest of Florence—which made the year begin on
March 25.

where the bishopric had been obtained by Arnulf, nephew of Guido of Milan. In that city, twelve men, headed by one Christopher, took the Patarine oath to fight the married clergy; the people joined them, and forced their oath on the bishop-elect before he was ordained. But, as in 1067, he seized a Patarine priest, a sedition broke out, in which the bishop was seriously injured. The inhabitants of Cremona, after Easter, sent ambassadors to the Pope, and received from him a reply, given by Bonizo, exhorting them not to allow a priest, deacon or sub-deacon, suspected of concubinage or simony, to hold a benefice or execute his ministry. The consequence of this letter was that all suspected clerks were excluded from their offices; and shortly after, the same course was followed at Piacenza. Asti, Lodi, and Ravenna also threw in their lot with the Patarines.

In 1067, Alexander II. sent legates to Milan to settle the disturbances therein. Adalbert of Bremen had fallen, and again the Papal party were in the ascendant. The fortunes of Milan fluctuated with the politics of those who held the regency in the minority of Henry IV.

Guido, now advanced in years, and weary of ruling so turbulent a diocese, determined to vacate a see which he had held for twenty-seven years; the last ten of incessant civil war. He burdened it with a pension to himself, and then made it over to Godfrey, the sub-deacon, along with the pastoral staff and ring. Godfrey crossed the Alps, took the oath of allegiance to the Emperor, promised to use his utmost endeavours to exterminate the Patarines, and to deliver

Herlembald alive into the hands of the Emperor,
laden with chains. Friend and foe, without scruple,
designate the followers of the Papal policy as
Patarines; it is therefore startling, a few years later,
when the Popes had carried their point, to find them
insisting on the luckless Patarines being given in
wholesale hecatombs to the flames, as damnable
heretics. It was an ungracious return for the battle
these heretics had fought under the banner of St.
Peter.

But Herlembald refused to acknowledge Godfrey,
he devastated the country with fire and sword where-
ever Godfrey was acknowledged, and created such
havoc that not a day passed in the holy Lenten fast
without the effusion of much Christian blood.
Finally, Herlembald drove the archbishop-elect to
take refuge in the strong fortress of Castiglione.
Guido, not receiving his pension, annulled his resignation, and resumed his state. But he unwisely trusted
to the good faith of Herlembald ; he was seized,[1] and
shut up in a monastery till his death, which took
place August 23, 1071.

The year before this, 1070, Adelheid, Margravine
of Turin, mother-in-law of the young Emperor, attacked the Patarines, and burnt the cities of Lodi and
Asti. On March 19, 1071, as Herlembald was besieging Castiglione, a terrible conflagration broke out
in Milan, and consumed a great part of the city and
several of the stateliest churches. Whilst the army
of Herlembald was agitated by the report of the fire,
Godfrey burst out Castiglione, and almost routed the

[1] " Gloriosus hac vice delusus," says Arnulf.

besiegers. Before the death of Guido, Herlembald, with the sanction of the Pope, had set up a certain Otto to be Archbishop, nominated by himself and the Papal legate, without consulting the electors of Milan or the Emperor, January 6, A.D. 1072.

Otto was but a youth, just admitted into holy orders, likely to prove a pliant tool in the strong hand of the dictator. It was the Feast of the Epiphany, and the streets were thronged with people, when the news leaked out that an archbishop had been chosen, and was now holding the customary banquet after election in the archiepiscopal palace.

The people were furious, rose and attacked the house, hunted the youthful prelate out of an attic, where he had taken refuge, dragged him by his legs and arms into the church, and compelled him to swear to renounce his dignity. The Roman legate hardly escaped with his robes torn.

Herlembald, who had been surprised, recovered the upper hand in Milan on the morrow, but not in the open country, which was swept by the imperial troops. The suffragan bishops of Lombardy assembled at Novara directly they heard of what had taken place in Milan, and consecrated Godfrey as their archbishop.

Otto appealed to Rome (January, 1072), and a few weeks later the Pope assembled a synod, and absolved Otto of his oath extorted from him at Milan, acknowledged him as archbishop, and struck Godfrey with interdict. Alexander II. died April 21, 1073, and the tiara rested on the brows of the great Hildebrand.

On June 24, Hildebrand, now Gregory VII., wrote
to the Margravine Beatrice to abstain from all relations with the excommunicated bishops of Lombardy;
on June 28, to William, Bishop of Pavia, to oppose
the usurper, the excommunicate Godfrey of Milan ;
on July 1, to all the faithful of Lombardy to refrain
from that false bishop, who lay under the apostolic
ban. From Capua, on September 27, he wrote to
Herlembald, exhorting him to fight valiantly, and
hold out Milan against the usurper Godfrey. Again,
on October 9, to Herlembald, bidding him be of good
courage ; he hoped to detach the young Emperor
from the party of Godfrey, and bade him receive
amicably those who, with true sentiments of contrition, came over to the Patarine, that is, the Papal
side.

On March 10, 1074, Gregory held one of the most
important synods, not of his reign only, but ever
held by any Pope. The acts of this assembly have
been lost or suppressed, but its most important
decisions were summed up in a letter from Gregory
to the Bishop of Constance. This letter has not been
printed in the Registrum ; but fortunately it has been
preserved by two contemporary writers, Paul of
Bernried, and Bernold of Constance, the latter of
whom has supplied a detailed apology for the law of
celibacy promulgated in that synod. Gregory absolutely forbade all priests sullied with the *crimen
fornicationis*, which embraced legitimate marriage,
either to say a mass or to serve at one ; and the
people were strictly enjoined to shun their churches
and their sacraments ; and when the bishops were

remiss, he exhorted them themselves to enforce the pontifical sentence.[1]

The results shall be described in the words of a contemporary historian, Sigebert of Gemblours. "Many," says he, "seeing in this prohibition to hear a mass said by a married priest a manifest contradiction to the doctrine of the Fathers, who believed that the efficacy of sacraments, such as baptism, chrism, and the Body and Blood of Christ, is independent of the dignity of the minister, thence resulted a grievous scandal; never, perhaps, greater, even in the time of the great heresies, was the Church divided by a greater schism. Some did not abandon their simony, others disguised their avarice under a more acceptable name; what they boasted they had given gratuitously, they in reality sold; very few preserved continence. Some through greed of lucre, or sentiments of pride, simulated chastity, but many added false oaths and numerous adulteries to their debaucheries. The laity seized the opportunity to rise against the clerical order, and to excuse themselves for dis-

---

[1] "Audivimus quod quidam Episcoporum apud vos commorantium, aut sacerdotes, et diaconi, et subdiaconi mulieribus commisceantur aut consentiant aut negligant. His præcipimus vos nullo modo obedire, vel illorum præceptis consentire, sicut ipsi apostolicæ sedis præceptis non obediunt neque auctoritati sanctorum patrum consentiunt." "Quapropter ad omnes de quorum fide et devotione confidimus nunc convertimur, rogantes vos et apostolicâ auctoritate admonentes ut quidquid Episcopi dehinc loquantur aut taceant, vos officium eorum quos aut simoniace promotos et ordinatos aut in crimine fornicationis jacentes cognoveritis, nullatenus recipiatis."—Letter to the Franconians (Baluze, *Misc.* vii. p. 125).

obedience to the Church. They profaned the holy mysteries, administering baptism themselves, and using the wax out of their ears as chrism. They refused on their death-beds to receive the *viaticum* from the married priests; they would not even be buried by them. Some went so far as to trample under foot the Host, and pour out the precious Blood consecrated by married priests."[1]

The affairs of the church of Milan continued in the same unsatisfactory condition. The contest between the Patarines and their adversaries had taken greater dimensions. The question which divided them was now less that of the marriage of the clergy than which of the rival archbishops was to be acknowledged. Godfrey was supported by the Emperor, Otto by the Pope. The parties were about even; neither Godfrey nor Otto could maintain himself in Milan; the former fortified himself in the castle of Brebbio, the latter resided at Rome. Henry IV., in spite of all the admonitions of the Pope, persisted in supporting the cause of Godfrey. Milan was thus without a pastor. The suffragan bishops wished to execute their episcopal functions in the city, and to consecrate the holy oils for the benediction of the fonts at Whitsuntide. Herlembald, when one of the bishops had sent chrism into the city for the purpose, poured it out on the ground and stamped on it, because it had been consecrated by an excommunicated prelate.

In March, 1075, another conflagration broke out in the city, and raged with even greater violence than the fire of 1071. Herlembald had again poured forth

[1] Pertz, viii. p. 362.

the oils, as he had the year before; and had ordered Leutprand, a priest, as Easter came, to proceed to the consecration of chrism. This innovation roused the alarm of the Milanese; the subsequent conflagration convinced them that it was abhorrent to heaven. All the adversaries of the Patarines assembled outside the city, and swore to preserve intact the privileges of St. Ambrose, and to receive only the bishop nominated or approved by the King. Then, entering the city, they fell unexpectedly on the Patarines. Leutprand was taken and mutilated, his ears and nose were cut off. The standard of St. Peter was draggled in the dust, and Herlembald fell with it, cut down by a noble, Arnold de Rauda. Every insult was heaped on the body of the "Defender of the Church," and the sacred banner was trampled under foot.

Messengers were sent to Henry IV. to announce the triumph, and to ask him to appoint a new Archbishop of Milan. Henry was so rejoiced at the victory, that he abandoned Godfrey, and promised the Milanese a worthy prelate. His choice fell on Tebald, a Milanese sub-deacon in his Court.

Pope Urban II. canonised Herlembald. Ariald seems never to have been formally enrolled among the saints, but he received honours as a saint at Milan, and has been admitted into several Italian Martyrologies, and into the collection of the Bollandists. Baronius wisely expunged Herlembald and Ariald from the Roman Martyrology; nevertheless, the disgraceful fact remains, that the ruffian Herlembald has been canonised by Papal bull.

The seeds of fresh discord remained. Leutprand, or Liprand, the priest, was curate of the Church of St. Paul;[1] having suffered mutilation in the riot, he was regarded in the light of a Patarine confessor. But no outbreak took place till the death of Anselm IV., Archbishop of Milan (September 30, 1101), at Constantinople, where he was on his way with the Crusaders to the Holy Land. His vicar, the Greek, Peter Chrysolaus, Bishop of Savonia, whom the Lombards called Grossulani, perhaps because of the coarse habit he wore (more probably as a corruption for Chrysolaus), had been left in charge of the see of Milan. On the news of the death of the Archbishop reaching that city, the Primicerius convoked the electors to choose a successor. The vote fell on Landulf, Ordinary of Milan; but he was not yet returned from Jerusalem, whither he had gone as a crusader. Grossulani declared the election informal. Thereupon the Abbot of St. Dionysius, at the head of a large party of the electors, chose Peter Grossulani. There is no evidence of his having used bribery in any form; but he may have acted unjustly in cancelling the election of Landulf. It is, however, fair to observe that Landulf, on his return, supported Grossulani; consequently, it is probable that the latter acted strictly in accordance with law and precedent.

But the election displeased Liprand and the remains of the Patarines. They appealed to Rome, but Grossulani, supported by the Countess Matilda

---

[1] The life of Liprand was written by Landulf the younger, his sister's son, in his *Hist. Mediolan.* 1095-1137.

and St. Bernard, abbot of Vallombrosa, overcame their objections. Pope Paschal II. ratified the election, and sent the pall to the Archbishop. Ardericus de Carinate had been sent to Rome on behalf of Grossulani. The people came out of the gates, on his approach, to learn the result. Ardericus, hanging the pall across his umbrella *(protensi virga)*, waved it over his head, shouting, " Ecco la stola ! Ecco la stola !" (Here is the pall !) and led the way into the cathedral, whither Grossulani also hastened, and ascending the pulpit in his pontifical habit, placed the coveted insignia about his neck.

Liprand was not satisfied. By means of private agitation, he disturbed the tranquillity of public feeling, and the Archbishop, to calm the minds of the populace, was obliged to convoke a provincial synod at Milan (1103), in which, in the presence of his suffragans, the clergy and the people, he said, " If anyone has a charge to make against me, let him speak openly at the present time, or he shall not be heard."

Liprand would not appear before the council and formally make charge, but he mounted the pulpit in the Church of St. Paul, and preached against the Archbishop as a simoniac. He declared his readiness to prove his charge by the ordeal of fire. The bishops assembled in council refused to suffer the attempt to be made.

However, Liprand was not deterred. " Look at my amputated nose and ears !" he cried, " I am a confessor for Christ. I will try the ordeal by fire to substantiate my charge. Grossulani is a simoniac, by gift of hand,

gift of tongue, and gift of homage." And he gave his
wolf-skin cloak and some bottles of wine in exchange
for wood, which the crowd carried off and heaped up
in a great pile against the wall of the monastery of St.
Ambrogio. The Archbishop sent his servants, and
they overturned the stack and scattered the wood.
Then the crowd of "boys and girls, men and women,"
poured through the main streets, roaring, "Away with
Grossulani, away with him!" and clamoured around
the doors of the archiepiscopal palace, so that Grossulani, fearing for his life, said, "Be it so, let the fellow
try the fire, or let him leave Milan." His servants with
difficulty appeased the people, by promising that the
ordeal should be undergone on the following Palm
Sunday evening. "I will not leave the city," said
Liprand; "but now I have no money for buying wood,
and I will not sell my books, as I keep them for my
nephew Landulf, now at school." So the magistrates
of the city prepared a pile of billets of oak wood.

On the appointed day Liprand, barefooted, in sackcloth, bearing a cross, went to the Church of Saints
Gervasius and Protasius and sang mass. Grossulani
also, bearing a cross, entered the same church and
mounted the pulpit, attended by Ariald de Marignano,
and Berard, Judge of Asti. Silence being made, and
Liprand having taken his place barefooted "on the
marble stone at the entrance to the choir, containing
an image of Hercules," Grossulani addressed the
people: "Listen, and I will silence this man in three
words." Then turning to Liprand, he asked, "You
have charged me with being a simoniac. To whom
have I given anything? Answer me."

Liprand, raising his eyes to the pulpit, pointed to those who occupied it and said, "Look at those three great devils, who think to confound me by their wit and wealth.[1] I appeal to the judgment of God."

Grossulani said, "But I ask what act of simony do you lay to my charge?"

Liprand answered, "Do you answer me, What is the lightest form of simony?"

The Archbishop, after some consideration, answered, "To refrain from deposing a simoniac."

"And I say that is simony which consists in deposing an abbot from his abbacy, a bishop from his bishopric, and an archbishop from his archbishopric."[2]

The people became impatient, and began to shout, "Come out, come out to the ordeal!" Then Liprand "jumped down from the stone, containing the image òf Hercules," and went forth accompanied by the multitude to the field where the pyre was made. There arose then a difficulty about the form of oath to be administered. Liprand, seeing that there was some hesitation, said, "Let me manage it, and see if I do not satisfy you all!" Whereupon he took hold of the hood of the Archbishop and shook it, and said

[1] "Proposuisti quod ego sum simoniacus per munus a manu. Modo dic : cui dedi ; Tunc presbyter super populum oculos aperuit, et digitum ad eos, qui stabunt in pulpito, extendit, dicens, Videte tres grandissimos diabolos, qui per ingenium et pecuniam suam putant me confundere."

[2] It is very evident from this discussion that Grossulani was innocent of true simony ; the whole charge against him was due to his having quashed the election of Landulf, and thus of having deposed, after a fashion, "an archbishop from his archbishopric."

in a loud voice, " That Grossulani, who is under this hood, he, and no other, has obtained the archbishopric of Milan simoniacally, by gift of hand, gift of tongue, and gift of service. And I, who enter on this ordeal, swear that I have used no charm, or incantation, or withcraft."

The Archbishop, unwilling to remain, remòunted his horse and rode to the Church of St. John " ad concham," but Ariald of Marignano remained to see that the ordeal was rightly carried out. When the pile was lighted, he said to the priest, " In heaven's name, return to your duty, and do not rush on certain death." But Liprand answered, " Get thee behind me, Satan," and signing himself, and blessing the fire with consecrated water, he rushed through the flames, barefooted, in sackcloth cassock and silk chasuble. He came out on the other side uninjured ; a sudden draught had parted the flames as he entered, and when he emerged his feet were not burnt, nor was his silk chasuble scorched.

The people shouted at the miracle, and Grossulani was obliged to fly from the city.

It was soon rumoured, however, that Liprand was suffering from a scorched hand and an injured foot. It was in vain for his friends to assure the people that his hand had been burnt when he was throwing the holy water on the flames before he entered them, and that his foot was injured not by the fire, but by the hoof of a horse as he emerged from the flames. One part of the mob began to clamour against Liprand that he was an impostor, the other to exalt him as a saint, and the streets became the scene of riot and bloodshed. At this juncture Landulf of Vereglate, who had been just elected to the vacant see, arrived from Jerusalem, and finding that the Archbishop had fled the city, he appealed to the people to cease from their riots, and promised to have Grossulani deposed, or at least the charges brought against him properly investigated at Rome. The tumults were with difficulty allayed, and the Archbishop, Landulf, and Liprand went to Rome (A.D. 1103). A Synod was convened and Liprand brought his vague accusations of simony against the Archbishop. Landulf refused to support him, so that it is hardly probable that he can have felt himself aggrieved by the conduct of Grossulani. Liprand, being unable to substantiate his charge of simony, was obliged to change the nature of his accusation, and charged the Archbishop with having forced him to submit to the ordeal of fire. The Pope and the Synod required the Archbishop to clear himself by oath ; accordingly Grossulani did so, in the following terms : " I, Grossulani, by the grace of God Archbishop, did not force Liprand to enter the fire." Azo, Bishop of Acqui, and Arderic, Bishop of Lodi, took the oath with him ; at the same time the pastoral staff slipped from the hands of the Archbishop and fell on the floor, a sign, the biographer of Liprand says, that he forswore himself.[1]

The Archbishop withdrew, his authority confirmed by the Holy See, and he returned to Milan, where he was well received.

[1] It is evident from the account of Landulf the younger himself, that the Archbishop did not force the priest to enter on the ordeal.

The Archbishop took an unworthy opportunity, in 1110, of ridding the city of the presence of Liprand for that priest having taken into his house and cured a certain Herebert of Bruzano, an enemy of the Archbishop, who was ill with fever. Grossulani deprived Liprand of his benefice, and the priest retired into the Valteline. Troubles broke out in Milan between the two parties, which produced civil war, and the Archbishop was driven out of the city, whereupon Liprand returned to it. The friends of Grossulani persuaded him to visit Jerusalem, and he started, after having appointed Arderic, Bishop of Lodi, his vicar (A.D. 1111). During his absence both parties united to reject him, and they elected Jordano of Cliva in his room (Jan. 1, A.D. 1112). Mainnard, Archbishop of Turin, hastened to Rome, and received the pall from the Pope, on condition that it should not be worn for six months. But the rumours having spread that Grossulani was returning from Jerusalem, Mainnard came to Milan, and placed the pall on the altar of St. Ambrose, whence Jordano took it and laid it about his shoulders.

On the return of Grossulani, civil war broke out again between the two factions, which ended in both Archbishops being summoned to Rome in 1116; and the Pope ordered Grossulani to return to his bishopric of Savonia, and confirmed Jordano in the archbishopric of Milan. But before this Liprand had died 3rd January, 1113. His sanctity was almost immediately attested by a miracle, in spite of the disparagement of his virtues by the party of the Archbishop Grossulani; for a certain knight of Piacenza, having swallowed a fish-bone which stuck in his throat, in sleep saw the priest appear to him and touch his throat, whereupon a violent fit of coughing ensued, in which the bone was ejected ; this was considered quite sufficient to estab-lish the claim of Liprand to be regarded as a saint.

The Anabaptist of Münster.

To the year 1524 Münster, the capital of Westphalia, had remained faithful to the religion which S. Swibert, coadjutor of S. Willibrord, first Bishop of Utrecht, had brought to it in the 7th century. But then Lutheranism was introduced into it.

Frederick von Wied at that time occupied the Episcopal throne. He was brother to Hermann, Archbishop of Cologne, who was afterwards deprived for his secession to Lutheranism.

The religious revolution in the Westphalian capital at its commencement presents the same symptoms which characterised the beginning of the Reformation elsewhere. The town council were prepared to hail it as a means of overthrowing the Episcopal authority, and establishing the municipal power as supreme in the city.

Already the State of Juliers had embraced the new religion, and faith had been shaken in Osnabrück, Minden, and Paderborn, when the first symptoms appeared in Münster.

Four priests, the incumbents of the parishes of St. Lambert, St. Ludger, St. Martin, and the Lieb-Frau Church, commonly called Ueberwasser, declared for the Reform. The contemporary historian, Kerssen-broeck, an eye-witness of all he describes, says of them, "They indulged in the most violent abuse of the clergy, they cursed good works, assured their auditors that such works would not receive the smallest recompense, and permitted every one to give way to all the excesses of so-called Evangelical liberty."[1] They stirred up their hearers against the religious orders, and the people clamoured daily at the gates of the monasteries and nunneries, insisting on being given food; and the monks and nuns were too much frightened to refuse those whom impunity rendered daily more exacting.[2] On the night of the 22nd March, 1525, they attacked the rich convent of nuns at Nizink, with intentions of pillaging it. They failed in this attempt, and the ringleaders were seized and led before the magistrates, followed by an excited and tumultuous crowd of men and women, "evangelically disposed," as the chronicler says. Hoping to ally the effervescence, the magistrates asked the cause of complaint against the nuns of Nizink, and then came out the true reason, for which religious prejudice had served as a cloak. They complained that the monks and nuns exercised professions to the prejudice of the artisans; and they demanded of the magistracy that their looms should be broken, the religious forbidden to work at trades, and their superabundant goods to be distributed among the poor. The orators of the band declared in conclusion "that if the magistrates refused to grant these requests, the people would disregard their orders, displace them by force of arms, and put in

[1] Kerssenbroeck, p. 114.
[2] *Ibid.* p. 115.

their stead men trustworthy and loyal, and devoted
to the interests of the citizens."[1] Alarmed at these
threats, the magistrates yielded, and promised to
take every measure satisfactory to the insurgents.[2]
On the 25th May, accordingly, the Friars of St. Francis
and the nuns of Nizink were ordered to give up their
looms and accounts. The friars yielded, but the
ladies stoutly refused. The magistrates, however,
had all the looms carried away, whilst a mob howled
at the gates, and agitators, excited by the four renegade priests, ran about the town stirring up the
people against the religious. " All the worst char
acters," says the old chronicler, " joined the rioters ;
the curious came to swell the crowd, and people of
means shut themselves into their houses." [3] For
Johann Grœten, the orator of the band, now proclaimed that having emptied the strong boxes of the
monks and nuns, they would despoil all those whose
fortunes exceeded two thousand ducats.

The rioters next marched to the town hall, where
the senators sat trembling, and they demanded the
immediate confirmation of a petition in thirty-four
articles that had been drawn up for them by their
leaders. At the same time the mob announced that
unless their petition was granted they would execute
its requirements with their own hands.

It asked that the canons of the cathedral should be
required to pay the debts of the bishop deceased ;
that criminal jurisdiction should be withdrawn from

1 Kerssenbroeck, p. 116.
2 *Ibid.* p. 117.
3 *Ibid.* p. 120.

the hands of the clergy ; that the monks and nuns should be forbidden to exercise any manufacture, to dry grain, make linen, and rear cattle ; that the burden of taxation should be shared by the clergy ; that rectors should not be allowed to appoint or dismiss their curates without consent of the parish ; that lawsuits should not be allowed to be protracted beyond six weeks ; that beer licences should be abolished, and tolls on the bridges done away with ; that monks and nuns should be allowed free permission to leave their religious societies and return to the world ; that the property of religious houses should be sold and distributed amongst the needy, and that the municipality should allow them enough for their subsistence ; that the Carmelites, the Augustinians, and the Dominicans should be suppressed ; that pious foundations for masses for the repose of souls should be confiscated ; and that people should be allowed to marry in Lent and Advent. The magistrates yielded at once, and promised to endeavour to get the consent of the other estates of the diocese to the legalising of these articles.[1]

On the morrow of the Ascension, 1525, the magistrates closed the gates of the town, and betook themselves to the clergy of the chapter to request them to accept the thirty-four articles. The canons refused at first, but, in fear of the people, they consented, but wrote to the bishop to tell him what had taken place, and to urge him to act with promptitude, and not to forget that the rights and privileges of the Church were in jeopardy.

[1] *Ibid.* p. 126.

It was one of the misfortunes in Germany, as it was in France, that the clergy were exempt from taxation. This precipitated the Revolution in France, and aroused the people against the clergy; and in Germany it served as a strong motive for the adoption of the Reformation.

The canons now fled the town, protesting that their signatures had been wrested from them by violence, and that they withdrew their consent to the articles. The inferior clergy remained at their post, and exhibited great energy and decision. They deprived Lubert Causen, minister of St. Martins, one of the most zealous fautors of Lutheranism in Münster, and the head of the reforming party. When his parishioners objected, a packet of love-letters he had written to several girls in the town, and amongst others some to a young woman of respectable position whom he had seduced, came to light, and were read in the Senate. The reformer had in his letters used scriptural texts to excuse and justify the most shameless libertinage.[1] Johann Tante, preacher at St. Lambert, and Gottfried Reining, of Ueberwasser, were also deprived. As for the Lutheran preacher at St. Ludger, Johann Fink, "his mouth was stopped by the gift of a fat prebendal stall, and from that moment he entirely lost his zeal for the gospel of Wittenberg, and never uttered another word against the Catholic religion."[2]

By means of the mediation of the Archbishop of Cologne, a reconciliation was effected. The articles

[1] Kerssenbroeck, p. 128.
[2] *Ibid.*

were abolished and the signatures annulled, and the members of the chapter returned to Münster, which had felt their absence by the decrease in trade, and the inconstant people " showed at least as much joy at their return as they had shown hatred at their departure."[1]

There can be no question but that the Reformation in Germany was provoked to a large extent by abuses and corruptions in the Church. To a much larger extent it was a revolt against the Papacy which had weakened and numbed the powers of the Empire throughout the Middle Ages from the time of the Emperor Henry IV. But chiefly as a social and political movement it was the revolt of municipalities against the authority of collegiate bodies of clergy and the temporal jurisdiction of prince-bishops, or of grand dukes and margraves and electors favouring the change because it allowed them at a sweep to confiscate vast properties and melt down tons of chalices and reliquaries into coin.

In Münster lived a draper, Bernhard Knipperdolling by name, who assembled the malcontents in his house, or in a tavern, and poured forth in their ears his sarcasms against the Pope, the bishops, the clergy and the Church. He was well known for his dangerous influence, and the bishop, Frederic von Wied, arrested him as he passed near his residence at Vecht. The people of Münster, exasperated at the news of the captivity of their favourite, obliged the magistrates and the chapter to ask the bishop to release him. Frederick von Wied yielded with reluct-

[1] *Ibid.* p. 138.

ance, using these prophetic words, "I consent, but I fear that this man will turn everything in Münster and the whole diocese upside down." Knipperdolling left prison, after having taken an oath to keep the peace; but on his return to Münster he registered a vow that he would terribly revenge his incarceration, and would make the diocese pay as many ducats as his captivity had cost him hellers.[1]

There was another man in Münster destined to exercise a fatal influence on the unfortunate city. This was a priest named Bernard Rottmann.[2] As a child he had been chorister at St. Maurice's Church at Münster, where his exquisite voice had attracted notice. He was educated in the choir school, then went to Mainz, where in 1524 he took his Master's degree, and returning to Münster, was ordained priest in 1529. He was then given the lectureship of the church in which, as a boy, he had sung so sweetly. He shortly exhibited a leaning towards Lutheranism, and the canons of St. Maurice, who had placed great hopes on the young preacher, thinking that he acted from inexperience and without bad intent, gave him a paternal reprimand, and provided him with funds to go to the University of Cologne, and study there dogmatic and controversial theology; at the same time undertaking to retain Rottmann in the receipt of his salary as lecturer, and to this they added a handsome pension to assist him in his studies.

The young man received this money, and then, instead of going to Cologne, betook himself to

[1] Kerssenbroeck, p. 143.

[2] *Ibid.* 148 ; Latin edition, p. 1517—9; Dorpius, f. 391 a.

Wittenberg, where he attached himself to Melancthon. On his return to Münster, the canons, unaware of the fraud that had been played upon them, reinstated Rottmann in the pulpit. He was too crafty to publish his new tenets in his discourses, and thus to insure the loss of his situation, but he employed his secret influence in society to spread Lutheranism. After a while, when he considered his party strong enough to support him, he threw off the mask, and preached boldly against the priests and the bishops, and certain doctrines of the Catholic Church. The more violent he became in his attacks, the more personal and caustic in his language, the greater grew the throng of people to hear him. Then he preached against Confession, which he called "the disturber of consciences," and contrasted it with Justification by Faith only, which set consciences at ease; he preached against good works, against the obligation to observe the moral law, and assured his hearers that grace was freely imputed to them, live as they liked, and that the Gospel afforded them entire freedom from all restraints. "The shameless dissolution which now began to spread through the town," says Kerssenbroeck, "proved that the mob adopted the belief in the impunity of sin; all those who were ruined in pocket, hoping to get the possessions of others, joined the party of innovators, and Rottmann was extolled by them to the skies."[1]

The Senate forbade the citizens to attend Rottmann's sermons, but their orders were disregarded. The populace declared that Master Bernard was the

---

[1] Kerssenbroeck, p. 152.

only preacher of the true Gospel, and they covered with slander and abuse those who strove to oppose his seductive doctrine. "Some of the episcopal councillors, however," says the historian, "favoured the innovator. The private secretary of the bishop, Leonhard Mosz, encouraged him secretly, and promised him his support in the event of danger."[1]

But the faithful clergy informed the bishop of the scandal, and before Mosz and others could interfere, a sentence of deprivation was pronounced against him.

Rottmann, startled by this decisive measure, wrote a series of letters to Frederick von Wied, which have been preserved by Kerssenbroeck, in which he pretended that he had been calumniated before "the best and most just of bishops," and excused himself, instead of boldly and frankly announcing his secession from the Catholic Church. In reply, the bishop ordered him to quit Münster, and charged his councillors to announce to him that his case would be submitted to the next synod. Rottmann then wrote to the councillors a letter which exhibits his duplicity in a clearer light. Frederick von Wied, hearing of this letter, ordered the recalcitrant preacher to quit the convent adjoining the church of St. Maurice, and to leave the town. Rottmann thereupon took refuge in the house of Knipperdolling and his companions. Under the protection of these turbulent men, the young preacher assumed a bolder line, and wrote to the bishop demanding a public discussion, and an-

[1] Kerssenbroeck, p. 152.

nouncing that shortly his doctrine would be published in a pamphlet, and thus be popularised.

On the 23rd of January, 1532, Rottmann's profession of faith appeared, addressed in the form of a letter to the clergy of Münster.[1] Like all the professions of faith of the period, it consisted chiefly of a string of negations, with a few positive statements retained from the Catholic creed on God, the Incarnation, &c. He denied the special authority of the priesthood, reduced the Sacraments to signs, going thereby beyond Luther; rejected doctrines of the Eucharistic Sacrifice, Purgatory, the intercession of saints, and the use of images, pilgrimages, vows, benedictions, and the like. It would certainly have been more appropriately designated a Confession of Disbelief. This pamphlet was widely circulated amongst the people, and the party of Lutheran malcontents, headed by Knipperdolling, and Herman Bispink, a coiner and forger of title-deeds, grew in power, in numbers, and in audacity.

On the 23rd of February, 1532, Knipperdolling and his associates assembled the populace early, and carried Rottmann in triumph to the church of St. Lambert. Finding the doors shut, they mounted the preacher on a wooden pulpit before the bone-house. The Reformer then addressed the people on the necessity of proclaiming evangelical liberty and of destroying idolatry; of overthrowing images and the Host preserved in the tabernacles. His doctrine might be summed up in two words: liberty for the Evangelicals to do what they liked, and compulsion

[1] *Ibid.* p. 165 *et seq.;* Latin edition, Mencken, p. 1520—8; Sleidan, French tr., p. 406.

for the Catholics. The sermon produced a tremendous effect; before it was concluded the rioters rushed towards the different churches, burst open the doors, tore down the altars, reliquaries, statues; and the Sacrament was taken from the tabernacles and trampled under foot. The cathedral alone, defended by massive gates, escaped their fury.[1]

Proud of this achievement, the insurgents defied all authority, secular and ecclesiastical, and installed Bernhard Rottmann as preacher and pastor of the Evangelical religion in St. Lambert's Church. "Thenceforth," says the Münster contemporary historian, "it may well be understood that they did not limit themselves to simple tumults, but that murders, pillage, and the overthrow of all public order followed. The success of this first enterprise had rendered the leaders masters of the city."

Bishop Frederick von Wied felt that his power was at an end. He was a man with no very strong religious zeal or moral courage. He resigned his dignity in the sacristy of the church of Werne, reserving to himself a yearly income of 2,000 florins. Duke Eric of Brunswick, Prince of Grubenhagen, Bishop of Paderborn and Osnabrück, was elected in his room. The nomination of Eric irritated the Lutheran party. He was a man zealous for his religion, and with powerful relations. Rottmann at once sent him his twenty-nine articles, and the artisans of Münster, who had embraced the cause of Rottmann, handed in a petition to the magistrates (April 16th, 1532) to re-

[1] Kerssenbroeck, p. 185; Bullinger, "Adversus Anabaptist." lib. ii. c. 8.

quest that compulsion might be used to force every one to become Lutheran, " because it seems to us," said they, " that this doctrine is in all points and entirely conformable to the Gospel, whilst that which is taught by the rest of the clergy is absurd, and ought to be rejected."[1]   The bishop-elect wrote to the magistrates, insisting on the dismissal of Rottmann, but in their answer they not only declined to obey, but offered an apology for his conduct.

The bishop wrote again, but received no answer. Wishing to use every means of conciliation, before adopting forcible measures, he sent a deputation to Münster to demand the expulsion of the preacher, but without success.

The people, becoming more insubordinate, determined to take possession of other churches. One of the most important is the church of Unsere Lieb-frau, or Ueberwasser, a church whose beautiful tower and choir attract the admiration of the traveller visiting Münster. This church and parish depended on the convent of Ueberwasser ; the rector was a man of zeal and power, a Dr. Martin, who was peculiarly obnoxious to the Lutheran party. A deputation was sent to the abbess, Ida von Merfelt, to insist on the dismissal of the rector and the substitution of an Evangelical preacher.[2]   The lady was a woman of courage ; she recommended the deputation to return to their shops and to attend to their own business, and announced that Dr. Martin should stay at his post ; and stay he did, for a time.

[1] Kerssenbroeck, pp. 189-90.
[2] *Ibid.* p. 203.

The bishop was resolved to try force of arms, when suddenly he died, May 9th, 1532, after having drunk a goblet of wine. Several writers of the period state that it was poisoned. A modern historian says he died of excess of drink—on what authority I do not know.[1] He had brought down upon himself the dislike of the Lutherans for having vigorously suppressed the reforming movement in Paderborn. The history of that movement in this other Westphalian diocese is too suggestive to be passed over. In 1527 the Elector John Frederick of Saxony passed through Paderborn and ordered his Lutheran preachers to address the people in the streets through the windows of the house in which he lodged, as the clergy refused them the use of the churches. Next year the agitation began by a quarrel between some of the young citizens and the servants of the chapter, and ended in the plundering and devastation of the cathedral and the residences of the canons. The leader of the Evangelical party in Paderborn was Johann Molner of Buren, a man who had been expelled from the city in 1531 for murder and adultery; he left, taking with him as his mistress the wife of the man he had murdered, and retired to Soest, "where," says a contemporary writer, Daniel von Soest, "he did not remain satisfied with this woman only." He returned to Paderborn as a burning and shining gospel light, and led the iconoclastic riot. Duke Philip of Grubenhagen supported his brother, and the town was forced to pay 2,000 gulden for the damage done, and to promise to pay damages

[1] Stürc, "Gerchichte v. Osnabrück." Osnab. 1826, pt. iii. p. 25.

if any further mischief took place, and this so cooled the zeal of the citizens of Paderborn for the Gospel that it died out.[1]

The chapter retired to Ludwigshausen for the purpose of electing the successor to Bishop Eric, who had only occupied the see three months ; their choice fell on Francis von Waldeck, Bishop of Minden, and then of Osnabruck. The choice was not fortunate ; it was dictated by the exigencies of the times, which required a man of rank and power to occupy the vacant throne, so as to reduce the disorder by force of arms. Francis of Waldeck was all this, but the canons were not at that time aware that he had himself strong leanings towards Lutheranism ; and after he became Bishop of Münster he would have readily changed the religion of the place, had it not been that such a proceeding would, under the circumstances, have involved the loss of his income as prince-bishop. Later, when the disturbances were at an end, he proposed to the Estates the establishment of Lutheranism and the suppression of Catholicism, as we shall see in the sequel. He even joined the Smalkald union of the Protestant princes against the Catholics in 1544.

With sentiments so favourable to the Reform, the new bishop would have yielded everything to the agitators, had they not assumed a threatening attitude, and menaced his temporal position and revenue, which were the only things connected with the office for which he cared.

[1] Vehse, "Geschichte der Deutschen Höfe." Hamburg, 1859, vol. xlvii. p. 4-6. Bessen, "Geschichte v. Paderborn; Paderb. 1820, vol. ii. p. 33.

The inferior clergy of Münster wrote energetically to him on his appointment, complaining of the innovations which succeeded each other with rapidity in the town. "The Lutheran party," said they in this letter, "are growing daily more invasive and insolent," and they implored the bishop to protect their rights and liberty of conscience against the tyranny of the new party, who, not content with worshipping God in their own way, refused toleration to others, outraged their feelings by violating all they held most sacred, and disturbed their services by unseemly interruptions.

Francis of Waldeck renewed the orders of his predecessor. The senate acknowledged the receipt of his letter, and promised to answer it on a future occasion.

However, the warmest partisans of Rottmann were resolved to carry matters to a climax, and at once to overthrow both the episcopal and the civil authority. Knipperdolling persuaded the butcher Modersohn and the skinner Redekker that, as provosts of their guilds, they were entitled to convene the members of their trades without the intervention of the magistrates. These two men accordingly convoked the people for the 1st July.[1] The assembly was numerously attended, and opened tumultuously. When silence was obtained, a certain Johann Windemuller rose and proclaimed the purpose of the convention. "The affair is one of importance," said he; "we have to maintain the glory of God, our eternal welfare, the happiness of all our fellow-citizens, and the develop-

[1] Kerssenbroeck, p. 207; Dorpius, f. 391 b. 392.

O

ment of our franchises ; all these things depend on
the sacred ecclesiastical liberty announced to us by
the worthy Rottmann. We must conclude an alliance against the oppressors of the Gospel, that the
doctrine of Rottmann, which is incontestably the true
one, may be protected." These words produced such
enthusiasm, that the audience shouted with one voice
that "they would defend Rottmann and his doctrine
to their last farthing, and the last drop of their blood."
Some of those present, by their silence, expressed
their displeasure, but a draper named Johann Mennemann had the courage to raise his voice against the
proposal. A furious band at once attacked him with
their fists, crying out that the enemies of the pure
Gospel must be destroyed ; "already the bold draper
was menaced with their daggers, when one of his
friends succeeded in effecting his escape from the
popular rage." However, he was obliged to appear
before the heads of the guilds and answer for his
opposition. Mennemann replied, that in weighty
matters concerning the welfare of the commonwealth, tumultuous proceedings were not likely
to produce good resolutions, and that he advised
the separation of the corporations, that the questions might be maturely considered and properly
weighed.[1]

The corporations of trades now appointed twenty-
six individuals, in addition to the provosts, to decide
on measures adapted to carry out the resolution.
This committee decided "that one religion alone
should be taught in the town for the future and for

[1] *Ibid* p. 208.

ever after ;" and that " if any opposition was offered by the magistrates, the whole body of the citizens should be appealed to." [1]

These decisions were presented to the senate on the 11th July, which replied that they were willing not to separate themselves from evangelical truth, but that they were not yet satisfied on which side it was to be found, and that they would ask the bishop to send them learned theologians who should investigate the matter.

This reply irritated Rottmann, Knipperdolling, and their followers. On the 12th July fresh messengers were sent to the Rath (senate) to know whether it might be reckoned upon. The answer was equivocal. A third deputation insisted on an answer of "Yes" or "No," and threatened a general rising of the people unless their demands were acceded to. [2] The magistrates, in alarm, promised their adhesion to the wishes of the insurgents, who demanded at once that "sincere preachers of the pure Gospel" should be installed in every church of Münster. The councillors accordingly issued orders to all the clergy of the city to adopt the articles of Bernard Rottmann, or to refute them by scriptural arguments, or they must expect the Council to proceed against them with the extremest rigour of the law.

Then, to place the seal on their cowardly conduct, they wrote to the prince-bishop on the 25th, to excuse themselves of complicity in the institution of Rottmann, but at the same time they undertook the defence of the Reformer, and assured the bishop

---

[1] Kerssenbroeck, p. 209. [2] *Ibid.* pp. 210, 211.

that his doctrine was sound and irrefutable. At the same time they opened a communication with the Landgrave Philip of Hesse, asking that bulwark of the Reformation to protect them. Philip wrote back, promising his intervention, but warning them not to make the Gospel an excuse for revolt and disorder, and not to imagine that Christian liberty allowed them to seize on all the property of the Church. At the same time he wrote to the prince-bishop to urge upon him not to deprive the good and simple people of Münster of their evangelical preachers.[1]

In the meantime the seditious members of the town guilds grew impatient; and on the 6th August they sent a deputation to the town council reminding it of its promise, and insisting on the immediate deprivation of all the Catholic clergy. The magistrates sought to gain time, but the deputation threatened them with the people taking the law into their own hands, rejecting the authority of the council, and electing another set of magistrates.

"The Rath, on hearing this," says Kerssenbroeck, "were filled with alarm, and they considered it expedient to yield, in part at least, to the populace, and to deprive the clergy of their rights, rather than to expose themselves rashly to the greatest dangers."[2]

They resolved therefore to forbid the Catholic clergy the use of the pulpits of the churches, and to address the people in any form. This was done at once, and all ceremonies "contrary to the pure word of God" were abolished, and the faithful in the different parishes

[1] Kerssenbroeck, pp. 212-23.   [2] *Ibid.* p. 227.

were required to receive and maintain the new pastors commissioned by the burgomaster and corporation to minister to them in things divine.

On the 10th August, a crowd, headed by Rottmann, the preacher Brixius, and Knipperdolling, fell upon the churches and completed the work of devastation which had been begun in February. The Cathedral and the Church of Ueberwasser alone escaped their Vandalism, because the fanatics were afraid of arousing too strong an opposition. The same day the celebration of mass and communion in one kind were forbidden under the severest penalties; the priests were driven out of their churches, and Rottmann, Brixius, Glandorp, Rolle, Wertheim, and Gottfried Ninnhoven, Lutheran preachers, were intruded in their room.[1]

The peace among these new apostles of the true Gospel was, however, subject to danger. Pastor Brixius had fallen in love with the sister of Pastor Rottmann, and the appearance of the girl proved to every one that the lovers had not waited for the ceremony of marriage. Rottmann insisted on this brother pastor marrying the young woman to repair the scandal. But no sooner was the bride introduced into the parsonage of St. Martin, of which Brixius was in possession, than the first wife of the evangelical minister arrived in Münster with her two children. Brixius was obliged to send away the new wife, but a coldness ensued between him and Rottmann; "however, fearing to cause dissension amongst their adher-

[1] *Ibid.* pp. 228-34.

ents by an open quarrel, they came to some arrangement, and Brixius retained his situation."[1]

These acts of violence and scandals had inspired many of the citizens with alarm. Those who were able sent their goods out of the town; the nuns of Ueberwasser despatched their title-deeds and sacred vessels to a place of safety. Several of the wealthy citizens and senators, who would not give up their religion, deserted Münster, and settled elsewhere. The two burgomasters, Ebroin Drost and Willebrand Plonies, resigned their offices and left the city never to return.[2] The provosts of the guilds next insisted on the severe repression of all Catholic usages and the performance of sacraments by the priests; they went further, and insisted on belief in the sacrifice of the altar and adoration of the Host being made penal. The clergy wrote to the bishop imploring his aid, and assuring him that their position was daily becoming more intolerable; but Francis of Waldeck recommended patience, and promised his aid when it lay in his power to assist them.

On the 17th September, 1532, he convoked the nobles of the principality at Wollbeck, gave them an account of the condition of Münster, and conjured them to assist him in suppressing the rebellion.[3] The nobles replied, that before adopting violent measures, it would be advisable to attempt a reconciliation. Eight commissioners were chosen from amongst the barons, who wrote to the magistrates, and requested them to send their deputies to Wollbeck on Monday, Septem-

[1] Kerssenbroeck, pp. 228, 229.   [2] *Ibid.* p. 230.
[3] *Ibid.* p. 248 *et seq.*

ber 23rd, "so as to come to some decision on what is necessary for the welfare of the republic." The envoys of the city appeared, and after the opening of the assembly, the grand marshal of the diocese described the condition of the city, and declared that if it pursued its course of disobedience, the nobility were prepared to assist their prince in re-establishing order. The delegates were given eight days to frame an answer. The agitation in Münster during these days was great. The evangelical preachers lost no time in exciting the people. The deputies returned to the conference with a vague answer that the best way to settle the differences would be to submit them to competent and enlightened judges; and so the matter dropped.

The bishop's officers now captured a herd of fat cattle belonging to some citizens of Münster, which were on their way to Cologne, and refused to surrender them till the preachers of disaffection were sent away.[1]

The party of Rottmann and Knipperdolling now required the town council to raise 500 soldiers for the defence of the town, should it be attacked by the prince-bishop—to strike 2000 ducats in copper for the payment of the mercenaries, such money to circulate in Münster alone—to order the sentinels to forbid egress to the Catholic clergy, should they attempt to fly —and to impose on the Catholic clergy a tax of 4000 florins a month for the support of the troops. As the clergy had been deprived of their benefices, forbidden to preach and minister the sacraments, this additional

[1] Kerssenbroeck, pp. 268-9.

act of persecution was intolerable in its injustice. The senate accepted these requisitions with some abatement—the number of soldiers was reduced to 300.[1]

The bishop, finding that the confiscation of the oxen had not produced the required results, adopted another expedient which proved equally ineffectual. He closed all the roads by his cavalry, declared the city in a state of blockade, and forbade the peasantry taking provisions into Münster. The artizans then marched out and took the necessary food; they paid for it, but threatened the peasants with spoliation without repayment, unless they frequented the market with their goods as usual. This menace produced its effect; Münster continued to be provisioned as before.[2]

Proud of their success, the innovators attacked Ueberwasser Church, and ordered the abbess to dismiss the Catholic clergy who ministered there, and to replace them by Gospel preachers. She declined peremptorily, and the mob then drove the priests out of the church and presbytery, and instituted Lutherans in their place.[3]

Notwithstanding the decrees of the senate, the priests continued their exhortations and their ministrations in such churches as the Evangelicals were unable to supply with pastors, of whom there was a lack. Brixius, the bigamist minister of St. Martin's, having found in one of them a monk preaching to a crowd of women, rushed up into the pulpit, crying out that the man was telling them lies; "but," says

[1] *Ibid.* p. 279 *et seq.*   [2] *Ibid.* p. 283 *et seq.*
[3] *Ibid.* pp. 284, 285.

Kerssenbroeck, " the devotees surrounded the unfortunate orator, beat him with their fists, slippers, wooden shoes and staves, so that he fled the church, his face and body black and blue." Probably these women bore him a grudge also for his treatment of Rottmann's sister, which was no secret. " Furious at this, he went next day to exhibit the traces of the combat to the senate, entreating them to revenge the outrage he had received—he a minister of the Holy Gospel ; but, for the first time, the magistrates showed some sense, and declared that they would not meddle in the matter, because the guilty persons were too numerous, and that some indulgence ought to be shown to the fair sex."[1]

The town council now sent deputies to the Protestant princes, Dukes Ernest and Francis of Lüneburg, the Landgrave Philip of Hesse, and Count Philip of Waldeck, brother of the prince-bishop, to promise the adhesion of the city to the Smalkald union, and to request their assistance against their bishop. The situation was singular. The city sought assistance of the Protestant union against their prince, desiring to overthrow his power, under the plea that he was a Catholic bishop. And the bishop, at heart a Lutheran, and utterly indifferent to his religious position and responsibilities, was determined to coerce his subjects into obedience, that he might retain his rank and revenue as prince, intending, when the city returned to its obedience, to shake off his episcopal office, to Lutheranize his subjects, and remain their sovereign prince, and possibly transform the ecclesi-

---

[1] Kerssenbroeck, p. 330.

astical into a hereditary principality, the appanage of a family of which he would be the founder. He had already provided himself with a concubine, Anna Pölmann, by whom he had children.

Whilst the senate was engaged in treating with the Protestant princes, negotiations continued with the bishop, at the diets convoked successively at Dulmen and Wollbeck, but they were as fruitless as before. The deputies separated on the 9th December, agreeing to meet again on the 21st of the same month.

At this time there arrived in Münster a formal refutation of the theses of Rottmann, by John of Deventer, provincial of the Franciscans at Cologne.[1] The magistrates had repeatedly complained that "the refusal of the Catholics to reply to Bernard Rottmann was the sole cause of all the evil." At the same time they had forbidden the Catholic clergy to preach or to make use of the press in Münster. This answer came like a surprise upon them. It was carried by the foes of the clergy to the magistrates. The news of the appearance of this counterblast created the wildest excitement. "The citizens, assembled in great crowds, ran about the streets to hear what was being said. Some announced that the victory would remain with Rottmann, others declared that he would never recover the blow."

The provosts of the guilds hastily drew up a petition to the senate to expel the clergy from the town, and to confiscate their goods; but the magistrates refused to comply with this requisition, which would have at once stirred up civil war.[2]

[1] Kerssenbroeck, p. 332.   [2] *Ibid.* pp. 335-7.

Rottmann mounted the pulpit on St. Andrew's day, and declared that on the following Sunday he would refute the arguments of John of Deventer. Accordingly, on the day appointed, he preached to an immense crowd, taking for his text the words of St. Paul (Rom. xiii. 12), "The night is far spent, the day is at hand." The sermon was not an answer to the arguments of John of Deventer, but a furious attack upon the Pope and Catholicism. Knipperdolling also informed the people that he would rather have his children killed and cooked and served up for dinner than surrender his evangelical principles and return to the errors of the past.[1]

On the 21st December, 1532, Francis of Waldeck assembled the diet of the principality, and asked its advice as to the advisability of proclaiming war against Münster, should the city persist in its obstinacy.[2] The clergy and nobles replied that, according to immemorial custom, the prince must engage in war at his own cost, and that they were too heavily burdened with taxes for the Turkish war to enable them to undertake fresh charges. Francis of Waldeck reminded them that he was obliged to pay a pension of 2000 florins to his predecessor, Frederick von Wied, and he affirmed that he also was not in a condition to have recourse to arms.

Whilst the prince, his barons and canons were deliberating, Rottmann had assumed the ecclesiastical dictatorship in the cathedral city, and had ordered, on his sole authority, the suppression of the observance of fast-days.

[1] *Ibid.* p. 338.　　[2] *Ibid.* p. 340 *et seq.*

The spirit of opposition and protestation that had been evoked already manifested itself in strange excesses. "Some of the Evangelicals refused to have the bread put into their mouths at Communion," says Kerssenbroeck, "but insisted on helping themselves from the table, or they stained themselves in taking long draughts at the large chalices. It is even said that some placed the bread in large soup tureens, and poured the wine upon it, and took it out with spoons and forks, so that they might communicate in both kinds at one and the same moment."[1]

The Reformer of Münster began to entertain and to express doubts as to the validity of the baptism of infants, which he considered had not the warrant of Holy Scripture. Melancthon wrote urgently to him, imploring him not to create dissensions in the Evangelical Church by disturbing the arrangement many wise men had agreed upon. "We have enemies enough," added Melancthon; "they will be rejoiced to see us tearing each other and destroying one another. . . . I speak with good intention, and I take the liberty of giving my advice, because I am devoted to you and to the Church."[2]

Luther wrote as well, not to Rottmann, but to the magistrates of Münster, praising their love of the Gospel, and urging them to beware of being drawn away by the damnable errors of the Sacramentarians, Zwinglians, *aliorumque schwermerorum.*[3] The senators received this apostolic epistle with the utmost respect and reverence imaginable; they communicated it to Rottmann and his colleagues, and ordered them

[1] Kerssenbroeck, p. 347.　　[2] *Ibid.* p. 348.　　[3] *Ibid.* p. 349.

to obey it. But the senate had long lost its authority; and this injunction was disregarded.[1] " Disorder and infidelity made progress ; the idle, rogues, spend-thrifts, thieves, and ruined persons swelled the crowd of Evangelists."[2]

However, it was not enough to have introduced the new religion, to satisfy the Evangelicals the Catholics must be completely deprived of the exercise of their religion. In spite of every hindrance, mass had been celebrated every Sunday in the cathedral. All the parish churches had been deprived of their priests, but the minster remained in the hands of the Catholics. As Christmas approached, many men and women pre-pared by fasting, alms, and confession, to make their communion at the cathedral on the festival of the Nativity.

The magistrates, hearing of their design, forbade them communicating, offering, as an excuse, that it would cause scandal to the partisans of the Reform. They also published a decree forbidding baptisms to be performed elsewhere than in the parish churches ; so as to force the faithful to bring their children to the ministrations of men whom they regarded with aversion as heretics and apostates.[3]

No envoys from the capital attended the reunion of the chambers at Wollbeck on the 20th December. But Münster sent a letter expressing a hope that the difference between the city and the prince might be terminated by mediation.

This letter gave the diet a chance of escaping from its very difficult position of enforcing the rule of the

[1] Kerssenbroeck, p. 351.   [2] *Ibid.* p. 351.   [3] *Ibid.* p. 353.

prince without money to pay the soldiers. The diet
undertook to lay the suggestion before the prince-
bishop, and to transmit his reply to the envoys of
Münster.

Francis of Waldeck then quitted his diocese of
Minden, and betook himself to Telgte,[1] a little town
about four miles from Münster, where he was to
receive the oath of allegiance and homage of his
subjects in the principality. The estates assembled
at Wollbeck, and all the leading nobles and clergy of
the diocese hastened to Telgte and assembled around
their sovereign on the same day. A letter was at
once addressed to the senate of Münster by the
assembled estates, urging it to send deputies to
Telgte, the following morning, at eight o'clock, to
labour together with them at the re-establishment of
peace.

The deputies did not appear ; the senate addressed
to the diet, instead, a letter of excuses. The estates
at once replied that in the interest of peace, they regretted the obstinacy with which the senate had refused to send deputies to Telgte ; but that this had
not prevented them from supplicating the bishop to
yield to their wishes ; and that they were glad to
announce that he was ready to submit the mutual
differences to the arbitration of two princes of the
Empire, one to be named by himself, the other by the
city of Münster. And until the arbitration took place,
the prince-bishop would provisionally suspend all
measures of severity, on condition that the ancient
usages should be restored in the churches, the

[1] *Ibid.* p. 354 *et seq.*   Sleidan, French tr. p. 407.

preachers should cease to innovate, and that the imprisoned vassals of the bishop should be released.

This missive was sent into the town on the 25th; the magistrates represented to the bearer "that it would be scandalous to occupy themselves with temporal affairs on Christmas-day," and on this pretext they persuaded him to remain till the morrow in Münster. Then orders were given for the gates of the town to be closed, and egress to be forbidden to every one.

Having taken these precautions, the magistrates assembled the provosts of the guilds, and held with them a conference, which terminated shortly before nine o'clock the same evening; after which the subaltern officers of the senate were sent round to rap at every door, and order the citizens to assemble at midnight, before the town-hall. A nocturnal expedition had been resolved upon; but the movement in the town had excited the alarm of the Catholics, who, thinking that a general massacre of those who adhered to the old religion was in contemplation, hid themselves in drains and cellars and chimneys.

Arms were brought out of the arsenal, cannons were mounted, waggons were laden with powder, shot, beams, planks and ladders. At the appointed hour, the crowd, armed in various fashions, assembled before the Rath-haus.[1] The magistrates and provosts then selected six hundred trusty Evangelicals, and united them to a band of three hundred mercenaries and a small troop of horse. The rest were dispersed upon

[1] Kerssenbroeck, p. 358 *et seq.* Sleidan, French tr. p. 408. Sleidan also gives the number as 900; Dorpius, f. 392 b.

the ramparts and were recommended to keep watch; then it was announced to the party in marching order that they were to hasten stealthily to Telgte and capture the prince-bishop, his councillors, the barons, and all the members of the estates then assembled in that little town.

However, the diet, surprised at not seeing their messenger return, conceived a slight suspicion. Whether he feared that his person was in danger so near Münster is not known, but fortunately for himself, the prince, that same evening, left Telgte for his castle of Iburg. The members of the diet, after long waiting, sent some men along the road to the capital to ascertain whether their messenger was within sight. These men returned, saying that the gates of Münster were closed and that no one was to be seen stirring.

The fact was singular, not to say suspicious; and a troop of horse was ordered to make a reconnaissance in the direction of Münster. It was already late at night, so, having given the order, the members of the diet retired to their beds. The horse soldiers beat the country, found all quiet, withdrew some planks from a bridge over the Werse, between Telgte and Münster, to intercept the passage, and then returned to their quarters, for the night was bitterly cold. On surmounting a hill, crowned by a gibbet, they, however, turned once more and looked over the plain towards the city. A profound silence reigned; but a number of what they believed to be will-o'-the-wisps flitted here and there over the dark ground. As, according to popular superstition in Westphalia, these little lights are to be seen in great abundance at Yuletide, the horsemen paid no attention to them, but continued their return. These lights, mistaken for marsh fires, were in fact the burning matches of the arquebuses carried by those engaged in the sortie. On their return to Telgte, the horse soldiers retired to their quarters, and in half-an-hour all the inhabitants of the town were fast asleep.

Meanwhile, the men of Münster advanced, replaced the bridge over the Werse, traversed the plain, and reached Telgte at two o'clock in the morning. They at once occupied all the streets, according to a plan concerted beforehand, then invaded the houses, and captured the members of the diet, clergy, nobles and commons. Three only of the cathedral chapter escaped in their night shirts with bare feet across the frozen river Ems. The Münsterians, having laid their hands on all the money, jewels, seals, and gold chains they could find, retreated as rapidly as they had advanced, carrying off with them their captives and the booty, but disappointed in not having secured the person of the prince. They entered the cathedral city in triumph on the morning of the 26th December, highly elated at their success, and nothing doubting that with such hostages in their hands, they would be able to dictate their own terms to the sovereign.

But the expedition of Telgte had made a great sensation in the empire. Francis of Waldeck addressed himself to all the members of the Germanic body, and appealed especially to his metropolitan, the Elector of Cologne, for assistance, and also to the Dukes of Cleves and Gueldres. The elector wrote at

P

once to Münster in terms the most pressing, because
some of his own councillors were among the prisoners.
He received an evasive answer. The Protestant
princes of the Smalkald league even addressed letters
to the senate, blaming energetically their high-handed
proceeding. Philip Melancthon also wrote a letter of
mingled remonstrance and entreaty.[1] The only result
of their appeals was the restoration to the prisoners of
their money and the jewels taken from them.

John von Wyck, syndic of Bremen, was despatched
by the senate of Münster to the Landgrave Philip of
Hesse, to ask him to undertake the office of mediator
between them and their prince. The Landgrave
readily accepted the invitation, and Francis of
Waldeck was equally ready to admit his mediation, as
he was himself, as has been already stated, a Lutheran
at heart. The people of Münster, finding that the
bishop was eager for a pacific settlement, insisted on
the payment of the value of the oxen he had confiscated, as a preliminary, before the subject of
differences was entered upon. The prince-bishop
consented, paid 450 florins, and allowed the Landgrave
of Hesse to draw up sixteen articles of treaty, which
met with the approval of both the senate and himself.

The terms of the agreement were as follows:[2]—

I. The prince-bishop was to offer no violence to the
inhabitants of Münster in anything touching religion.
"The people of Münster shall keep the pure Word of
God," said the article; "it shall be preached to them,

---

[1] Kerssenbioeck, p. 368.　　　[2] *Ibid.* p. 392 *et seq.*

without any human additions by their preachers, in the six parish churches. These same preachers shall minister the sacraments and order their services and ceremonies as they please. The citizens shall submit in religious matters to the judgment of the magistrates alone, till the questions at issue are decided by a General Council."

II. The Catholics were to exercise their religion freely in the cathedral and in the capitular churches not included in the preceding article, *until Divine Providence should order otherwise.* The Lutheran ministers were forbidden to attack the Catholics, their dogmas and rights, *unless the Word of God imperiously required it ;*—a clause opening a door to any amount of abuse. As the speciality of Protestantism of every sort consists in negation, it would be impossible for an Evangelical pastor to hold his position without denouncing what he disbelieved.

Artice III. interdicted mutual recriminations. Article IV., in strange contradiction with Article I., declared that the town of Münster should obey the prince-bishop as legitimate sovereign in matters spiritual and temporal. The bishop in the Vth Article promised to respect the privileges of the subject.

The VIth Article forbade any one making an arbitrary use of the Word of God to justify refusal of obedience to the magistrates. Article VII. reserved to the clergy their revenues, with the exception of the six parish churches, of which the revenues were to be employed for the maintenance of the Evangelical pastors. By the VIIIth Article the senate promised not to interfere with the collation to benefices not in their hands by right. The IXth Article allowed the citizens to deprive their pastors in the Lutheran churches, without the intervention of the bishop. The rest of the Articles secured a general amnesty, permission to the refugees to return, and to the imprisoned members of the diet to obtain their freedom.

This treaty was fair enough in its general provisions. If, as was the case, a large number of the citizens were disposed to adopt Lutheranism, no power on earth had any right to constrain them, and they might justly claim the free exercise of their religion. But there were suspicious clauses inserted in the 1st and 2nd Articles which pointed to the renewal of animosity and the re-opening of the whole question.

This treaty was signed on the 14th February, 1533, by Philip of Hesse, as mediator, Francis, Count of Waldeck, Prince and Bishop of Münster, the members of chapter, the representatives of the nobles of the principality, and the burgomasters and senators of Münster, together with those of the towns of Coesfeld and Warendorf, in their own name and in behalf of the other towns of the diocese. The captive estates were liberated on the 18th February. How the magistrates and town kept the other requirements of the treaty we shall soon see.

The senate having been constituted supreme authority in spiritual things by the Lutheran party, now undertook the organisation of the Evangelical Church in the city ; and a few days after the treaty had been signed, it published an " Evangelical Constitution," consisting of ten articles, for the government of the new Church.[1]

The 8th article had a threatening aspect. "The ministers of the Divine Word shall use their utmost endeavours to gain souls to the true faith, and to direct them in the ways of perfection. *As for those who shall refuse to accept the pure doctrine*, and those who shall blaspheme and be guilty of public crimes, the senate will employ against them all the rigour of the laws, and the sword of justice.

Rottmann was appointed by the magistrates Superintendent of the Lutheran Church in Münster, a function bearing a certain resemblance to that of a bishop.[2] Then, thinking that a bishop should be the husband of one wife at least, Rottmann married the widow of Johann Vigers, late syndic of Münster. "She was a person of bad character," says Kerssenbroeck, "whom Rottmann had inspired during her husband's life with Evangelical principles and an adulterous love."[3] It is asserted, with what truth it is impossible at this distance of time to decide, that Vigers was drowned in his bath at Ems, in a fit, and that his wife allowed him to perish without attempting to save him. Anyhow, no sooner was he dead, than she returned full speed to Münster and married her lover.[4]

The reformer and his adherents had been given their own way, and the senate hoped they would rest satisfied, and that tranquillity would be re-established in the city. But their hopes were doomed to disappointment.

---

[1] Kerssenbroeck, p. 398 *et seq.*   [2] *Ibid.* p. 402.
[3] *Ibid.* p. 403.   [4] *Ibid.* p. 404.

Certain people, if given an inch, insist on taking an ell; of these people Rottmann was one. Excited by him, the Evangelicals of the town complained that the magistrates had treated the Papists with too great leniency, that the clergy had not been expelled and their goods confiscated according to the original programme. It was decided tumultuously that the elections must be anticipated; and on the 3rd March, the people deposed the magistrates and elected in their room the leaders of the extreme reforming party.[1] Knipperdolling was of their number; only four of the former magistrates were allowed to retain office, and these were men whom they could trust. Hermann Tilbeck and Kaspar Judenfeld were named burgomasters; Heinrich Modersohn and Heinrich Redekker were chosen provosts or tribunes of the people.[2]

Next to the senate came the turn of the parishes. On the 17th March, under the direction of Rottmann, the people proceeded to appoint the ministers to the churches in the town. Their choice was not happy; it fell on those most unqualified to exercise a salutary influence, and restrain the excitement of a mob already become nearly ungovernable.[3]

The new senate endeavoured to strengthen the Evangelical cause by uniting the other towns of the diocese in a common bond of resistance. They invited these towns to send their deputies to meet those of the capital at a little inn between Münster and Coesfeld, on the 20th March. The assembly took place; but so

---

[1] Kerssenbroeck, p. 404.　　[2] *Ibid.* p. 405.　　[3] *Ibid.* p. 406.

far from the other cities agreeing to support Münster, their deputies read those of the capital a severe lecture, and refused to throw off their old religion and their allegiance to the bishop.[1]

On the 24th March, 1533, the burgomaster Tilbeck, accompanied by the citizen Kerbink, went to Ueberwasser, summoned the abbess before him, and ordered her to maintain at the expense of the abbey the preachers lately appointed to the church in connection with the convent. She was forced to submit.[2]

On the 27th of the same month one of the preachers invaded the church of St. Ledger, still in the hands of the Catholics, at the head of his congregation, broke open the tabernacle, drew out the Host, broke it, and blowing the fragments into the air, screamed to the assembled multitude, "Look at your good God flying away."

The same day the treaty was violated towards the Franciscans. Some of the senators ordered them to quit their convent, their habit, and their order, unless they desired still more rigorous treatment, "because the magistrates were resolved to make the Church flourish again in her ancient purity, and because they wanted to convert the convent into a school."[3]

The superior replied that he and his brethren followed strictly the rule of their founder, and that this house belonged to them by right of succession, and that they were no charge to the town. He said that if a building was needed for an Evangelical

[1] Kerssenbroeck, p. 407 *et seq.*　　[2] *Ibid.* p. 413.
[3] *Ibid.* p. 413.

school, he was ready to surrender to the magistrates a portion of the convent buildings ; all he asked in return was that he and his brethren should be allowed to live in tranquillity. This proposal saved the Franciscans for a time. The Evangelical school was established in their convent, "but at the end of a month it had fallen into complete disorder, whereas the old Papist school had not lost one of its pupils, and was as flourishing as ever."[1]

Whilst the senators menaced the monasteries, Knipperdolling and his friend Gerhardt Kibbenbroeck pillaged the church of S. Lambert. Scarcely a day now passed without some fresh act of violence done to the Catholics, or Vandalism perpetrated on the churches.

On the 5th April the prior and monks of Bispinkhoff were forbidden by the magistrates to hear confessions in their own church. The same day the Lutherans broke the altar and images in the church of Ueberwasser, and scraped the paintings off the walls.

On Palm Sunday, April 6th,[2] at Ueberwasser, some of the nuns, urged by the preachers in their church, cast off their vows, and joining the people, chanted the 7th verse of the 124th Psalm according to Luther's translation—

> " Der Strich ist entzwei,
> Und wir sind frei."

" The snare is broken, and we are delivered ; " and then they received Communion with the pastors.

On the 7th the mob pillaged the church of the

---

[1] Kerssenbroeck, p. 415.   [2] *Ibid.* p. 416.

Servites, and defaced it. Next day the Franciscans, who had made the wafers for the Holy Sacrament for the churches in the diocese, were forbidden to make them any more. On the 9th Knipperdolling, heading a party of the reformed, broke into the cathedral during the celebration of the Holy Eucharist, rushed up to the altar, and drove away the priest, exclaiming, "Greedy fop, haven't you eaten enough good Gods yet?" Two days later the magistrates ordered the chapter to surrender into their hands their title deeds and sacred vessels. On the 14th, Belkot, head of the city tribunal of Münster, entered the church of S. Ledger, and carried off all its chalices, patens, and ciboriums, whilst others who accompanied him destroyed the altars, paintings, and statuary, and profaned the church in the most disgusting manner. The unhappy Catholics, unable to resist, uttered loud lamentations, and did not refrain from calling the perpetrators of the outrage "robbers and sacrilegious," for which they were summoned before the magistrates, and threatened with imprisonment unless they apologised.[1]

As the news of the conversion of the city of Münster to the Gospel spread, strangers came to it from all parts, to hear and to learn, as they gave out, pure Evangelical truth.

Amongst these adventurers was a man destined to play a terribly prominent part in the great drama that was about to be enacted at Münster. This was John Bockelson, a tailor, a native of Leyden, in Holland. He had quitted his country and his wife secretly to hear Rottmann. He entered Münster

---

[1] *Ibid.* 417.

on the 25th July, and lodged with a citizen named Hermann Ramers. Having been instructed in the Gospel according to Luther, he went to preach in Osnabrück, but from thence he was driven. He then returned to his own home. There he became an Anabaptist, under the instruction of John Matthisson, who sent him with Gerrit Buchbinder as apostles of the sect to Westphalia in the month of November, 1533.

The time had now arrived when the Lutheran party, which had so tyrannically treated the Catholics in the city of Münster, was itself to be despotically put down and trampled upon by a sect which sprang from its own womb.

Rottmann had for some while been wavering in his adhesion to Lutheranism.[1] He doubted first, and then disbelieved in the Real Presence, which Luther insisted upon. He thought that the reformation of the Wittenberg doctor was not sufficiently thoroughgoing in the matter of ceremonial; then he doubted the scriptural authority for the baptism of infants. Two preachers, Heinrich Rott and Herman Strapedius, fell in with his views. The former had been a monk at Haarlem, but had become a Lutheran preacher. He regarded the baptism of infants as one of those things which are indifferent to salvation. Strapedius was more decided; he preached against infant baptism as an abomination in the sight of God. He was named by the people preacher at S. Lambert's, the head

---

[1] Kerssenbroeck, p. 429 *et seq.*; Sleidan, French tr. p. 409 ; Bullinger, "Adv. Anabapt.," 116, ii. c. 8.

church of the city, in spite of the opposition of the authorities.[1]

The Lutheran senate of Münster, which a few months previously had been elected enthusiastically by the people, now felt that before these fiery preachers, drifting into Anabaptism, their power was in as precarious a position as was that of those whom they had supplanted. Alarmed at the rapid extension of the new forms of disbelief, they twice forbade Rottmann to preach against the baptism of infants and the Real Presence, and ordered him to conform in his teaching to authorised Lutheran doctrine. He treated their orders with contempt. Then they summoned him before them : he appeared, but on leaving the Rathhaus, preached in the square to the people with redoubled violence.

The senate, at their wits' end, ordered a public discussion between Rottmann and the orthodox Lutherans, represented by Hermann Busch. The discussion took place before the city Rath, and the senate decided that Busch had gained the day, and they therefore forbade all innovation in the administration of baptism and the Lord's Supper.

Rottmann and his colleague disregarded the monition, and continued their sermons against the rags of Popery which still disfigured the Lutheran Church. Several of the ministers in the town, whether from conviction or from interest, finding that their congregations drained away to the churches where the stronger-spiced doctrine was preached, joined the movement. It was simply a carrying of negation beyond the pillars

[1] Kerssenbroeck, pp. 431, 432 ; Dorp., f. 322-3.

of Hercules planted by Luther. Luther had denied of the sum total of Catholic dogmas, say ten, and had retained ten. The Anabaptist denied two more, and retained only eight. On the 10th August a tumultuous scene took place in the church of S. Giles.[1] A Dutch preacher began declaiming against baptism of children. Johann Windemoller, ex-senator, a vehement opponent of Anabaptist disintegration of Lutheran doctrine, who was in the congregation, rushed up the pulpit stairs, and pulled the preacher down, exclaiming, "Scoundrel! how dare you take upon you the office of preacher—you who, a few years ago, were thrust into the iron-collar, and branded on the cheek for your crimes? Do you think I do not know your antecedents? *You* talk of virtue, you gibbet-bird? You who are guilty of so many crimes and impieties? Go along with you, take your doctrine and your brand elsewhere."

Windemoller was about to turn the pastor out of the church, when a number of women, who had joined the Anabaptist party, fell, howling, upon Windemoller, crying that he wanted to deprive them of the saving Gospel and Word of Truth, and they would have strangled him had he not beat a precipitate retreat. The same afternoon, some citizens who brought their children to this church to be baptized were driven from the doors with shouts of derision.

The magistrates played a trump card, and ordered Rottmann to leave the town, together with the ministers who followed his teaching.[2] Bernard Rottmann replied much in the same strain as he had answered the bishop,

[1] Kerssenbroeck, p. 434.   [2] *Ibid.* p. 436.

stating that his doctrine was strictly conformable to the pure word of God, and that he demanded a public discussion, in which his doctrines might be tested by Scripture alone, without human additions. Finally he protested that he would not abstain from preaching, nor desert his flock, whether the senate persisted in its sentence or not. Five ministers signed this defiant letter—Rottmann, Johann Clopris, Heinrich Roll, Gottfried Strahl, and Denis Vinnius. These men at once hastened to collect the heads of the corporations and provosts together, and urge them to take their part against the Rath. They were quite prepared to do so, and the magistrates yielded on condition that Bernard and his following of preachers should abstain from speaking on the disputed questions of infant baptism and the Eucharist. Rottmann consented, in his own name and in that of his friends, in a paper dated October 3rd, 1533.[1] The senate was, however, well aware that its power was tottering to its fall, and that the preachers had not the remotest intention of fulfilling their engagement. They saw that these men were gradually absorbing into themselves the supreme authority in the city, and that a magistracy which opposed them could at any moment be by them dismissed their office. In alarm they wrote to the prince-bishop, and sent him messengers to lay before him the precarious condition of the affairs in the capital, imploring him to consider the imminence of the peril, and to send them learned theologians who could combat the spread of erroneous doctrine, and introduce those conformable to the pure word of God.[2]

[1] *Ibid.* pp. 437-9   [2] *Ibid.* p. 441.

It was a singular state of affairs indeed. The magistrates had appealed to the pure word of God, as understood by Luther, against Catholicism, and now the Anabaptists appealed to the same oracle, with equal confidence against Lutheranism; the two parties leaned on the same support—who was to decide which party Scripture upheld?

The answer of Francis of Waldeck was such as might have been expected from a man endowed with some common sense. He reminded the magistrates that it was their own fault if things had come to such a pass; he feared that now the evil had gained the upper hand, and that gentleness was out of place; a decided face could alone secure to the magistrates moral authority. He was ready to support them if they would maintain their allegiance for the future. He would send them a learned theologian, Dr. Heinrich Mumpert, prior of the Franciscans of Bispinkhoff, to preach against error in the cathedral.

The senate was in a dilemma. They had no wish to return to Catholicism, and they dreaded the progress of schism. They stood on an inclined plane. Above was the rock of an infallible authority; below, faith shelved into an abyss of negation they shrank from fathoming. If they looked back, they saw Catholicism; if they looked forward, they beheld the dissolution of all positive belief. Like all timorous men they shrank from either alternative, and attempted for a little' longer to maintain their slippery position. They declined the offer of the Catholic doctor, and turned to the Landgrave Philip of Hesse for assistance. The Landgrave at once acceded to the request of the magistrates, and sent them Theodore Fabricius and Johann Melsinger, guaranteeing to their senate their orthodoxy.[1]

While these preachers were on their way, disorder increased in Münster. The faction of Rottmann grew apace, and spread into the Convent of Ueberwasser, where the nuns were daily compelled to hear the harangues of two zealous Evangelical pastors, who exerted themselves strenuously to demolish the faith of the sisters down to the point fixed as the limit of negation by Luther. But these pastors having become infected with Rottmann's views, continued the work of destruction, and lowered the temple of faith two additional stages.

The result of these sermons on the excitable nuns was that the majority broke out into revolt, and refused to observe abstinence and practise self-mortification; and proclaimed their intention of returning to the world and marrying. The bishop wrote to them, imploring them to consider that they were all of them members of noble families, and that they must be careful in no way to dishonour their families by scandalous behaviour. The mutineers seemed disposed to yield, but we shall presently see that their submission was only temporary.[2]

On the 15th October, the senate wrote to the bishop, and informed him that they would not permit the prior Mumpert to preach in the cathedral.[3] They acknowledged that according to the treaty of Telgte,

---

[1] Kerssenbroeck, p. 443; Sleidan, p. 410; Dorpius, f. 393 b.
[2] Kerssenbroeck, p. 443.   [3] *Ibid.* p. 444.

the city had consented to allow the Catholics the use
of the cathedral, "until such time as the Lord shall
dispose otherwise," but, they said, at the time of the
conclusion of the treaty, there was no preacher at the
minster; which was true, for the Catholic clergy had
been forbidden the use of the pulpit; and they declared
that "in all good conscience, they could not permit
the institution of one whose doctrine and manner of
life were not conformable to the gospel."

Francis of Waldeck, without paying attention to
this refusal, ordered Mumpert to preach and celebrate
the Eucharist in the cathedral church, on Sunday,
26th October, 1533. The prior obeyed. The fury of
the Evangelicals was without limits; and in a second
letter, more insolent than the first, the magistrates told
the bishop that "they would not suffer a fanatical friar
to come and teach error to the people." The bishop's
sole reply was a command to the prior to continue his
course.

At this moment the learned divines sent by Philip
of Hesse arrived in the city, and hearing of the sermons
in the minster, to which the people flocked, and which
were likely to produce a counter-current in a Catholic
direction, they insisted, as a preliminary to their mission, that the mouth of the Catholic preacher should
be stopped. "We pray you," said they to the magistrates, "to forbid this man permission to reside in the
town, lest our pure doctrine be choked by his abominable sermons. An authority claiming to be Christian
should not tolerate such a scandal."

The senate hastened to satisfy the Hessian theologians, by not merely ordering the Catholic preacher

to leave the city, but by outlawing him, so that he was obliged in haste to fly a place where his life might be taken by any unscrupulous persons with impunity.[1]

Francis of Waldeck, justly irritated, wrote to Philip of Hesse, remonstrating at the interference of his commissioners in the affairs of another man's principality.[2] The Landgrave replied that, so far from deserving reproach, he merited thanks for having sent to Münster two divines of the first class, who would preach there the pure Word of God, and would strangle the monster of Anabaptism. With the outlawry of the Catholic preacher, the struggle between Catholicism and Lutheranism closed ; the struggle for the future was to be between Lutheranism and Anabaptism ; a struggle desperate on the part of the Lutherans, for what basis had they for operation ? The Catholics had an intrenched position in the authority of a Church, which they claimed to be invested with divine inerrancy, by commission from Christ ; but the Lutheran and Anabaptist fought over the pages of the Bible, each claiming Scripture as on his side. It was a war within a camp, to decide which should pitch the other outside the rampart of the letter.

Fabricius and Melsinger fought for Infant Baptism and the Real Presence, Rottmann and Strapedius against both. " Do you call this the body and blood of Christ ? " exclaimed Master Bernard one day, whilst he was distributing the Sacrament ; and flinging it on the ground, he continued, " Were it so, it would get up from the ground and mount the altar of itself without

---

[1] Kerssenbroeck, p. 444 *et seq.*   [2] *Ibid.* p. 457 *et seq.*

Q

my help. Know by this that neither the body nor blood of Christ are here."[1]

Peter Wyrthemius, a Lutheran preacher, was interrupted, when he attempted to preach, by the shouts and jeers of the Anabaptists, and was at last driven from his pulpit.

Rottmann kept his promise not to preach Anabaptist doctrine in the pulpit, but he printed and circulated a number of tracts and pamphlets, and held meetings in private houses for the purpose of disseminating his views.[2] His reputation increased rapidly, and extended afar. Disciples came from Holland, Brabant, and Friesland, to place themselves under his direction; women even confided to him the custody of their children.

The most lively anxiety inspired the senate to make another attempt to regain their supremacy in the direction of affairs.

On the 3rd or 4th November, the heads of the guilds and the provosts and patricians of the city were assembled to deliberate, and it was resolved that Rottmann and his colleagues should be expelled the town and the diocese; and to remove from them the excuse that they feared arrest when they quitted the walls of Münster, the magistrates obtained for them a safe-conduct, signed by the bishop and the upper chapter.[3]

Next day, the magistrates and chief citizens reassembled in the market square, and voted that "not only should the Anabaptist preachers be exiled, but

---

[1] Dorpius, f. 394. [2] Kerssenbroeck, p. 448.
[3] *Ibid.* p. 449.

also those of the magistrates who had supported them; and that this sentence should receive immediate execution."[1]

This was too sweeping a measure to pass without provoking resistance. The burgomaster, Tilbeck, who felt that the blow was aimed at himself, exclaimed, angrily: "Is this the reward I receive for having prudently governed the republic? But we will not suffer the innocent to be oppressed, and we shall treat you in such a manner as will calm your insolence."

These words gave the signal for an open rupture.

Knipperdolling and Hermann Krampe, both members of the senate, drew their swords and ranged themselves beside the burgomaster, calling the people to arms. The mob at once rushed upon the senators. The servants of the chapter and the clergy in the cathedral close, hastened carrying arms to the assistance of the magistrates. Both parties sought a place of defence, each anticipating an attack. The Lutherans occupied the Rath-haus and barricaded the doors. The Anabaptists retired behind the strong walls of the cemetery of St. Lambert. The night was spent by both parties under arms, and a fight appeared imminent on the morrow. Then the syndic Johann von Wyck persuaded the frightened senate to moderate their sentence, and hurrying to the Anabaptists, he urged them to be reconciled to the magistrates. An agreement was finally concluded, whereby Rottmann was forbidden for the future to preach, and every one was to be allowed to believe what he liked, and to disbelieve what he chose.

[1] Kerssenbroeck, p. 450 *et seq.*

Master Bernard, however, evaded his obligation by holding meetings in private houses at night, to which his followers were summoned by the discharge of a gun.[1] Considering that it was now necessary that his adherents should have their articles of belief, or rather of disbelief, as a bond of union and of distinction between themselves and the Lutherans, he drew up a profession of faith in nineteen articles. That which he had published nine months before was antiquated, and represented the creed of the Lutheran faction, against which he was now at variance.

This second creed contained the following propositions :—

The baptism of children is abominable before God.

The habitual ceremonies used at baptism are the work of the devil and of the Pope, who is Antichrist.

The consecrated Host is the great Baal.

A Christian (that is, a member of Rottmann's sect) does not set foot in the religious assemblies of the impious (*i.e.,* of the Catholics and Lutherans).

He holds no communication and has no relations with them ; he is not bound to obey their authorities ; he has nothing in common with their tribunals ; nor does he unite with them in marriage.

The Sabbath was instituted by the Lord God, and there is no scriptural warrant for transferring the obligation to the Sunday.

Papists and Lutherans are to be regarded as equally infamous, and those who give faith to the inventions of priests are veritable pagans.

[1] Kerssenbroeck, p. 453 *et seq.*

During fourteen centuries there have been no true Christians. Christ was the last priest; the apostles did not enjoy the priestly office.

Jesus Christ did not derive His human nature from Mary.[1]

Every marriage concluded before re-baptism is invalid.

Faith in Christ must precede baptism.

Wives shall call their husbands lords.

Usury is forbidden.

The faithful shall possess all things in common.

The publication of this formulary of faith, if such it may be called, which is a string of negative propositions, increased the alarm of the more sober citizens, who, feeling the insecurity of property and life under a powerless magistracy, prepared to leave the town. Many fled and left their Lutheranism behind them. Lening, one of the preachers sent by the Landgrave of Hesse, ran away.

Fabricius had more courage. He preached energetically against Rottmann, assisted by Dr. Johann Westermann, a Lutheran theologian of Lippe.[2]

According to Kerssenbroeck, however, half the town followed by the Anabaptist leader, and brought their goods and money to lay them at his feet. Those

---

[1] This is corroborated by the Acta, Handlungen, &c., fol. 385. "*The Preachers:* Do you believe that Christ received His flesh off the flesh of Mary, by the operation of the Holy Ghost? *John of Leyden:* No; such is not the teaching of Scripture." And he explained that if the flesh had been taken from Mary, it must have been sinful, for she was not immaculate.

[2] Kerssenbroeck, p. 456; Sleidan, p. 411.

who had nothing of their own, in a body joined the society which proclaimed community of goods.

The bishop again wrote to the magistrates, urging them to permit the Catholic preacher, Mumpert, the use of the cathedral pulpit, but the senate refused, and continued their vain efforts to build their theological system on a slide. At their request, Fabricius and Westermann drew up (November 28, 1533) a symbol of belief in opposition to that formulated by Rottmann, and it was read and adopted by the Lutherans in the Church of St. Lambert. A large number of the people gave in their adhesion to this last and newest creed, and the magistrates, emboldened thereby, made a descent upon the house of the ex-superintendent, and confiscated his private press, with which he had printed his tracts.[1]

It was then that the two apostles, Buchbinder and Bockelson, sent by Matthisson into Westphalia, appeared in the city. They remained there only four days, during which they re-baptised the preachers and several of their adepts, and then retired prophesying their speedy return and the advent of the reign of grace.

Rottmann, highly exasperated against Fabricius for having drawn up his counter-creed, went on the 30th November to the churchyard of St. Lambert, and standing in an elevated situation, preached to the people on his own new creed, whilst Fabricius was discoursing within to his congregation on his own profession of faith.

When service was over Fabricius came out, and was

[1] *Ibid.* p. 456.

immediately attacked by Rottmann with injurious expressions, which, however, so exasperated the congregation of the Lutheran, that they fell upon the late superintendent of the Evangelical Church, and threatened him with their sticks and fists.

On the 1st December, Fabricius complained in the pulpit of the insult he had received, and appealed to the people to judge between his doctrine and that of Master Bernard by the difference there was between their respective behaviour.[1]

A new Anabaptist orator now appeared on the stage; he was a blacksmith's apprentice, named Johann Schrœder. On the 8th December he occupied the position in the cemetery of St. Lambert from which Rottmann had been forced to fly, and defied the Lutherans to oppose him with the pure Word of God. He denounced them as still in darkness, as wrapped in the trappings of Popery, and as enemies to the Gospel of Christ and Evangelical liberty. Then he dared Fabricius to meet him in a public discussion, and prove his doctrine by the text of Scripture.[2]

The magistrates resolved on one more attempt to arrest the disorder. On the 11th November they informed Rottmann that, unless he immediately left the city, they would decree his outlawry. Rottmann sent a message to them in reply, "That he would not go; that he was not afraid; and that exile was to him an empty word, for, wherever he was, the heavenly Father would cover him with His wings." He took no further notice of the order, except only that he instituted a

[1] Kerssenbroeck, p. 461.　　[2] *Ibid.* p. 461.

bodyguard of armed citizens to accompany him wherever he went. On the Sunday following, December 14th, he betook himself, surrounded by his guard, to the church of the Servites, where he intended to preach. But finding the doors locked, he placed himself under a lime-tree near the building and pronounced his discourse, without any one venturing to lay a hand upon him.[1]

The magistrates were equally unsuccessful in silencing the blacksmith Schrœder. This man, having preached again on the 15th December, was taken by the police and thrown into prison. Next day the members of the Blacksmiths' Guild marched to the Rath-haus, armed with their hammers and with bars of iron, to demand the release of their comrade. A violent dispute arose between the senators and the exasperated artisans. The former declared that Schrœder, whose trade was to shoe horses and not to preach, had deserved death for having incited to sedition. The reply of the blacksmiths was very similar to that made by the senate to the bishop when he ordered the expulsion of Rottmann. "Schrœder," said they, "has been urged on by love of truth, and he has preached with so much zeal that he has made himself hoarse. He has been guilty neither of murder nor of any crime worthy of death. How dare you maltreat this one who has given edifying instruction to his fellow citizens? Must nothing be done without your authorisation?" Upon the heels of the arguments came menaces. The senate yielded again, and promised to release Schrœder on the morrow.

[1] *Ibid.* p. 163 ; Dorpius, f. 394 a.

"Not to-morrow," shouted the blacksmiths; "restore our comrade to us immediately, or we will burst open the prison doors."

The magistrates bowed to the storm, taking, however, the worse than useless precaution of making Schrœder swear, before they knocked off his chains, that he would not attempt to revenge on them his captivity.[1]

On the 21st December, Rottmann resumed the use of his pulpit in the church of the Servites, treating the orders of the senate with supreme contempt. Westermann, tired of a struggle with the swelling tide, deserted Münster, leaving Fabricius alone to fight against the growing power of the Anabaptists.

The year 1534 opened under gloomy auspices at Münster. In the first few days of January, the new sect dealt the Lutherans the same measure these latter had dealt the Catholics a twelvemonth before. They invaded their churches and disturbed divine worship.

Fabricius attacked Rottmann violently in a sermon preached on the 4th January, and offered to have a public discussion with him on the moot points of doctrine. The senate accepted the proposition with transport, but Rottmann refused. "Not," said he, "that I am afraid of entering the lists against this Lutheran, but that men are so corrupt that they would certainly condemn that side which had for its support right and the word of Scripture."[2]

On the same day that Rottmann sent in his refusal, a band of women tumultuously entered the town-hall

[1] Kerssenbroeck, p. 464.   [2] *Ibid.* pp. 466, 467.

and demanded that "the miserable foreign vagabond Fabricius, who could not even speak the dialect of the country, and who, inspired by an evil spirit, preaches all kinds of absurdities in a tongue scarcely intelligible, should be driven out of the city. Set in his place the worthy Rottmann," said the women; "he is prudent, eloquent, instructed in every kind of knowledge, and he can speak our language. Grant us this favour, Herrn Burgmeistern, and we will pray God for you." The burgomasters requested the ladies not to meddle with matters that concerned them not, but to return to their families and kitchens. This invitation drove them into a paroxysm of rage, and they shouted at the top of their shrill voices: "Here are fine burgomasters! They are neglecting the interests of the town! Here are tender fathers of their country who attend to nothing! You are worse than murderers, for *they* kill the body, but *you* assassinate souls by depriving them of the Evangelical Word which is their nourishment." The women then retired, but returned next day reinforced by others, and among them were six nuns who had deserted the convent of Ueberwasser and exhibited greater violence than the rest.

The women entered the hall where the senators were sitting and demanded peremptorily that Rottmann should be instituted to the church of St. Lambert. They were turned out of the hall without much ceremony, but they waited the exit of the magistrates when their session was at an end; then they bespattered them with cow and horse dung, and cursed them as Papists. "At first you favoured our holy enterprise, but you have returned to Popery like dogs to their vomit. Since you have devoured the good Hessian God which Fabricius offers you in communion, you oppress the pure Word of God. To the gallows, to the gallows with you all!" The senators fled to their houses, pursued by the women, covered with filth, and deafened by their yells.[1]

Rottmann and his colleagues exercised an extraordinary influence over the people; they persuaded the rich ladies and citizens' wives of substance to sell their goods, give up their jewels, and cast everything they had into a common fund. The prompt submission of so many proves that the number of fanatics who were sincere in their convictions was considerable. These proceedings led to estrangement in families. Kerssenbroeck relates that the wife of one of the senators, named Wardemann, having been re-baptised by Rottmann, "was so vigorously confirmed in her faith by her husband, who had been informed by a servant maid of the circumstance, that she could not walk for several weeks." Other women, who had given up their jewels and money to Rottmann, were also severely chastised by their husbands.[2]

The magistrates, afraid to touch Rottmann's person, hoped to weaken him by dismissing his assistants. They therefore, on the 15th January, 1534, ordered their officers to take the Anabaptist preachers, Clopris, Roll, and Strahl, and to turn them out of the town, with orders never to re-enter it. The mandate was executed; but the ministers returned by another gate,

[1] Kerssenbroeck, p. 468. [2] *Ibid.* p. 472.

and were conducted in triumph to their parsonages by the whole body of the Anabaptists.[1]

The fugitive nuns of Ueberwasser, to the number of eight, were re-baptised by Rottmann on the 11th January, and became some of his most devoted adherents. Their conduct in the sequel was characterised by the most shameless lubricity.

The prince-bishop at this time published a decree against the Anabaptists, outlawed Rottmann and five other preachers of that sect in Münster, and ordered his officers to check the spread of the schism through the other towns of his principality.

On the 23rd January, Rottmann having noticed some Catholics and Lutherans amongst his audience in the church of the Servites, abruptly stopped his sermon, saying that it was not meet to cast the pearls of the new revelation before swine.[2] Then he descended from the pulpit, and refused to remount it again. But probably the real cause of this sudden cessation was, that the views of the leader were undergoing a third change, and he was unwilling to announce his new doctrine to an audience of which all were not prepared to receive it. He continued to assemble the faithful in private houses, and to hold daily assemblies, in which they were initiated into the further mysteries of his revelation. In every parish a house was provided for the purpose, and none were admitted without a pass-word. In these gatherings the mystic was able to give full development to his views without the restraint of an only partially sympathising audience.

[1] Kerssenbroeck, p. 473.   [2] *Ibid.* p. 476.

On the evening of the 28th January, at seven o'clock, the Anabaptists stretched chains across the streets, assembled in armed bands, closed the city gates, and placed sentinels in all directions. A terrible anxiety reigned in the city. The Lutherans remained up and awake all night, a prey to fear, with their doors and windows barricaded, waiting to see what these preparations signified. The night passed, broken only by the tramp of the sectarian fanatics, and lighted by the glare of their torches.

Dawn broke and nothing further had taken place, when suddenly two men, dressed like prophets, with long ragged beards, ample garments, and flowing mantles, staff in hand paced through the town solemnly, up one street and down another, raising their eyes to heaven, sighing, and then looking down with an expression of compassion on the multitude, which bowed before them and saluted them as Enoch and Elias. After having traversed the greater part of the town, the two men entered the door of Knipperdolling's house.[1]

The names of these prophets were John Matthisson and John Bockelson. The first was the chief of the Anabaptist sect in Holland. The part which the second was destined to play in Münster demands that his antecedents should be more fully given. Bockelson was the bastard son of Bockel, bailiff of the Hague, and a certain Adelhaid, daughter of a serf of the Lord of Zoelcken, in the diocese of Münster. This Adelhaid purchased her liberty afterwards and married her seducer. John was brought up at Leyden, where he

---

[1] Kerssenbroeck, p. 476.

was apprenticed to a tailor. He visited England,
Portugal, and Lubeck, and returned to Leyden in his
twenty-first year. He then married the widow of a
boatman, who presented him with two sons. John
Bockelson was endowed by nature with a ready wit
and with a retentive memory. He amused himself by
learning nearly the whole of the Bible by heart, and by
composing obscene verses and plays. In addition to
his business of tailoring, he opened a public-house under the sign of " The Three Herrings," which became a
haunt of women of bad repute. The passion for change
came over Bockelson after leading this sort of life for
a while, and he visited Münster in 1533, as we have
already seen, and thence passed to Osnabrück, from
which place he was expelled. After wandering about
Westphalia for a while he returned to Leyden. Next
year, in company with Matthisson, the head of the
Anabaptists, he visited Münster, which the latter declared prophetically was destined to be the new Jerusalem, the capital of a regenerate world, where the
millennial kingdom was to be set up.[1]

The two adventurers reached their destination on
the 13th January, and Knipperdolling received them
into his house. Some of the preachers were informed
of their arrival, but were required to keep the matter
secret till the time ordained of God should come for
their revealing themselves to the world.

A council was being held in the house of Knipperdolling, when the prophets entered it after having
finished their peregrination of the town. Rottmann,

[1] Kerssenbroeck, part ii. p. 51 *et seq.;* Heresbach, p. 31 ;
Hast, p. 324.

Roll, Clopris, Strapedius, Vinnius, and Strahl were engaged in a warm discussion. Some of the party were of opinion that the moment had arrived, now that all the Anabaptists were under arms, for a general purification of the city by the massacre or expulsion of Catholics and Lutherans; the others thought that the hour of vengeance had not yet struck, and that the day of the Lord must not be antedated. The quarrel was appeased by the appearance of the two prophets, who were hailed as messengers sent from heaven to announce the will of God. Then Matthisson and his companion knelt down and wept, and having meditated some moments, they uttered their decision in voices broken by sobs. " The time for cleansing the threshing-floor of the Lord is not yet come. The slaughter of the ungodly must be delayed, that souls may be gathered in, and that souls may be formed and educated in houses set apart, and not in churches which were lately filled with idols. But," said they in conclusion, " the day of the Lord is at hand."

These words reconciled the council. On the evening of the 29th, the Anabaptists laid aside their arms and returned to their homes.[1] The events of the night had utterly dispelled the last traces of courage in the magistrates; they did not venture to notice the threatening aspect of the armed fanatics, or to remonstrate with them for barricading the streets. To avert all possible danger from themselves was their only object; and to effect this they published an act of toleration, permitting every man to worship God and

---

[1] Kerssenbroeck, part i. p. 477 *et seq.*

perform his public and private devotions as he thought proper.

The power of Rottmann had become so great, through the events just recorded, that a false prophecy did not serve to upset his authority. On the 6th February, at the head of a troop of his admirers, he invaded the Church of Ueberwasser, "to prevent the Evangelical flame kindled in the hearts of the nuns from dying out."[1]   Having summoned all the sisters into the church, he mounted the pulpit and preached to them a sermon on matrimony, in which he denounced convents and monasteries, in which the most imperious laws of nature were left unfulfilled, and " he urged the nuns to labour heartily for the propagation of the human race ;" and then he completely turned the heads of the young women, by announcing to them with an inspired air, that their convent would fall at midnight, and would bury beneath its ruins every one who was found within its walls. "This salutary announcement has been made to me," said he, "by one of the prophets now present in this town, and the Heavenly Father has also favoured me with a direct and special revelation to the same effect."[2]

This was enough to complete the conversion of the nuns, already shaken in their faith by the sermons they had been compelled to listen to for some time past. In vain did the Abbess Ida and two other sisters implore them to remain and despise the prophecy. The infatuated women, in paroxysms of fear and excitement, fled the convent and took refuge in the

[1] Kerssenbroeck, p. 479.   [2] Hast, p. 329 *et seq.*

house of Rottmann, where they changed their clothes, and then ran about the town uttering cries of joy.

The prophecy of Rottmann had been repeated by one to another throughout Münster. No one slept that night. Crowds poured down the streets in the direction of Ueberwasser, and the square in front of the convent was densely packed with breathless spectators, awaiting the ruin of the house.

Midnight tolled from the cathedral tower. The crowd waited another hour. It struck one, and the convent had not fallen. Master Bernard was not the man to be disconcerted by so small a matter. "Prophecies," cried he, "are always conditional. Jonah foretold that Nineveh should be destroyed in forty days, but since the inhabitants repented, it remained standing. The same has taken place here. Nearly all the nuns have repented, have quitted their cloister and their habit, have renounced their vows —thus the anger of the Heavenly Father has been allayed."[1]

The preacher Roll was next seized with prophetic inspiration. He ran through the town, foaming at the mouth, his eyes rolling, his hair and garments in disorder, his face haggard, uttering at one moment inarticulate howls, and at another, exhortations to the impenitent to turn and be saved, for that the day of the Lord was at hand.[2]

A young girl of eighteen, the daughter of a tailor named Gregory Zumberge, was next seized. "On the 8th February she was possessed with a sort of oratori-

[1] Kerssenbroeck, p. 479.   [2] Dorpius, p. 394.

R

cal fury, and she preached with fire and extraordinary volubility before an astonished crowd."

The same day the spirit fell on Knipperdolling and Bockelson; they ran about the streets with bare heads and uplifted eyes, repeating incessantly in shrill tones, "Repent, repent, repent, ye sinners; woe, woe!" Having reached the market-place, they fell into one another's arms before a crowd of citizens and artizans who ran up from all directions. At the same moment, the tailor, Gregory Zumberge, father of the preaching damsel, arrived with his hair flying, his arms extended, his face contorted, and a wild light playing in his eyes, and cried, "Lift up your heads, O men, O dear brothers! I see the majesty of God in the clouds, and Jesus waving the standard of victory. Woe to ye impious ones who have resisted the truth! Repent, repent! I see the Heavenly Father surrounded by thousands of angels menacing you with destruction! Be converted! the great and terrible day of the Lord is come. . . . God will truly purge His floor, and burn the chaff with unquenchable fire. . . . Renounce your evil ways and adopt the sign of the New Convenant, if you wish to escape the wrath of the Lord."

"It is impossible," says the oft-quoted writer, who was eye-witness in the town of all he describes, "impossible to imagine the gestures and antics which accompanied this discourse. Now the tailor leaped about on the stones and seemed as though about to fly; then he turned his head with extraordinary rapidity, beating his hands together, and looking up to heaven and then down to earth. Then, all at once,

an expression of despair came over his face, and he
fell on the pavement in the form of a cross, and
rolled in the mud. A good number of us young
fellows were there," continues Kerssenbroeck, "much
astonished at their howling, and looking attentively at
the sky to see if there really was anything extraordinary to be seen there; but not distinguishing anything,
we began to make fun of the illuminati, and this decided them to retire to the house of Knipperdolling."[1]

There a new scene commenced. The ecstatics left
doors and windows wide open, that all that passed
within might be seen and heard by the dense crowd
which packed the street without. Those in the street
saw Knipperdolling place himself in a corner, his face
to the wall, and carry on in broken accents a familiar
conversation with God the Father. At one moment
he was seen to be listening, then to be replying,
making the strangest gestures. This went on for some
time, till another actor appeared. This was a blind
Scottish beggar, very tall and gaunt—a zealous Anabaptist. He was fantastically dressed in rags, and
wore high-heeled boots to add to his stature. Although
blind, he ran about exclaiming that he saw strange
visions in the sky. This was enough to attract a
crowd, which followed him to the corner of the
König's Strasse, when, just as he was exclaiming,
"Alas, alas! Heaven is going this instant to fall!" he
tumbled over a dung-heap which was in his way. This
accident woke him from his ecstasy, and he picked
himself up in great confusion, and never prophesied
again.[2]

[1] Kerssenbroeck, p. 483. [2] *Ibid.* p. 479.

But his place was speedily supplied by another man named Jodocus Culenburg, who, in order to convey himself with greater rapidity whither the Spirit called him, rode about the town on a horse, announcing in every street that he heard the peal of the Last Trumpet. Several women also were taken with the prophetic spirit, and one, named Timmermann, declared that "the King of Heaven was about to appear like a lightning-flash, and would re-establish Jerusalem." Another woman, whose cries and calls to repentance had caused her to lose her voice, ran about with a bell attached to her girdle, urging the bystanders with expressive gestures to join the number of the elect and be saved.[1]

These fantastic scenes had made a profound impression on many of the citizens of Münster. A nervous affection accompanying mystic excitement is always infectious. The agitation of minds and consciences became general; men and women had trances, prayed in public, screamed, had visions, and fell into cataleptic fits. In those days people knew nothing of physical and psychological causes; the general excitement was attributed by them to supernatural agency. It was simply a question whether these signs were produced by the devil or by the Spirit of God. The Catholics attributed the signs to the agency of Satan; the Lutherans were in nervous uncertainty. Were they resisting God or the devil? Fear lest they should be found in the ranks of those fighting against the Holy Spirit drew off numbers of the timorous and most conscientious to swell the ranks of the mystical sect.

[1] *Ibid.* p. 484.

Münster was exhibiting on a large scale what is reproduced in our own land in many a Wesleyan and Ranter revival meeting.

The time had now come, thought Rottmann, for the destruction of the enemies of God.   Secret notice was sent to the different Anabaptist congregations to be prepared to strike the blow on the 9th of February. Accordingly, early in the morning, 500 fanatics seized on the gates of the city, the Rath-haus, and the arms it contained; cannons were planted in the chapel of St. Michael, the tower of St. Lambert's church, and in the market place; barricades of stones, barrels, and benches from the church were thrown up.   The common danger united Catholics and Lutherans; they saw clearly that the intention of their adversaries was either to massacre them, or to drive them out of the town.   They retreated in haste to the Ueberwasser quarter, and took up their position in the cemetery, planted cannons, placed bodies of armed men in the tower of the cathedral, and retook two of the city gates.   They also arrested several of the senators who had joined the Anabaptist sect, but they had not the courage to lay their hands on the burgomaster, Tilbeck, who was also of that party.   Two of the preachers, Strahl and Vinnius, were caught, and were lodged in the tower of Ueberwasser church.[1]

Messages were sent to the villages and towns around announcing the state of affairs, and imploring assistance.   The magistrates even wrote in the stress of their terror to the prince-bishop, asking him to come speedily to their rescue from a position of imminent

[1] Dorpius, f. 394.

peril. Francis of Waldeck at once replied by letter, promising to march with the utmost rapidity to Münster, and demanding that one of the gates might be opened to admit him. This letter was taken to Hermann Tilbeck; but the burgomaster, intent on securing the triumph of the fanatics, with whom he was in league, suppressed the letter, and did not mention either its arrival or its contents to the senate. He, however, informed the Anabaptists of their danger, and urged them to come to terms with the Lutherans as speedily as possible.

At the same time the pastor, Fabricius, unable to restrain his religious prejudices, even in the face of danger, sped among the Lutheran ranks, inciting his followers against the Catholics, and urging them to make terms with the fanatics rather than submit to the bishop. "Beware," said he, "lest, in the event of your gaining a victory, the Papists should recover their power, for it is they who are the real cause of all these evils and disorders."

Whilst the preacher was sowing discord in the ranks of the party of order, Rottmann and the two prophets, Matthisson and Bockelson, roused the enthusiasm of their disciples to the highest pitch, by announcing to them a glorious victory, and that the Father would render His elect invulnerable before the weapons of their adversaries.

The Anabaptist women ran about the streets making the most extraordinary contortions and prodigious leaps, crying out that they saw the Lord surrounded by a host of angels coming to exterminate the worshippers of Baal.

[1] Kerssenbroeck, p. 405 *et seq.* Monfort, "Tumult. Anabap.," p. 15 *et seq.*; Bullinger, lib. ii. c. 8.

Thus passed the night. At daybreak Knipper-dolling recommenced his course through the streets, uttering his doleful wail of "Repent, repent! woe, woe!" Approaching too near the churchyard wall of Ueberwasser, he was taken and thrown into the tower with Strahl and Vinnius.

At eight o'clock the drossar of Wollbeck arrived at the head of a troop of armed peasants to reinforce the party of order, and several ecclesiastics entered the town to inform the magistrates that the prince-bishop was approaching at the head of his cavalry.

Before the lapse of many hours the city might have been pacified and order re-established, had it not been for the efforts of Tilbeck the burgomaster, and Fabricius the divine. Mistrust of their allies had now fully gained possession of the Lutherans, and the burgomaster took advantage of the hesitation to dismiss the drossar of Wollbeck and his armed band, and to send to the prince, declining his aid. By his advice, also, the Anabaptists agreed to lay down their arms and make a covenant with the senate for the establishment of harmony. Hostages were given on either side and the prisoners were liberated. Peace was finally concluded on these conditions: 1st. That faith should be absolutely free. 2nd. That each party should support the other. 3rd. That all should obey the magistrates.

The treaty having been signed, the two armed bodies separated, the cannons were fired into the air, the drossar of Wollbeck and the ecclesiastics withdrew, with grief at their hearts, predicting the approaching ruin of Münster. The prince-bishop was near the town with his troops when the fatal news was brought him. He shed tears of mortification, turned his horse and departed.[1]

Peace was secured for the moment by this treaty, but order was not re-established. No sooner had the armed Anabaptists quitted the market-place than it swarmed with women who had received from Rottmann the sign of the New Covenant. " The madness of the pagan bacchantes," says the eye-witness of these scenes, Kerssenbroeck,[2] " cannot have surpassed that of these women. It is impossible to imagine a more terrible, crazy, indecent, and ridiculous exhibition than they made. Their conduct was so frenzied that one might have supposed them to be the furies of the poets. Some had their hair disordered, others ran about almost naked, without the least sense of shame ; others again made prodigious gambles, others flung themselves on the ground with arms extended in the shape of a cross ; then rose, clapped their hands, knelt down, and cried with all their might, invoking the Father, rolling their eyes, grinding their teeth, foaming at the mouth, beating their breasts, weeping, laughing, howling, and uttering the most strange inarticulate sounds . . . . . Their words were stranger than their gestures. Some implored grace and light for us, others besought that we might be struck with blindness and damnation. All pretended that they saw in heaven some strange sights ; they saw the Father descending to judge their holy cause, myriads of angels, clouds of blood, black and blue fires falling upon the

---

[1] Same authorities ; Sleidan, p. 411.
[2] Kerssenbroeck, p. 495 *et seq.*

city, and above the clouds a rider mounted on a white horse, brandishing his sword against the impenitent who refused to turn from their evil ways. . . . But the scene was constantly varying. Kneeling on the ground, and turning their eyes in one direction, they all at once exclaimed together, with joined hands, ' O Father ! Father ! O most excellent King of Zion, spare the people !' Then they repeated these words for some while, raising the pitch of their voices, till they attained to such a shriek that a host of pigs could not have produced a louder noise when assembled on market-day.

"There was on the gable of one of the houses in the market-place a weathercock of a peculiar form, lately gilt, which just then caught the sun's rays and blazed with light. This weathercock caused the error of the women. They mistook it for the most excellent King of Zion. One of the citizens discovering the cause, climbed the roof of the house and removed this new sort of majesty. A calm at once succeeded to the uproar ; ashamed and full of confusion, the visionaries dispersed and returned to their homes. Unfortunately the lesson did not restore them to their senses."

Shortly after the treaty was signed, the burgomaster, Tilbeck, openly joined the Anabaptists, and was re-baptised with all his family by Rottmann.[1]

The more sensible and prudent citizens, including nearly all the Catholics and a good number of Lutherans, being well aware that the treaty was, in fact, a surrender of all authority into the hands of the fanatics, deserted the town in great numbers, carrying

[1] Kerssenbroeck, p. 496.

with them all their valuables. The emigration began on 12th February. The Anabaptists ordered that neither weapons nor victuals should be carried out of the gates, and appointed a guard to examine the effects of all those who left the city. The emigration was so extensive, that in a few days several quarters of the town were entirely depopulated.[1]

Then Rottmann addressed a circular letter to the Anabaptists of all the neighbouring towns to come and fill the deserted mansions from which the apostates had fallen. "The Father has sent me several prophets," said he, "full of His Spirit and endowed with exalted sanctity; they teach the pure word of God, without human additions, and with sublime eloquence. Come then, with your wives and children, if you hope for eternal salvation; come to the holy Jerusalem, to Zion, and to the new temple of Solomon. Come and assist us to re-establish the true worship of God, and to banish idolatry. Leave your worldly goods behind, you will find here a sufficiency, and in heaven a treasure."[2]

In response to this appeal, the Anabaptists streamed into the city from all quarters, from Holland, Friesland, Brabant, Hesse, Osnabrück, and from the neighbouring towns, where the magistrates exerted themselves to suppress a sect which they saw imperilled the safety of the commonwealth.

In a short while the deserted houses were peopled by these fanatics. Bernhard Krechting, pastor of Gildehaus, arrived at the head of a large portion of his

---

[1] *Ibid.* Dorpius, ff. 394-5.
[2] Kerssenbroeck, p. 502; Mencken, p. 1545.

parishioners. Hermann Regewart, the ex-Lutheran preacher of Warendorf, sought a home in the new Jerusalem. Rich and well-born persons, bitten with the madness, arrived; such were Peter Schwering and his wife, the wealthiest citizens of Coesfeld; Werner von Scheiffort, a country gentleman; the Lady von Becke with her three daughters, of whom the two eldest were broken nuns, and the youngest was betrothed to the Lord of Dörlö; and the Grograff of Schoppingen, Heinrich Krechting, with his wife, his children, and a number of the inhabitants of that town, with carts laden with their effects. The Grograff took up his abode in Kerssenbroeck's house, along with his family and servants, and, as the chronicler bitterly remarks, he took care to occupy the best part of the mansion.[1]

Amongst those who escaped from the town were the syndic, Von Wyck, who had led the opposition against the bishop, and the burgomaster, Caspar Judenfeld. The latter retired to Hamm and was left unmolested, but Von Wyck had played too conspicuous a part to escape so easily. By the orders of the prince-bishop he was arrested and executed at Vastenau.[2]

Münster now became the theatre of the wildest orgies ever perpetrated under the name of religion. It is apparently a law that mysticism should rapidly pass from the stage of asceticism into that of licence. At any rate, such has been the invariable succession of stages in every mystic society that is allowed unchecked to follow its own course. In the Roman

[1] Kerssenbroeck, p. 503.   [2] *Ibid.* p. 505.

Church those thus psychologically affected are locked up in convents. The religious passion verges so closely on the sexual passion that a slight additional pressure given to it bursts the partition, and both are confused in a frenzy of religious debauch. The Anabaptist fanatics were rapidly approaching this stage. The prophet Matthisson led the way by instituting a second baptism, administered only to the inner circle of the elect, which was called the baptism of fire.

The adepts were sworn to secrecy, and refused to explain the mode of administration. But public curiosity was aroused, and by learning the password, some were enabled to slip into the assembly and see what took place. Amongst these was a woman who was an acquaintance of Kerssenbroeck, and from whose lips he had an account of the rite. "Matthisson," says he, "secretly assembled the initiated of both sexes during the night, in the vast mansion of Knipperdolling. When all were assembled, the prophet placed himself under a copper chandelier, hung in the centre of the ceiling, lighted with three tapers." He then made an instruction on the new revelation of the Divine will, which he pretended had been made to him, and the assembly became a scene of frantic orgies too horrible to be described.

The assemblies in which these abominations were perpetrated, prepared the way for the utter subversion of all the laws of decency and morality, which followed in the course of a few months.

When Carnival arrived, a grand anti-Catholic procession was organised, to incite afresh the hostility of the people to the ancient Church, its rites and

ceremonies.   First, a company of maskers dressed
like monks, nuns, and priests in their sacred vest-
ments, led the way, capering and singing ribald
songs.   Then followed a great chariot, drawn by six
men in the habits of the religious orders.   On the
box sat a fellow dressed as a bishop, with mitre and
crosier, scourging on the labouring monks and friars.
On the car was a man represented as dying, with a
priest leaning over him, a huge pair of spectacles on
his nose, administering to the sick man the last sacraments of the Church, and addressing him in the most
absurd manner, loudly, that the bystanders might
hear and laugh at his farcical parody of the most
sacred things of the old religion.   The next car was
drawn by a man dressed as a priest in surplice and
stole.   The other cars contained groups suitable for
turning into ridicule devotion to saints, belief in
purgatory, the mass, &c.[1]

The prophets now decided that it was necessary to
be prepared in the event of a siege.   They, therefore,
commissioned the preacher Roll to visit Holland
and raise the Anabaptists there, urge them to arm
and to march to the defence of the New Jerusalem.
Roll started from Münster on the 21st of February,
but the Spanish Government in the Netherlands,
alarmed at what was taking place in the capital of
Westphalia, ordered a strict watch to be kept on the
movements of the fanatics, and Roll was seized and
executed at Utrecht.

The next step taken by the prophets was to discharge the members of the senate from the perform-

[1] Kerssenbroeck, p. 509.

ance of their office, because they had been elected "according to the flesh," and to choose to fill their room another body of men "elected according to the Spirit." Bernard Knipperdolling and Gerhardt Kippenbroeck, both drapers, were appointed burgo-masters.

One of the first acts of the new magistrates was to forbid the removal of furniture, articles of food, and money from the town, and to permit a general pillage of all the churches and convents in the city. The Anabaptist mob first attacked the religious houses, and carried off all the sacred vessels, the gold, the silver, and the vestments. Then they visited the chapel of St. Anthony, outside the gate of St. Maurice, and after having sacked it completely, they tore it down. They burnt the church of St. Maurice, then fell upon the church of St. Ledger, but had not the patience to complete its demolition. Thence they betook themselves to the cathedral, broke it open, and destroyed altars, with their beautiful sculp-tured and painted oak retables, miracles of delicate workmanship and Gothic beauty, the choir stalls, statues, paintings, frescoes, stained glass, organ, vest-ments, and carried off the chalices and ciboriums. The great clock, the pride of Münster, as that of Strasburg is of the Alsatian capital, was broken to pieces with hammers. A valuable collection of MSS., collected by the poet Rudolf Lange, and presented to the minister, together with the rest of the volumes in the library, were burned. Two noble paintings, one of the Blessed Virgin, the other of St. John the Baptist, on panel, by Franco, were split up and

turned into seats for privies to the guard-house near
the Jews' cemetery. The heads and arms were
broken off the statues that could not be overthrown
—statues of apostles, prophets, and sibyls, which
decorated the interior of the cathedral and the neighbouring square. The tabernacle was broken open,
and the Blessed Sacrament was danced and stamped
on. The font was shattered with crowbars, in token
of the abhorrence borne by the fanatics to infant
baptism ; the tombs of the bishops and canons were
destroyed, and the bodies torn from their graves, and
their dust was scattered to the winds.[1]

But whilst this was taking place in Münster,
Francis von Waldeck was preparing for war. On
the 23rd February he held a meeting at Telgte to
consolidate plans, and now from all sides assistance
came. The Elector of Cologne, the Duke of Cleves,
even the Landgrave of Hesse, now exasperated at
the ill-success of his endeavours to establish tranquillity and to effect a compromise, the Duke of
Brunswick, the Regent of Brabant, the Counts of
Lippe and Berntheim, and many other nobles and
cities sent soldiers, artillery, and munitions.

The bishop appointed the generals and principal
officers, then he made all the soldiers take an oath of
fidelity to himself, and concluded with them an agreement, consisting of the following ten articles :

1. The soldiers are to be faithful to the prince, and
to obey their officers.

2. The towns, arms, and munitions taken in war
shall belong to the prince.

[1] Kerssenbroeck, p. 510 ; Sleidan, p. 411 ; Dorpius, f. 395.

3. If, after the capture of the city, the prince-bishop permits its pillage by the troops, he shall not be obliged to pay them any prize-money.

4. If the pillage be accorded, the town hall is not to be touched.

5. The prince shall have half the plunder.

6. The nobles, canons, and those who have escaped from the city shall be allowed the first bid for their articles when offered for sale.

7. No fixtures shall be removed by the soldiery.

8. After the capture of the town, the custody of the gates and ramparts shall be confided to those whom the prince-bishop shall appoint.

9. The city taken, and its pillage permitted, the soldiers shall be allowed eight days for distribution and sale of the plunder. The soldiers shall receive their pay with punctuality.

10. The heads of the revolt shall, as far as possible, be taken alive and delivered up to the bishop for a recompense.[1]

The Anabaptists were not afraid at these preparations; they made ready vigorously for the defence of the New Zion. As a preliminary, a body of five hundred burnt the convent of St. Maurice, outside the city gates, and levelled all the houses of the suburbs, which obscured the view, and might serve as cover for the besiegers.

On the 26th February Matthisson preached in the afternoon to a congregation summoned by the discharge of a culverin. At the end of the sermon he

---

[1] Kerssenbroeck, p. 513 *et seq.* Sleidan, lib. x. pp. 412-3; Heresbach, p. 36.

assumed an inspired air, and announced that he had an important revelation to communicate. Having arrested the attention of his hearers, he said in a solemn tone, " The Father requires the purification of the New Jerusalem and of His temple ; for our re-public, which has begun so prosperously, cannot grow and endure if a prey to the confusion produced by the presence of impious sects. My advice is that we kill without further delay the Lutherans, the Papists, and all those who have not the right faith, that there may remain in Zion but one body, one society, which is truly Christian, and which can offer to the Father a pure and well-pleasing worship. There is but one way of preserving the faithful from the contagion of the impious, and that is to sweep them off the face of the earth. Nothing is easier than the execution of this scheme. We form the majority in a strong city, abundantly supplied with all necessaries ; there is nothing to fear from within or from without."[1]

This suggestion would have been carried into im-mediate execution by the frenzied sectarians, had it not been for the intervention of Knipperdolling, who, fearing that a general massacre of Lutherans and Catholics would combine the forces of the Smalkald union and of the Imperialists against the city, urgently insisted on milder measures. " Let us be content," said he, " with driving, to-morrow, out of the city those miserable creatures who refuse the sign of the New Covenant ; thus shall we thoroughly purge the floor of the Lord, and nothing that is impure will remain in the New Jerusalem."[2]

[1] Kerssenbroeck, p. 516.   [2] *Ibid.* p, 517 ; Sleidan, p. 412.

S

This advice was accepted, and it was unanimously decided that the morrow should witness the expulsion of Catholics and Lutherans. The 27th Feburary was a bitterly cold day. A hard frost had set in, the north wind blew, cutting to the bone all exposed to the blast, the country was white with snow, and the streams were crusted over with ice. At every gate was a double guard; the squares were thronged with armed fanatics, and in and out among them passed the prophets, staff in hand, uttering maledictions on the Lord's enemies, and words of encouragement to those sealed on their brows and hands.

Matthisson sought out those who did not belong to the sect, and with menacing gestures and flaring eyes called them to repentance before the door was shut. "Turn ye, turn ye, sinners," he cried in his harsh tones. "Judgment is preparing for you. The elements are in league against you; your iniquities have made nature rise to scourge you. The sword of the Lord's anger is hung above your heads. Turn, ye sinners, and receive the sign of our alliance, that ye be not cast out from the chosen people!" Then he flung himself down in the great square, and called on the Father; and lying with arms extended on the frozen ground, and his face pinched with cold turned towards the sky, he fell into a trance. The Anabaptists knelt around him, and lifting their hands to heaven besought the Father to reveal His will by the mouth of the prophet whom He had sent.

Then Matthisson, slowly returning from his ecstasy, like one awaking out of a dream, said, "This is the will and order of the Father: the miscreants, unless

they be converted and be baptised, must be expelled
this place. This holy city shall be purified of all that
is unclean, for the conversation of the ungodly
corrupts and defiles the people of God. Away with
the sons of Esau! this place, this New Zion, this
habitation belongs to the sons of Jacob, to the true
Israel."

The enthusiasm of Matthisson communicated itself
to the assembly. The Anabaptists separated to
sweep the streets, sword and pike in hand, and drove
the ungodly beyond their walls, shouting, " The lot is
ours ; the tares must be gathered from among the
wheat ; the goats from the sheep; the unholy from
the godly ; away, away !" Doors were burst open,
and the fanatics invaded every house, driving before
them men, women, and children, from garret and
cellar, wherever concealed, in spite of their cries and
entreaties. Men of all professions, men and women
of every age were banished ; they were not allowed
to take anything with them. The sword of the Lord
was brandished against them ; the hale and the in-
firm, the master and the servant, none were spared.
Those who lagged were beaten ; those who were sick
and unable to fly were carried to the market-place
to be rebaptised by Rottmann.

Through the gates streamed the terrified crowd,
shivering, half clothed, mothers clasping their babes
to their breasts, children sustaining between them
their aged parents, all blue with cold, as the fierce wind
thick strewn with sleet rushed upon them at the
corners, and over the bare plain without the city walls,
growling and cruel, as though it too were wrought up

into religious frenzy, and came as an auxiliary to the savage work.

Thousands traversed the frozen plans, uncertain whither to fly for refuge, uttering piteous cries lamentations, or low moans; whilst from the walls of the heavenly city thundered a salvo of joy, and the Anabaptists shouted, because the Lord's day of vengeance had come, and the millennium was set up on earth.

"Never," says Kerssenbroeck, "never did I see anything more afflicting. The women carried their naked nurslings in their arms, and in vain sought rags wherewith to clothe them; miserable children, hanging to their fathers' coats, ran barefooted, uttering piercing cries; old people, bent by age, tottered along calling down God's vengeance on their persecutors; lastly, some sick women driven from their beds during the pangs of maternity fell in labour in the snow, deprived of all human succour."[1]

Amongst those expelled was Fabricius, the Lutheran divine, who escaped in disguise. He was so greatly hated by the sectarians, that had he been recognised, he would not have been suffered to quit the city alive.

The Frau Werneche, a rich lady, too stout to walk, and unable to find a conveyance, was obliged to remain in Münster. Rottmann insisted on her receiving the sign of the New Covenant.

"I have been baptised already, as were my ancestors," said the good woman. Rottmann replied that if she persisted in her impiety she must be slain

[1] Kerssenbroeck, p. 5222.

with the sword, lest the wrath of the Father should
be kindled against the Holy City. The poor lady,
who had no desire for martyrdom, cried out, im-
patiently, "Well, then, be it so! baptise me in the
name of all the devils of hell, for I have already been
baptised in the name of God." Rottmann, not very
particular, administered the rite, and the stout lady
remained in Münster.

The apostle now sent letters into all the country,
announcing the glad tidings of the approaching reign
of Christ on earth, and inviting the Anabaptists of the
neighbourhood to flock into Zion. One of these
epistles of Rottmann has been preserved.[1]

"Bernard, servant of Jesus Christ in His Church of
Münster, salutes affectionately his very dear
brother Henry Schlachtschap. Grace and peace
from God, and the strength of the Holy Spirit,
be with you and with all the faithful.

"Dear Brother in Christ,—

"The marvellous works of God are so great and
so diverse that it would not be possible for me to
describe them all, had I a hundred tongues. I am,
therefore, unable to do so with my single pen. The
Lord has splendidly assisted us. He has delivered
us out of the hands of our enemies, and has driven
them from the city. Seized by a panic terror, they
fled in multitudes. This is the beginning of what the
Lord announced by His prophets—that all the saints
would assemble in this New Zion. These prophets
have charged me to write to you, that you may order
all the brethren to hasten to us with all the gold and

---

[1] Kerssenbroeck, p. 520; Dorpius, f. 395.

silver they can collect; as for their other goods, let them be left to the sisters, who will dispose of them, and then join us here also. Beware of doing anything after the flesh; do all in the Spirit. The rest by word of mouth. Health in the Lord."

This appeal had all the more success because several executions had taken place at Wollbeck and Bevergern and other places, together with confiscation of goods, and this had struck alarm into the Anabaptists scattered throughout the principality. Numbers, therefore, answered the appeal, and went up, as the tribes of the Lord, to Jerusalem, out of Leyden, Coesfeld, Warendorf, and Gröningen. The vacated houses were re-occupied, the Münster Baptists selecting for themselves the best. Knipperdolling, Kippenbroeck, and others, took possession of the residences of the canons; servants installed themselves in the dwellings of their masters as if they were their own; and the deserted monasteries were given up as hostels to receive the influx from the country, till houses could be provided for them.[1]

On the 28th February, Francis von Waldeck left Telgte at the head of his army and invested the capital. Batteries were planted, seven camps were established for the infantry, and six for the cavalry around Münster. These camps were in connection with one another, for mutual support in the event of a sortie, and were rapidly fortified.

Thus began the siege which was to last sixteen months minus four days, during which a multitude of untrained, undisciplined fanatics, commanded by a

[1] Kerssenbroeck, p. 523.

Dutch tailor-innkeeper, held out against a numerous and well-armed force. But there was an element of strength in the besieged that lacked in the besiegers. Those within the walls were members of a vast confraternity, which ramified over Germany, Switzerland, and the Low Countries, its members bound together by a common enthusiasm, in more or less direct relation with the chiefs who commanded in the Westphalian capital. In spite of the siege, news from without was constantly brought into the city, and messengers were sent out to stir up the members of the society in other countries and provinces to rise and march to the relief of the city which, they all believed, was destined to be their religious capital. The Münster brothers looked for a speedy deliverance wrought by the efficacy of the arms of their brothers in Holland, Juliers, Cleves, and Brabant. The Low Countries swarmed with Anabaptists who had organised communities in Amsterdam, Leyden, Utrecht, Haarlem, Antwerp, and Ghent; they had arms stored in cellars and garrets, and waited only the proper moment to rise in a body, massacre their opponents, and deliver the Holy City. Several attempts to rise were made, but the vigilance of the Spanish Government in the Netherlands prevented the rising; and the hopes of the besieged were never realised.

On the other hand, the army of the prince-bishop was composed of mercenaries, of soldiers from different provinces and principalities, speaking different dialects, with different interests, and differing also in faith. The Lutheran troops would not cordially unite with the Catholics, and the latter mistrusted their Protestant allies, whose sympathies they believed lay with the Anabaptist besieged. And the head of the whole army was a Catholic prelate with Lutheran proclivities, who knew nothing of war, had an empty purse, and desired to reduce his own subjects by the aid of foreign mercenaries, with little expense to himself, and damage to his subjects.

The Anabaptists organised their defence with prudence. They elected captains and standard-bearers, and divided all the citizens capable of bearing arms into regiments and companies. Every one was given his place and his functions, and it was decided that the magistrates should be required to mount guard when it came to their turn. Boys were drilled and taught the use of the arquebus; women prepared brands steeped in pitch and sulphur to fling at the enemy, and they melted lead from the roofs into bullets. Mines were dug and charged with powder, fresh bastions were thrown up, and curtains were erected before the gates, into which were built the tombs and sarcophagi of the bishops and canons.[1]

The newly-elected senate, though composed of the most zealous Anabaptists, was powerless before Matthisson. A sect governed by the inspiration of the moment, professing to be guided by the Spirit speaking through the mouths of prophets, ready to spring into the maddest excesses at the dictates of visionaries, could not long submit to the government of a magistracy whose power was temporal. The way was rapidly preparing for the establishment of a spiritual despotism.

[1] Kerssenbroeck, p. 531 *et seq.*; Hast, p. 344.

It was in vain for the senate to pass an order without the sanction of Matthisson, in vain for them to attempt resistance to the execution of his mandates. One day he announced that it was the will of the Father that all the goods of the citizens who had fled, or had been expelled, should be collected into one place, that they might be distributed amongst the saints, as every man had need. He thereupon despatched men to bring together all that was left behind in the city by the refugees, and convey the articles to houses which he designated in every parish. He was promptly obeyed. Garments, linen, beds, furniture, crockery, food, wine—everything was brought away in carts. The jewels, the gold, and the silver, were deposited in the chancery. Then the prophet ordered three days of prayer to be instituted, " that God might reveal to him the persons chosen by Him to keep guard over the accumulated treasure."[1]

When the three days were at an end, Matthisson announced that the Father had indicated to him seven individuals who were to be the deacons to serve tables in the New Jerusalem. He therefore appointed the men to distribute out of the common store to those who needed that which would satisfy their necessities.[2]

It must not, however, be supposed that, with the expulsion of the impious from the holy city, all opposition had disappeared. A very considerable number of citizens, shopkeepers, and merchants, rather than desert their houses, abandon their goods to pillage, and lose their trade, had consented to be re-

[1] Kerssenbroeck ; Dorpius, f. 395.   [2] *Ibid.* p. 585.

baptised. The reign of the prophets was becoming to them daily more irksome. A blacksmith, named Hubert Rüscher, or Trutling, had the courage to oppose Matthisson, to charge him with being a false prophet, and an impostor.[1] The prophet, feeling the danger of his position, saw that a measure, decided and terrible, must be adopted to suppress the murmurs, and frighten those who desired to shake off his yoke. "Judgment must begin at the house of God," said Matthisson ; and he ordered the immediate execution of the smith. Tilbeck, the burgomaster, and Redecker, a magistrate, interposed, but were, by order of the prophet, cast into prison. Then Bockelson, bursting through the crowd, announced with frantic gesture that the Father had commissioned him to slay with the sword he bore all those who withstood the will of Heaven as interpreted by the prophets whom He had sent. Then brandishing his weapon, he rushed upon the blacksmith, but Matthisson forestalled him, by running his halbert through the body of the unfortunate man. Finding that he still breathed, he despatched him with a carbine, crying, "So perish all who are guilty of similar crimes." Then, at his command, the multitude chanted a hymn of praise, and dispersed, silent and trembling, to their homes.[2]

Matthisson took immediate advantage of the power this bold stroke had given him to deal another blow.

---

[1] Kerssenbroeck, p. 535 *et seq.*; Monfortius, p. 19 ; Sleidan and Dorpius call the man Truteling ; Sleidan, p. 412 ; Dorpius, f. 395 b.

[2] Monfortius, p. 19.

When the treasure of the enemies of Zion had been confided to the care of deacons, the faithful had kept their own goods. But this was to be no longer tolerated. The prophet issued a decree, requiring all, old and young, male and female, under pain of death, to bring all their possessions in gold and silver, under whatever form it might be, into the treasury; "Because," said he, "such things profit not the true Christian."

The majority of the citizens obeyed, in fear and trembling; but many buried their vessels and ornaments of precious metal, and declared that they possessed no jewels.[1] However, the amount of money, chains, rings, brooches, and cups, brought together was very considerable. It was placed in the chancery, and confided to four of Matthisson's most devoted adherents.

A few days after, he summoned all the inhabitants into the Cathedral square, where, in a long discourse, he announced that the wrath of God was excited against those who had allowed themselves to be re-baptised on the 26th of February, out of human considerations, because they did not desire to leave their homes and their effects, or out of fear; and he advised them all to betake themselves to the church of St. Lambert, to entreat the Father to pardon them for having lied to the Holy Ghost, and soiled by their presence the city of the children of God; "and if the Father does not remit your offence," concluded he in a loud and terrible voice, "you must perish by the sword of the Just One."

[1] Kerssenbroeck, p. 538.

In an agony of terror, the unfortunate citizens crowded the church, and the doors were fastened behind them. They passed several hours within, weeping, groaning, and deploring their lot, a prey to inexpressible terror.[1]

At length Matthisson entered, accompanied by armed men, and the prisoners, supposing they were about to be slaughtered, fell at his feet and embraced his knees, entreating him, with tears, as the favourite of God, to mediate with Him and obtain their pardon. The prophet replied that he must consult the Father; he knelt down, and fell into an ecstasy. After a few moments he rose, leaped with joy, and declared that the Father, though greatly irritated, had granted his prayer, and suffered the penitents to live. Then the poor creatures were purified, hymns of praise were sung, and they were pronounced admitted into the household of the true Israel. The doors were thrown open, and they were allowed to disperse.

On the 15th of March, a new decree appeared, forbidding the faithful to possess, read, or look at any books except the Bible, and requiring all the books, in print or MS., and all legal documents that were found in the town, to be brought to the Cathedral square, and there to be consigned to the flames. Thus perished many a treasure of inappreciable value.

In the meantime the appeal of Rottmann to the Anabaptists of the Low Countries to come and deliver Zion had produced its effect. Thousands assembled in the neighbourhood of Amsterdam, crossed the

---

[1] Kerssenbroeck, p. 539.

Zuyder Zee, landed at Zwoll, and marched towards
Münster, pillaging and burning churches and convents.
But Baron Schenk von Teutenburg, imperial lieutenant, met them, utterly routed them, cut to pieces a
large number, and made many prisoners.[1]

The prophets of Münster, warned of their advance,
but ignorant of their dispersion, reckoned on an
approaching deliverance, and continued their follies.
On Good Friday, April 3, 1534, they organised a
general festival, with bells pealing, and a mock procession carrying candles. The treaty concluded with
the prince-bishop, through the intervention of Philip
of Hesse, was attached to the tail of an old horse,
and the beast was driven out of the gate of St. Maurice
in the direction of the enemy's camp.[2]

Easter approached, and with it great things were
expected. A rumour circulated that a mighty deliverance of Israel would be wrought on the Feast of
the Resurrection. Whether Matthisson started the
report or was carried away by it, it is impossible to
decide; but it is certain that, on the eve, he announced
in an access of enthusiasm, after a trance, that he had
received orders from the Father to put to flight the
armies of the aliens with a handful of true believers.[3]

Accordingly, on the morrow, carrying a halbert, he
headed a few zealots who shared his confidence; the
gate of St. Ludgar was thrown open, and he rushed
forth with his followers upon the army of the prince-
bishop; whilst the ramparts were crowded by the
inhabitants of Münster, shouting and praying, and

[1] Kerssenbroeck, p. 541, 542 ; Bullinger, ii. c. 10.
[2] *Ibid.* p. 542.   [3] *Ibid,* 542; Hast, p. 348.

expecting to see a miracle wrought in his favour. But he had not advanced very far before a troop of the enemy surrounded his little band, and, in spite of a desperate resistance, he and his companions were cut to pieces.[1]

John Bockelson, seeing that the confidence of the Anabaptists was shaken by the failure of this prediction and the fall of the great prophet, lost not a moment in establishing his own supremacy. He called all the people together, and declared to them that Matthisson had died by the just judgment of God, because he had disobeyed the commandment of the Father to go forth with a very small handful, and because he had relied on his own strength instead of on Divine aid. "But," added he, "he neglected all those precautions he ought to have taken, solemn prayer and fasting, after the example of Judith; and he forgot that victory is in the hands of God; he was proud and vain, therefore was he forsaken of the Lord. His terrible end was revealed to me eight days ago by the Holy Ghost; for, as I was sleeping in the house of Knipperdolling, after having meditated on the Divine Law, Matthisson appeared to me pierced through by the lance of an armed man, with all his bowels gushing forth. Then was I frightened beyond measure at this terrible spectacle; but the armed man said to me, 'Fear not, well-beloved son of the Father, but be faithful to thy calling, for the judgment of God will fall upon Matthisson; and when he is dead, marry his widow.' These words cast me into

---

[1] Kerssenbroeck, 542; Sleidan, p. 413; Bullinger, lib. ii. c. 9; Heresbach, p. 138; Buissierre, p. 310.

profound amazement, for I have already a legitimate wife at Leyden. Nevertheless, that I might have a witness worthy of confidence to this extraordinary revelation, I trusted the secret to Knipperdolling ; he is present, let him be brought forth."[1]

Thereupon Knipperdolling stepped forward and declared by oath that Bockelson had spoken the truth, and he mentioned the place, the day, and the hour when the revelation was confided to him.

From that moment Bockelson passed with the people not only as a prophet, but as a favourite of Heaven, one specially chosen of the Father, and was held in far higher estimation, accordingly, than had been the fallen prophet. He was seized with inspiration. On the 9th of April, he declared that "the Father ordered, under pain of incurring his dire wrath, that every exalted thing should be laid low, and that the work was to begin at the church steeples." Consequently three architects of the town were ordered to demolish them. They succeeded in pulling down all the spires in Münster. That of Ueberwasser church was singularly beautiful. It was reduced to a stump ; and the modern visitor to the ancient Westphalian capital has cause to deplore its loss. The towers were only saved to be used as positions for cannon to play upon the besigers.[2]

Bockelson had another vision, which served to consolidate his power. "The Father," said he, "had appeared to him, and had commanded him to appoint

---

[1] Kerssenbroeck, p. 543 ; Monfort, p. 24.
[2] Bullinger, ii. c. 8 ; Sleidan, p. 271 ; Dorpius, f. 396.

Knipperdolling to be the executioner of the new republic."

This was not precisely satisfactory to Knipperdolling; he aimed at a higher office, but he dissembled his irritation, and accepted the sword offered him by John of Leyden with apparent transports of joy.[1] Four under-executioners were named to assist him, and to accompany him wherever he went.

The nomination of Knipperdolling was the prelude to other important changes. Bockelson aspired to exercise absolute power, without opposition or control. To arrive at his ends, a wild prophetic scene was enacted. He ran, during the night, through the streets of Münster stark naked, uttering howls and crying, " Ye men of Israel who inhabit this holy Zion! fear the Lord, and repent for your past lives. Turn ye, turn ye! The glorious King of Zion, surrounded by multitudes of angels, is about to descend and judge the world, at the peal of His terrible trumpet. Turn, ye blind ones, and be converted."[2]

Exhausted with his run and his shouts, and satisfied with having thoroughly alarmed the inhabitants, he returned to the house of Knipperdolling, who was also in a paroxysm of inspiration, foaming, leaping, rolling on the ground, and performing many other extravagant actions. Bockelson, on entering, cast himself down in a corner and pretended to have lost the power of speech; and as the crowd, assembled

---

[1] Kerssenbroeck, p. 545 ; Heresbach, p. 139 ; Sleidan, p. 413 ; Dorpius, f. 396.

[2] Kerssenbroeck, p. 596; Monfort, pp. 25, 26; Heresbach, p. 99 *et seq.*

round him, asked him the meaning of what had taken place, he signed to them to bring him tablets, on which he wrote, "By the order of the Father, I remain dumb for three days."

At the expiration of this period he convoked the people, and declared to them that the Father had revealed to him that Israel must have a new constitution, with new laws and new magistrates, divinely appointed. The former magistracy had been elected by men, but the new one was to be designated by the Holy Ghost. Bockelson then dissolved the senate, and, as the mouthpiece of God, he declared the names of the new officers, to the number of twelve, who were to bear the title of The Elders of the Tribes of Israel, in whose hands all power, temporal and spiritual, was to be placed. Those appointed were, as might have been expected, the prophet's most devoted adherents.[1] Hermann Tilbeck, the old burgomaster, was brought out of prison, and it was announced to him that he was to be of the number of elders; but perhaps a little cooled in this enthusiasm by his sojourn in chains, he burst into tears, and in accents of humility prayed, "Oh, Father! I am not worthy so great an honour; give me strength and light to govern with wisdom."

Rottmann, who, since the arrival of the prophet, had played but a subordinate part, judged the occasion favourable for thrusting himself into prominence. He therefore preached a long sermon, in which he declared that God was the author of the new constitution, and then, calling the elders before him by name, he committed to each a drawn sword, with the words,

---

[1] Dorpius, f. 396 b.

T

'Receive with this weapon the right of life or death which the Father has ordered me to confer upon you, and use the sword conformably to the Lord's will." Then the proceedings closed with the multitude singing the *Gloria in excelsis* in German, on their knees.

The senate resigned its functions without apparent regret or opposition, and the twelve elders assumed the plenitude of power. They abolished the laws and formulated new ones, published edicts, resolved difficulties, judged causes, subject to no control save the will of the prophet; but that will they regarded as identical with the Divine will, as superior to all law, and every one obeyed its smallest requirements.

Immediately after the installation of the government, an edict in ten parts was published.[1] The first part, divided into thirteen articles, contained the moral law; the second part, in thirty-three articles, contained the civil law.

The first part forbade thirteen crimes under pain of death: blasphemy, disobedience, adultery, impurity, avarice, theft, fraud, lying and slander, idle conversation, disputes, anger, envy, and discontent against the government.

The second part required every citizen to conform his life and belief to the Word of God; to fulfil exactly his duties to others and to the State. It ordered a strict system of vigilance against night surprises by the enemy, and required one of the elders to sit in rotation every day as judge to try cases brought

[1] Kerssenbroeck, pt. ii. pp. 1-9; Monfortius, pp. 26, 27; Hast, p, 352 *et seq.*

before him; also, that whatsoever was decided by the elders as necessary for the welfare of the New Jerusalem should be announced to the assembly-general of Israel, by the prophet John of Leyden, servant of the Most High; that Bernard Knipper-dolling, the executioner, should denounce to the elders the crimes committed within the holy city; and that he might exercise his office with greater security he was never to go forth unaccompanied by his four assistants.

It ordered that henceforth repasts should be taken publicly and in common; that every one should accept what was set before him, should eat it modestly, in silence; that the brothers and the sisters should eat at separate tables; and that, during the meal, portions of the Old Testament should be read to them.

The next articles named the individuals who were to execute the offices of butcher, shoemaker, smith, tailor, brewer, and the like, to the Lord's people. Two articles forbade the introduction of new fashions, and the wearing of garments with holes in them. Article XXIX. ordered every stranger belonging to another religion, who should enter the city of Münster, to be examined by Knipperdolling. No communication of any sort with strangers was permitted to the children of Zion.

Article XXXII. forbade, under pain of death, desertion from the military service, or exchange of companies without the sanction of the elders.

Article XXXIII. required that in the event of a decease, all the goods and chattels of the defunct should be taken to Knipperdolling, who would convey them to the elders, and they would distribute them as they judged fitting.

That some of these provisions were indicative of great prudence is not to be doubted. All food having been seized upon and being served out publicly to all the citizens alike, and in moderation, the capabilities of prolonging the defence were greatly increased; and the military dictatorship and strict discipline within the city maintained by the prophet, enabled the Anabaptists to preserve an invulnerable front to an enemy torn by faction and with divided responsibilities.

To increase the disaffection and party strife in the hostile camp, the people of Münster sent arrows amongst the besiegers, to which were attached letters, one of which has been preserved by Kerssenbroeck.[1] It is an exhortation to the enemy to beware lest by attacking the people of the Lord, who held to the pure Word of God, they should be regarded by him as in league with Antichrist, and urging them to repentance.

Besiegers and besieged heaped on each other reciprocal insults, exhibiting themselves to one another in postures more expressive of contempt than decent.[2]

A chimney-sweep, named William Bast, had about this time a vision ordering him to burn the cities of the ungodly. Bast announced his mission to the elders and to the prophet, and was bidden go forth in the Lord's name. He accordingly left Münster, eluded the vigilance of the enemy's sentinals, and reached

[1] Kerssenbroeck, pt. ii. p. 9.   [2] *Ibid*, pp. 11, 12.

Wollbeck, where was the powder magazine of the Episcopal army. He fired several houses, and the flames spread, but were fortunately extinguished before they reached the powder. Bast had escaped to Dreusteindorf, where also he attempted to execute his mission, but was caught, brought back to Wollbeck, and burnt alive.

In the meantime various sorties had taken place, in which the besiegers suffered, being caught off their guard. On May 22nd, the prince-bishop, finding the siege much more serious than he had anticipated, began to bombard the town; but as fast as the walls gave way, they were repaired by the women and children at night.

A general assault was resolved on for the 26th May; of this the besieged were forewarned by their spies. Unfortunately for the investing army, the soldiers of Guelders got drunk on the preceding day in anticipation of their victory, and marched reeling and shouting against the city as the dusk closed in. The Anabaptists manned the walls, and easily repulsed their tipsy assailants; but in the meantime the rest of the army, observing the march of the men of Guelders, and hearing the discharge of firearms, rushed to their assistance, without order; the Münsterians rallied, repulsed them with great carnage, and they fled in confusion to the camp. The Anabaptists had only lost two officers and eight soldiers in the fray; and their success convinced them that they were under the special providence of God, which had rendered them invincible.[1] They, therefore, repaired their walls

[1] Kerssenbroeck, pp. 15, 16; Sleidan, p. 413.

with energy, erected several additional bastions, and continued their sorties.

On the 30th May, a party of the fanatics issued from a subterraneous passage upon the sentinels opposite the Judenfeld gate, spiked nineteen cannon, and laid a train of gunpowder from the store, which they reached, to the mouth of their passage. The troops stationed within sight marched hastily to repulse the sortie, when the train was fired, the store exploded, and a large number of soldiers were destroyed.[1]

The prince-bishop next adopted an antiquated expedient, which proved singularly inefficacious. He raised a huge bank against the walls, by requisitioning the services of the peasants of the country round. The besieged poured a shower of bullets amongst the unfortunate labourers, who perished in great numbers, and the mole remained unfinished.[2]

Francis of Waldeck, discouraged, and at the end of his resources, sent his deputies to the Diet of Neuss on the 25th June, to announce to the Archbishop of Cologne and the Duke of Juliers his failures, and to ask for additional troops. The two princes replied that they would not abandon their ally in his difficulties, and they promised to bear a part of the cost of the siege, advanced 40,000 florins for the purchase of gunpowder, promised to despatch forces to his assistance, and sent at once prudent advisers.[3] The prince was, in fact, utterly incompetent as a general and incompetent as a bishop. The pastoral staff has a crook at the head and a spike at the bottom. Litur-

---

[1] Kerssenbroeck, pp. 15, 16.   [2] *Ibid*, p. 21.
[3] Hast, p. 357; Sleidan, p. 413.

giologists assure us that this signifies the mode in which a bishop should exercise discipline—the gentle he should restrain or direct with mercy, the rebellious he should treat with severity. To the former he should be lenient, with the latter prompt. Francis of Waldeck wielded gracefully and effectively neither end of his staff.

He shortly incurred a risk, and but for the fidelity of one of his subjects in Münster, he would have fallen a victim to assassination.

A young Anabaptist maiden, named Hilla Phnicon, of singular beauty, conceived the notion that she had been called by God to be the Judith of this new Bethulia, and was to take the head from off the shoulders of the great, soft, bungling Holophernes, Francis of Waldeck.[1]

Rottmann, Bockelson, and Knipperdolling encouraged the girl in her delusion, and urged her not to resist the inspirations of the Father. Accordingly, on the 16th June, Hilla dressed herself in the most beautiful robes she could procure, adorned her hair with pearls, and her arms with bracelets, selecting from the treasury of the city whatever articles she judged most conducive to the end ; the treasury being for the purpose placed at her disposal by order of the prophet. Furnished with a linen shirt steeped in deadly poison, which she had herself made, as an offering to the prince, she left Münster, and delivered herself up into the hands of the drossar of Wollbeck, who, after having dispoiled her of her jewels, questioned her as to her object in deserting the city. She

[1] Kerssenbroeck, p. 26 *et seq.*

replied with the utmost composure, that she was a native of Holland, and that she had lived in Münster with her husband, till the change of religion had so disgusted her that she could endure it no longer, and that she had fled on the first opportunity, and that her husband would follow her on a suitable occasion. "It is to ask pardon for him that I am come," said she; "and he will be able to indicate to his highness a means of entering the city without loss."

The perfect self-possession of the lady convinced the drossar of her sincerity, and he promised to introduce her to the prince at Iburg within two days. Everything seemed to favour the adventuress; but an unexpected event occurred on the 18th, the day appointed for the audience, which spoiled the plot.

The secret had been badly kept, and it was a matter of conversation, hope, and prayer in Münster. A citizen named Ramers, who had remained in the city, and had been rebaptised rather than lose his business and give up his house to pillage, having heard of it, escaped from the town on the 18th, and revealed the projects of Hilla to one of the generals of the besieging army. The unfortunate young woman was thereupon put to the question, and confessed. She was conducted to Bevergern and decapitated. At the moment when she was being prepared for execution, she assured the bystanders that they would not be able to take her life, for the prophet John "chosen friend of the Father, had assured her that she would return safe and sound to Zion."

The bishop sent for Ramers, provided for his

necessities, and ordered that his house and goods should be spared in the event of the capture of Münster.

As soon as one danger disappeared, another rose up in its place. The letters attached to arrows fired by the Anabaptists into the hostile camp, as well as their secret agents, had wrought their effect. The Lutheran auxiliaries from Meissen complained that they were called to fight against the friends of the Gospel, and on the night of the 30th June they deserted in a body.[1] Other soldiers escaped into Münster and offered their arms to the Anabaptists. Disaffection was widely spread. Disorder, misunderstandings, and ill-concealed hatred reigned in the camp. The besieged reckoned among their assailants numerous and warm friends, and were regularly informed of all the projects of the general. Their emissaries bearing letters to the Anabaptists in other territories easily traversed the ranks of the investing army, and when they had accomplished their mission they returned with equal ease to the gates of Münster, which opened to receive them.

One of the soldiers of the Episcopal army, who had taken refuge in Münster, was lodged in the house of Knipperdolling, in which also dwelt John Bockleson. The deserter observed that the Leyden prophet was wont to leave his bedroom at night, and he ventured to watch his conduct and satisfy himself that it was not what it ought to be.[2] He mentioned to others what he had observed. The scandal would

---

[1] Kerssenbroeck, p. 36.
[2] *Ibid*, p. 38 ; H. Montfort. p. 28.

soon get wind.   One only way remained to cut it
short.   John Bockleson consulted with Rottmann and
the other preachers, and urged that polygamy should
be not only sanctioned but enjoined on the elect.

Some of those present having objected to this new
doctrine, the prophet cast his mantle and the New
Testament on the ground, and solemnly swore that
this which he enjoined was the direct revelation of the
Almighty.   He threatened the recalcitrant ministers,
and at last, half-persuaded and wholly frightened,
they withdrew their objections; and he appointed
the pastors three days in which to preach polygamy
to the people.[1]   The new doctrine having been
ventilated, an assembly of the people was called, and
it was formerly laid down by the prophet as the will
of God, that every man was to have as many wives as
he wanted.[2]

The result of this new step was to bring about a
reaction which for a moment threatened the prophet's
domination with downfall.

On the 30th July, Heinrich Mollenhecke, a blacksmith, supported by two hundred citizens, burghers
and artisans, declared openly that he was resolved to
put down the new masters of Münster, and to restore
everything upon the ancient footing.   With the
assistance of his companions, he captured Bockleson, Knipperdolling, and the preachers Rottmann,
Schlachtscap, Clopris, and Vinnius, and cast them
into prison.   Then a council was held, and it was
resolved that the gates should be opened to the
bishop, the old magistracy should be restored, and

---

[1] Sleidan, p. 414 ; Dorp. f 396.   [2] Kerssenbroeck, p. 38.

.the exiled burgesses should be recalled, and their property restored to them : and that all this should be done *on the morrow*. Had it been done on the spot we should have heard no more of John of Leyden. The delay saved him and ruined the reactionary party. It allowed time for his adherents to muster.[1] Mollenhecke and his party, when they met on the following morning to execute their design, were attacked and surrounded by a mulitude of fanatics headed by Heinrich Redecker. The blacksmith had succeeded in collecting only a handful. " No pen can describe the rage with which their adversaries fell upon them, and the refinements of cruelty to which they became victims. After having overwhelmed them with blows and curses, they were imprisoned, but they continued inflicting upon them such horrible tortures that the majority of these unfortunates would have a thousand times preferred death."[2] Ninety-one were ordered to instant execution. Twenty-five were shot, the other sixty-six were decapitated by Knipperdolling to economize powder, and lest the sound of the discharge of firearms within the city should lead the besiegers to believe that fighting was going on in the streets. Some had their heads cut off, others were tied to a tree and shot, others again were cut asunder at the waist, and others were slowly mutilated. Knipperdolling himself executed the men, so many every day, in the presence of the prophet, till all were slain.[3]

[1] Kerssenbroeck, p. 39 *et seq* ; Heresbach, pp. 41, 42 ; H. Montfort., pp. 29, 30 ; Bullinger, lib. ii. c. 9, p. 56.
[2] Kerssenbroeck, p. 40.   [3] *Ibid.* p. 41 ; Dorpius, f. 536 b.

"The partisans of the emancipation of the flesh having thus obtained the mastery in Münster," says the eye-witness, "it was impossible, a few days later, to discover in the capital of Westphalia the last and feeble traces of modesty, chastity, and self-restraint."

Three men, John Œchinckfeld, Henry Arnheim, and Hermann Bispinck, having, however, the hardihood to assert that they still believed that Christian marriage consisted in the union of one man with one woman, were decapitated by order of John of Leyden.[1]

With the death of these men disappeared every attempt at resistance.

The horrors which were perpetrated in Münster under the name of religious liberty almost exceed belief. The most frantic licence and savage debauchery were practised. The prophet took two wives, besides his favourite sultana, the beautiful Divara, widow of Matthisson, and his lawful wife at Leyden. These were soon discovered to be too few, and the harem swelled daily.[2]

"We must draw a veil," says Kerssenbroeck, "over what took place, for we should scandalise our readers were we to relate in detail the outrageous scenes of immorality which took place in the town, and the villanies which these maniacs committed to satisfy their abominable lusts. They were no more human beings, they were foul and furions beasts. The hideous word *Spiritus meus concupiscit carnem tuam*

---

[1] H. Montfort. p. 29; C. Heresbach, p. 42.

[2] Kerssenbroeck, p. 42. Dorpius confirms the horrible account given by Kerssenbroeck from what he saw himself, f. 498.

was in every mouth; those who resisted these magic words were shut up in the convent of Rosenthal; and if they persisted in their obstinacy after exhortation, their heads were cut off. In one day four were simultaneously executed on this account. On another occasion a woman was sentenced to be decapitated, after childbirth, for having complained of her husband having taken to himself a second wife."[1]

Henry Schlachtscap preached that no man after the Ascension of Christ had lived in true matrimony, if he had contracted marriage on account of beauty, wealth, family, and similar causes, for that true marriage consisted solely in that which was instigated by the Spirit.

A new prophet now appeared upon the scene, named Dusentscheuer, a native of Warendorf. He rushed into the market-place uttering piercing cries, and performing such extraordinary antics that a crowd was speedily gathered around him.

Then, addressing himself to the multitude, he exclaimed, " Christian brothers, the celestial Father has revealed to me, and has commanded me to announce to you, that John Bockelson of Leyden, the saint and prophet of God, must be king of the whole earth; his authority will extend over emperors, kings, princes, and all the powers of the world; he will be the chief authority; and none shall arise above him. He will occupy the throne of his father David, and will carry the sceptre till the Lord reclaims it from him."[2]

[1] Kerssenbroeck, p. 43 *et seq.*
[2] *Ibid*, p. 47; Sleidan, p. 419; Bullinger, lib. ii. p. 56; Montfort., p. 31; Heresbach, pp. 136-7, " Historia von d. Münsterischen Widerteuffer," f. 328 b; Dorpius, f. 397.

Bockelson and the twelve elders were present. A profound silence reigned in the assembly. Dusentscheuer, advancing to the elders, demanded their swords of office; they surrendered them into his hands; he placed eleven at the feet of Bockelson, and put the twelfth into his hand, saying—"Receive the sword of justice, and with it the power to subjugate all nations. Use it so that thou mayst be able to give a good account thereof to Christ, when He shall come to judge the quick and the dead."[1] Then drawing from his pocket a phial of fragrant oil, he poured it over the tailor's head, pronouncing solemnly the words, "I consecrate thee in the presence of thy people, in the name of God, and by His command, and I proclaim thee king of the new Zion." When the unction was performed, Bockelson cast himself in the dust and exclaimed, "O Father! I have neither years, nor wisdom, nor experience, necessary for such sovereignty; I appeal to Thy grace, I implore Thy assistance and Thy all-powerful protection! . . . . Send down upon me, therefore, Thy divine wisdom. May Thy glorious throne descend on me, may it dwell with me, may it illumine my labours; then shall I be able to accomplish Thy will and Thy good pleasure, and thus shall I be able to govern Thy people with equity and justice."

Then, turning himself towards the crowd, Bockelson declared that he had long known by revelation the glory that was to be his, but he had never mentioned it, lest he should be deemed ambitious, but had awaited in patience and humility the accomplishment

[1] Kerssenbroeck.

of God's holy will. He concluded by saying that, destined by the Father to reign over the whole world, he would use the sword, and slay all those who should venture to oppose him.[1]

Nevertheless murmurs of disapprobation were heard. "What!" thundered the Leyden tailor, "you dare to resist the designs of God! Know then, that even were you all to oppose me, I should nevertheless become king of the whole earth, and that my royalty, which begins now in this spot, will last eternally."

The new prophet Dusentscheuer and the other preachers harangued the people during three consecutive days on the new revelation, read to the people the 23rd chapter of Jeremiah and the 27th of Ezekiel, and announced that in the King John the prophecies of the old seers were accomplished, for that he was the new David whom God had promised to raise up in the latter days. They also read aloud the 13th chapter of St. Paul's Epistle to the Romans, and accompanied the lecture with commentaries on the necessity and divine obligation of submission to authority.[1]

At the expiration of these three days, Dusentscheuer requested John of Leyden to complete the spoliation of the inhabitants, so that everything they possessed might be placed in a common fund. "It has been revealed to me," said he, "that the Father is violently irritated against the men and women because they have abused grievously their food and drink and clothing. The Father requires for the

[1] Kerssenbroeck, p. 47 ; and the authors before quoted.

future, that no one of either sex shall retain more than two complete suits and four shirts; the rest must be collected and placed in security. It is the will of the Lord that the provisions of beef and pork found in every house shall also be seized and be consecrated to the general use."[1]

The order was promptly obeyed. Eighty-three large waggons were laden with confiscated clothes, and all the provisions found in the city were brought to the king, who confided the care and apportionment of them to Dusentscheuer.

Bockelson now organised his court with splendour. He appointed his officers, chamberlain, stewards, marshals, and equerries, in imitation of the Court of the Emperor and Princes of Germany. Rottmann was named his chaplain; Andrew von Coesfeld, director of police; Hermann Tilbeck, grand-marshal; Henry Krechting, chancellor; Christopher Waldeck, the bishop's son, who had fallen into his power, was in derision made one of the pages; and a privy council of four, composed of Bernard Krechting, Henry Redecker, and two others of inferior note, was instituted under the presidency of Christian Kerkering. John had also a grand-master of the kitchen, a cup-bearer, taster, carver, gentlemen of the bedchamber, &c.[2]

But John Bockelson not only desired to be surrounded by a court; he determined also to display all the personal splendour of royalty. Accordingly, at his

---

[1] Kerssenbroeck, p. 49.

[2] *Ibid.* p. 55 Montfort., pp. 31-3; Sleidan, p. 418; Bullinger, p. 57; Heresbach, pp. 137-8.

order, two crowns of pure gold were made, one royal, the other imperial, encrusted with jewels. Around his neck hung a gold chain enriched with precious stones, from which depended a globe of the same metal transfixed by two swords, one of gold, the other of silver. The globe was surmounted by a cross which bore the inscription, "Ein König der Gerechtigkeit über all" (a King of Righteousness over all). His sceptre, spurs, baldrick and scabbard were also of gold, and his fingers blazed with diamonds. On one of the rings, which was exceedingly massive, was cut, "Der König in dem nyen Tempel furet dit zeichen vur sein Exempel" (the King of the new Temple bears this symbol as his token). The royal garments were magnificent, of crimson and purple, and costly stuffs of velvet, silk, and gold and silver damask, with superb lace cuffs and collars, and his mantle lined with costly furs. The elders, the prophets, and the preachers followed suit, and exchanged their sad-coloured garments for robes of honour in gay colours. The small house of Knipperdolling no longer contented the tailor-king; he therefore furnished, and moved into, a handsome mansion belonging to the noble family of Von Büren. The house next door was converted into the palace of his queens, and was adorned with royal splendour. A door of communication, broken through the partition wall, allowed King John to visit his wives at all hours.

He now took to himself thirteen additional wives, and a large train of concubines. Among his sixteen legitimate wives was a daughter of Knipperdolling. Divara of Haarlem remained the head queen, though

U

she was the oldest. The rest were all under twenty, and were the most beautiful girls of Münster. They all bore the title of queens, but Divara alone had a court, officers, and bodyguard, habited in a livery of chestnut brown and green ; the livery of the king being scarlet and blue.[1]

The king usually had his meals with his wives, and during the repasts he examined them with great attention, feasting his eyes on their beauty. The names of the sixteen queens were inscribed on a tablet on which the king, after dinner, designated the lady who had attracted his favour.[2]

The King of Zion had abolished the names of the days of the weeks, and had replaced them by the seven first letters of the alphabet. He ordered that whenever a child was born in the town, it should be announced to him, and then he gave it a name, whose initial letter corresponded with the letter of the day on which it entered the world. But, as Kerssenbroeck observes, the debauchery which reigned in Münster had the result of diminishing the births, so that the number of children born during the latter part of the siege was extraordinarily small.

Bockelson had only two children by all his wives, and both were daughters. Divara was the first to

---

[1] Kerssenbroeck, p. 55 *et seq.* ; and the authors above cited. Kerssenbroeck gives long details of the dress, ornaments, and manner of life of the king ; also " Historia von d. Münsterischen Widerteuffer," f. 329.

[2] Kerssenbroeck gives the names of all the wives except one, which he conceals charitably, as the poor child—she was very young—fell ill, but recovered, and was living respectably after the siege with her relatives in the city.

give birth; the event took place on a Sunday, designated by the letter A; it was given the name of Averall (for Ueberall—Above all); the second child, born on Monday, was called Blydam (the Blythe).[1]

Thrice in the week Bockelson sat in judgment in the market-place on a throne decked in purple silk, and richly adorned with gold. He betook himself to this place of audience with great pomp. A band of musical instruments headed the pageant, then followed the councillors in purple, and the grand-marshal with the white wand in his hand. John, wearing the royal insignia, mounted on a white horse, splendidly capar- isoned, followed between two pages fantastically dressed, one bearing a Bible, the other a naked sword, symbols of the spiritual and temporal jurisdiction exercised by his majesty. The bodyguard surrounded his royal person, to keep off the crowd and to protect him from danger. Knipperdolling, Rottmann, the secretary Puthmann, and the chancellor Krechting followed; then the executioner and his four assist- ants, a train of courtiers, and servants closed the pro- cession. The whole ceremony was as regal, as punctiliously observed, as at a royal court where the traditions date from many centuries.[2]

When the king reached the market-place, a squire held the horse, he slowly mounted the steps of the throne, and inclining his sceptre, announced the open- ing of the audience.

[1] Kerssenbroeck, p. 59.

[2] Kerssenbroeck, p. 62; H. Montfort., p. 33; Hast, p. 363 *et seq.;* Sleidan, p. 415; "Historia von de Münsterischen Wider- teuffer," f. 328 b.

Then the plaintiffs approached, prostrated themselves flat upon the ground twice, and spoke. The
majority of the cases were matrimonial complaints,
often exceedingly indecent; "the greatest abominations formulated in the most hideously cynical terms
before the most cynical of judges." Capital sentences,
or penalties little less severe, were pronounced against
insubordinate wives.[1]

The same ceremonial was observed whenever his
majesty went to hear the preaching in the market-
square, with the sole exception, that on this occasion
he was accompanied by the sixteen queens, magnificently dressed. Queen Divara rode a palfrey capari-
soned in furs, led by a page; the court and the fifteen
other queens followed on foot. On reaching the
market-place, the ladies entered a house opposite the
throne, and assisted at the sermon, sitting at the
windows.

The pulpit and the throne were side by side; a
long broad platform united them. When the sermon
was concluded, the king, his queens, court, ministers,
and the preacher, assembled on the platform and
danced to the strains of the royal band.

It was from this platform that King John, as
sovereign pontiff, blessed polygamous marriages,
saying to the brides and the bridegrooms, "What God
hath joined let no man put asunder; go, act according
to the divine law, be fruitful and multiply, and

[1] Kerssenbroeck. Sleidan says, "Almost every case and
complaint brought before him concerned married people and
divorces. For nothing was more frequent, so that persons who
had lived together for many long years now separated for the
first time."—p. 415-6.

replenish the earth." This sanction was necessary for the validity of these unions.

John, wishing to exercise all the prerogatives of royalty, struck coins of various values, bearing on one side the inscription, "Das Wort is Fleisch geworden und wohnet unter uns" (The Word was made flesh and dwelt among us); or "Wer nicht gebohren ist aus Wasser und Geist der kann nicht eingehen—" the rest on the reverse—" In das Reich Gottes. Den es ist nur ein rechter König über alle, ein Gott, ein Glaube, eine Tauffe" (who is not born of Water and the Spirit, cannot enter into the Kingdom of God. For there is only one true King over all, one God, one Faith, one Baptism). And in the middle, " Münster, 1534."

Whilst the city of Münster was thus passing from a republic to a monarchy, the siege continued ; but the besiegers made no progress. Refugees informed the prince-bishop of what had taken place within the walls.

On the 25th August he assembled the captains and the princes and nobles who had come into the camp to observe the proceedings, to request them to advise him how to put an end to all these horrors and abominations. It was proposed that a deputation should be sent into the town to propose a capitulation on equitable terms; and in the event of a refusal to offer a general assault. [1]

On the 28th August an armistice of three hours' duration was concluded, and the deputation obtained a safe-conduct authorising them to enter the city.

[1] Kerssenbroeck, p. 65 *et seq.;* Montfort, pp. 27, 28.

But instead of being brought before the inhabitants of the town, to whom they were commissioned to make the propositions, they were introduced to the presence of Bockelson and his court.

The envoys informed King John of the terms proposed by the bishop. They were extremely liberal. He promised a general amnesty if the place were surrendered, and arms laid down.

King John replied haughtily, that he did not need the clemency of the prince-bishop, for that he stood strengthened by the almighty and irresistible power of God. " It is your pretended bishop," said he, " who is an impious and obstinate rebel, he who makes war without previous declaration against the faithful servants of the celestial Father. Never will I lay down my arms which I have taken up for the defence of the Gospel ; never in cowardly fashion will I surrender my capital: on the contrary, I know how to defend it, even to the last drop of my blood, if the honour of God requires it." [1]

The bishop, when he learnt that his deputies had been refused permission to address the citizens, attached letters, sealed with his Episcopal seal, to arrows, which were shot into the town. In these letters he promised a general pardon to all those who would leave the party of the Anabaptists, and escape from the town before the following Thursday.

But Bockelson forbade, on pain of death, any one touching or opening one of these letters, and ordered the instant decapitation of man, woman, or child who testified anxiety to leave Münster.

[1] Kerssenbroeck, p. 21.

The bishop and the princes resolved on attempting
an assault without further delay. John of Leyden
received information of their purpose through his
spies. He at once mounted his white horse, convoked
the people, and announced to them that the Father
had revealed to him the day and hour of the projected
attack; he appointed his post to every man, gave
employment to the women and children, and displayed, at this critical moment, the zeal, energy, and
readiness which would have done credit to a veteran
general.[1]

The assault was preluded by a bombardment of
three days. The battlements yielded, breaches were
effected in the walls, the roofs of the houses were
shattered, the battered gates gave way, and all promised
success. But the besieged neglected no precaution.
During the night the walls were repaired and the
gates strenghtened. Women laboured under the
orders of the competent directors during the hours of
darkness, thus allowing their husbands to take their
requisite repose. They carried stones and the
munitions of war to the ramparts, and learning to
handle the cross-bow, they succeeded in committing
no inconsiderable amount of execution among the
ranks of the Episcopal army. Other women prepared lime and boiling pitch " to cook the bishop's
soup for him." [2] On the 31st August, at daybreak,
the roar of the Hessian devil, as a large cannon belonging to the Landgrave Philip was called, gave the
signal. Instantly the city was assaulted in six places.
The ditches were filled, petards were placed under

[1] Kerssenbroeck, p. 68.   [2] *Ibid.* p. 70.

the gates, the palisades were torn down, and ladders were planted. But however vigorous might be the attack, the defence was no less vigorous. Those on the walls threw down the ladders with all upon them, and they fell bruised and mangled into the fosse, the heads of those who had reached the battlements were crushed with stones and cudgels, and their hands, clasping the parapet, were hacked off. Women hurled stones upon the besiegers, and enveloped them in boiling pitch, quicklime, and blazing sulphur.

Repulsed, they returned to the charge eight or ten times, but always in vain. The whole day was consumed in ineffectual assaults, and when the red sun went down in the west, the clarions pealed the retreat, and the army, dispirited and bearing with it a train of wounded, withdrew, leaving the ground strewn with dead.

Had the Anabaptists made a night assault, the defeat and dispersion of the Episcopal troops would have been completed. But instead, they sang a hymn and spent the night in banqueting.

The prince-bishop, despondent and at his wits' end for money, called his officers to a consultation on the 3rd September, and it was unanimously resolved to turn the investment into an effective blockade. This resolution was submitted to the electors of Cologne and Saxony, the Duke of Cleves, and the Landgrave of Hesse, and these princes approved of the design of Francis von Waldeck.

It was determined to raise seven redoubts, united by ramparts and a ditch, around the city, so as completely to close it, and prevent the exit of the besieged and the entrance of provisions. It was decided that the defence of this circle of forts should be confided to a sufficient number of tried soldiers, and that the rest of the army should be dismissed.

Accordingly, on the 7th September, all the labourers of the country round were engaged, under the direction of the engineer Wilkin von Stedingen, in raising the walls and digging the trenches. The work was carried on with vigour by relays of peasants; nevertheless, the undertaking was on so great a scale, that several months must elapse before it could be completed.[1]

The cost of this terrible siege had already risen to 600,000 florins, the treasury was empty, and the country could bear no further taxes. Francis of Waldeck appealed to the Elector Palatine, the Electors of Cologne, Mainz, and Trèves, to give help and subsidies; he had recourse also to the princes and nobles of the Upper and Lower Rhine; and it was decided that a diet should assemble on the 13th December, 1534, to make arrangements for the complete subjugation of the insurgent fanatics. All the princes, Catholic and Protestant, trembled for their crowns, for the Anabaptist sect ramified throughout the country, and if John of Leyden were successful in Münster, they might expect similar risings in their own principalities.[2]

Whilst the preparations for the blockade were in progress, John Bockelson, inflated with pride, placed no bounds to his prodigality, his display, and his

---

[1] Kerssenbroeck, p. 75 *et seq.*; Heresbach, p. 132.
[2] *Ibid.* p. 75; Bussierre, p. 372; Hast, p. 366.

despotism. He frequently pronounced sentences of death. Thus Elizabeth Holschers was decapitated for having refused her husband what he demanded of her; Catherine of Osnabrück underwent the same sentence for having told one of the preachers that he was building his doctrines upon the sand; Catherine Knockenbecher lost her head for having taken two husbands. Polygamy was permitted, but polyandry was regarded as an unpardonable offence.[1]

However, the people chafed at the tyranny they were subjected to, and murmurs, low and threatening, continued to make themselves heard; whereupon, by King John's order, Dusentscheuer announced from the pulpit, " that all those who should for the future have doubts in the verities taught them, and who should venture to blame the king whom the Father had given them, would be given over to the anointed of the Lord to be extirpated out of Israel, decapitated by the headsman, and condemned to eternal oblivion."

Amongst those who viewed with envy the rise and splendour of the tailor-king was Knipperdolling. He had opened his home to the prophet, had patronised him, introduced him to the people of Münster, and now the draper was eclipsed by the glory of the tailor. Thinking that the time was come for him to assume the pre-eminence, he made an attempt to dethrone Bockelson.

On the 12th of September he was seized with the spirit of prophecy, became as one possessed, rushed through the town howling, foaming at the mouth, making prodigious leaps and extravagant gestures,

---

[1] Kerssenbroeck, p. 75; Bussierre, p. 372.

and crying in every street, "Repent! repent!" After having carried on these antics for some time, Knipperdolling dashed into the market-place, cast himself down on the ground, and fell into an ecstasy.

The people clustered around him, wondering what new revelation was about to be made, and the king, who was then holding audience, looked on uneasily at the crowd drifting from his throne towards his lieutenant-general, whose object he was unable to divine, as this performance had not been concerted between them.

He was not left long in uncertainty, for Knipperdolling, rising from the ground with livid face, scrambled up the back of a sturdy artisan standing near, and crawled on all fours "like a dog," says Sleidan, over the heads of the throng, breathing in their faces, and exclaiming, "The celestial Father has sanctified thee; receive the Holy Ghost." Then he anointed the eyes of some blind men with his spittle, saying, "Let sight be given you." Undiscomfited by the failure of this attempt to perform a miracle, he prophesied that he would die and rise again in three days; and he indicated a corner of the market-place where this was to occur. Then making his way towards the throne, he began to dance in the most grotesque and indecent manner before the king, shouting contemptuously, "Often have I danced thus before my mistresses, now the celestial Father has ordered me to perform these dances before my king."[1]

John was highly displeased at this performance; and he ran down the steps of his throne to interrupt

[1] Kerssenbroeck, p. 81 *et seq.*; Sleidan, p. 416.

him. But Knipperdolling nimbly leaped upon the dais, seated himself in the place of majesty, and cried out, " The Spirit of God impels me : John Bockelson is king according to the flesh, I am king according to the Spirit ; the two Testaments must be abolished and extirpated. Man must cease from obeying terrestrial laws ; henceforth he shall obey only the inspirations of the Spirit and the instincts of nature."

John of Leyden sprang at him, dragged him from the throne, beat his head with his golden sceptre, and administering a kick to the rear of his lieutenant, sent him flying head over heels from the platform, and then calmly enthroning himself, he gave orders for the removal and imprisonment of the rebel.

He was obeyed.[1]

Knipperdolling, left to cool in the dungeon, felt that his only chance of life was to submit. He therefore sent his humble apology to the king, and assured him that he had been possessed by an evil spirit, which had driven him, against his judgment and conscience, into revolt. " And," said he, "last night the Father revealed to me that one must venerate the royal majesty, and that John is destined to reign over the whole earth."

He was at once released, for Bockelson needed him, and the failure of this attempt only secured the king's hold over him. He sent him a letter of pardon, concluding with the royal signature in this eccentric fashion :—

> " In fide persiste salvus
> Carnis curam agit Deus.

[1] Kerssenbroeck, Hast p. 366.

Johannes Leydanus.
Potentia Dei, robur meum."[1]

Another event took place at Münster, which distracted the thoughts of the people from the events of the siege, and the attempt of Knipperdolling to dethrone the king.

The prophet Dusentscheuer, on the same day, the 12th September, sought the King of Zion in his palace, and said to him with an inspired air, " This is the commandment of the Lord to me : Go and say unto the chief of Israel, that he shall prepare on the Mount Zion (that is, the cathedral square) a great supper for all Christian brethren and sisters, and after supper he shall commission the teachers of my Word to go forth to the four quarters of the world, that they may teach all men the way of my righteousness, and that they may be brought into my fold."

The king accepted the message with respect, and gave orders for its immediate execution.

On the 13th September, Dusentscheuer called together the elect, traversing the streets playing upon a flute. At noon 1700 men, capable of bearing arms, 400 old men and children, and 5000 women assembled on Mount Zion.

Bockelson left his palace, habited in a scarlet tunic over which was cast a cloth of silver mantle, on his head was his crown, and his sceptre was in his right hand. Thirty-two knights, magnificently dressed, served as his bodyguard. Then came Queen Divara and the rest of the wives of the court.

[1] Persist secure in Faith. God takes care of the Flesh. John of Leyden. The Power of God is my strength.

When the king had taken his place, the Grand Marshal Tilbeck made the people sit down. Tables had been arranged along the sides of the great square under the trees, with an open space in the centre.

When all were seated, the king and his familiars distributed food to those invited. They were given first boiled beef and roots, then ham with other vegetables, and finally roast meat. When the plates had been removed, thin round cakes of fine wheat flour were brought in large baskets, and John, calling the faithful up before him, communicated them with the bread, saying, " Take and eat this, and show forth the Lord's death." Divara followed, holding the chalice in her jewelled hands ; she made the communicants drink from it, repeating the words to each, "Drink this, and show forth the Lord's death." Then all sang the *Gloria in excelsis* in German, and this fantastic parody of the communion was over. Bockelson now ordered all his subjects to arrange themselves in a circle, and he demanded if they would faithfully obey the Word of God. All having assented, Dusentscheuer mounted the pulpit and said, " The Father has revealed to me the names of twenty-seven apostles who are to be sent into every part of the world ; they will spread everywhere the pure doctrine of the celestial kingdom, and the Lord will cover them with the shadow of His wings, so that not a hair of their head shall be injured. And when they shall arrive at a place where the authorities refuse to receive the Gospel, there they shall leave a florin in gold, they shall shake off the dust of their garments, and shall go to another place." Then the prophet designated the chosen apostles—he saw himself of the number—and he added, " Go ye into all the cities and preach the Word of God." The twenty-seven stepped forward, and the king, mounting the pulpit, exhorted the people to prepare for a grand sortie.[1]

The banquet was over for the people; but John, his wives and court, and those who had been on guard upon the walls, to the number of 500, now sat down.

The second banquet was much more costly than the first. In the midst of the feast, Bockelson, rising, said that he had received an order from the Father to go round and inspect the guests. He accordingly examined those present, and recognising amongst them a soldier of the Episcopal army, who had been made prisoner, he confronted him sternly, and asked—

" Friend, what is thy faith ? "

"My faith," replied the soldier, who was half drunk, " is to drink and make love."

" How didst thou dare to come in, not having on the wedding garment ? " asked the king, in a voice of thunder.

[1] Kerssenbroeck, p. 86 ; Montfort., p. 34 ; Dorpius, f. 397 b ; Heresbach, p. 139, *et seq.;* Bullinger, lib. ii. c. 10 ; Sleidan, p. 417 ; this author sets the number of communicants at 5,000, the " Newe Zeitung " at 4,000, f. 329. This authority adds that the communicants distributed the sacrament they had received amongst themselves saying, " Brother and sister, take and eat thereof. As Christ gave Himself for me, so will I give myself for thee. And as the corn-wheat is baked into one, and the grape branches are pressed into one, so we being many are one." Also, " Letter of the Bishop to the Electors of Cologne," *ibid.* p. 390.

"I did not come of my own accord to this de-bauch,"[1] answered the prisoner; "I was brought here by main force."

At these words, the king, transported with rage, drew his sword and smote off the head of the unfortunate reveller.

The night was spent in dancing.[2]

Whilst the king was eating and drinking, the twenty-seven apostles were taking a tender farewell of their 124 legitimate wives,[3] and making their preparations to depart.

When all was ready, they returned to Mount Zion; Bockelson ascended the pulpit, and gave them their mission in the following terms :—"Go, prepare the way; we will follow. Cast your florin of gold at the feet of those who despise you, that it may serve as a testimony against them, and they shall be slain, all the sort of them, or shall bow their necks to our rule."

Then the gates were thrown open, and the apostles went forth, north and south, and east and west. The blockade was not complete, and they succeeded in traversing the lines of the enemy.

However, the prince-bishop notified to the governors of the towns in his principality to watch them

---

[1] The expression used was somewhat broad—Hurenhochzeit.

[2] Kerssenbroeck, p. 88 *et seq.;* Heresbach, p. 139; Dorp. f. 398.

[3] Evidence of Heinrich Graess. Dorpius says that the number of apostles was twenty-eight, and gives their names and the places to which they were sent, f. 398.

and arrest them, should they attempt to disseminate their peculiar doctrines.[1]

We shall have to follow these men, and see the results of their mission, before we continue the history of the siege of Münster. In fact, on their expedition and their success, as John Bockelson probably felt, everything depended. As soon as the city was completely enclosed no food could enter: already it was becoming scarce; therefore an attack on the Episcopal army from the flank was most essential to success; the palisades and ramparts recently erected sufficiently defending the enemy against surprises and sorties from the town.

Seven of the apostles went to Osnabrück, six to Coesfeld, five to Warendorf, and eight, amongst whom was Dusentscheuer himself, betook themselves to Soest.[2]

On entering Soest, Dusentscheuer and his fellow-apostles opened their mission by a public frenzied appeal to repentance. Then, hearing that the senate had assembled, they entered the hall and preached to the city councillors in so noisy a fashion that the magistrates were obliged to suspend their deliberations. The burgomaster having asked them who they were, and why they entered the town-hall unsummoned and unannounced, "We are sent by the king of the New Zion, and by order of God to preach

---

[1] Kerssenbroeck, p. 89 *et seq.;* Heresbach, pp. 89, 101, 141 ; Montfort., p. 35 ; Bullinger, lib. ii. c. 10 ; Sleidan, pp. 417-8 ; Hast, p. 368 ; " Historia v. d. Münst. Widerteuffer." p. 329 a.

[2] For the acts of these apostles, Kerssenbroeck, p. 92 *et seq.;* Menck. p. 1574; Montfort., p. 36 *et seq.;* Sleidan, p. 418 ; Bullinger, lib. ii. c. 10 ; Heresbach, p. 149.

the Gospel," was the reply of Dusentscheuer; "and to execute this mission we need neither passports nor permission. The kingdom of Heaven suffereth violence, and the violent take it by storm." "Very well," said the burgomaster collectedly. "Guards, remove the preachers and throw them into prison." A few days after several of them lost their heads on the block.

John Clopris, at the head of four evangelists, entered Warendorf. They took up their abode in the house of an Anabaptist named Erpo, one of the magistrates of the town, and began to preach and prophesy in the streets. The first day they rebaptised fifty persons. Clopris preached with such fervour and persuasive eloquence, that the whole town followed him ; the senate received the sign of the covenant in a body, and this was followed by a rebaptism of half the population.

Alarmed at what was taking place, and afraid of a diversion in his rear, Francis of Waldeck wrote to the magistrates ordering them to give up the apostles of error. They refused, and the prince at once invested the town and bombarded it. The magistrates sent offers of capitulation, which the prince rejected ; they asked to retain their arms and their franchises. Francis of Waldeck insisted on unconditional surrender, and they were constrained to yield. Some of the senators and citizens who had repented of their craze, or who had taken no part in the movement, seized the apostles and conducted them to the townhall. Clopris and his fellows cast down their florins of gold and declared that they shook off the dust of their feet against the traitors, and that they would carry the pure Word of God and the living Gospel elsewhere; but escape was not permitted, and they were delivered over to the prince-bishop.

Francis of Waldeck at once placed sentinels in the streets, ordered every citizen to deliver up his weapons, took the title-deeds of the city, withdrew its franchises, and executed four of the apostles and three of the ringleaders of the senators. Clopris was sent to Cologne, and was burnt there on the 1st February, 1535, by the Elector. The bishop then raised a fortress to command the town, and placed in it a garrison to keep the Warendorfians in order. Seventeen years after, the greater part of the franchises were restored, and all the rest in 1555.

The apostles of the east, under Julius Frisius, were arrested at Coesfeld, and were executed.[1]

Those of the north reached Osnabrück. Denis Vinnius was at their head. They entered the house of a certain Otto Spiecher, whom they believed to be of their persuasion, and they laid at his feet their gold florins bearing the title and superscription of King John, as tokens of their mission. Spiecher picked up the gold pieces, pocketed them, and then

---

[1] The "Newe Zeitung v. d. Widerteuffer. zu Münster," f. 329 b, 330 a, gives a summary of the confessions of these men, and their account of the condition of affairs in the city. They said that every man there had five, six, seven, or eight wives, and that every girl over the age of twelve was forced to marry; that if one wife showed resentment against another, or jealousy, or complained, she was sentenced by the king to death.

informed his visitors that he did not belong to their sect, and that the only salvation for their necks would be reticence on the subject of their mission.

But this was advice Vinnius and his fellow-fanatics were by no means disposed to accept. They ran forth into the streets and market-place, yelling, dancing, foaming, and calling to repentance. Then Vinnius, having collected a crowd, preached to them the setting up of the Millennial kingdom at Münster. Thereupon the city-guard arrived with orders from the burgomaster, arrested the missionaries, and carried them off to the Goat-tower, where they shut them in, and barred fast the doors.[1]

The rabble showed signs of violence, threatened, blustered, armed themselves with axes and hammers, and vowed they would batter open the prison-gates unless the true ministers of God's Word, pure from all human additions, were set at liberty. The magistrates replied with great firmness that the first man who attempted to force the doors should be shot, and no one caring to be the first man, though very urgent to his neighbours to lead the assault, the mob sang a psalm and dispersed, and the ministers were left to console themselves with the promises of Dusentscheuer that not a hair of their head should fall.

A messenger was sent by the magistrates post haste to the prince-bishop, and before morning the evangelists were in his grasp at Iburg.

As they were led past Francis of Waldeck, one of them, Heinrich Graess, exclaimed in Latin, " Has not the prince power to release the captive?" and the

---

[1] Kerssenbroeck, p. 100 *et seq.*

prince, disposed in his favour, sent for him. Graess then confessed that the whole affair was a mixture of fanaticism and imposture, the ingredients being mixed in pretty equal proportions, and promised, if his life were spared, to abandon Anabaptism, and, what was more to the point, to prove an Ahitophel to the Absalom in Zion.

Graess was pardoned, Strahl died in prison, the other four were brought to the block.

Graess was the sole surviving apostle of the seventy-seven, and the miserable failure of their mission had rudely shaken out of him all belief in its divine character, and he became as zealous in unmasking Anabaptism as he had been enthusiastic in its propagation.

There is no reason to believe that the man was an unprincipled traitor. On the contrary, he appears to have been thoroughly in earnest as long as he believed in his mission, but his confidence had been shaken before he left the city, and the signal collapse of the mission sufficed to convince him of his previous error, and make him resolute to oppose it.

Laden with chains, he was brought to the gates of Münster one dark night and there abandoned. In the morning he was recognised by the sentinels, and was brought into the city, and led in triumph before the king, by a vast concourse chanting German hymns.[1]

And thus he accounted for his presence :—" I was last night at Iburg in a dark dungeon, when suddenly

[1] Kerssenbroeck, p. 103 *et seq.*; Montfort., pp. 40-1; Hast, p. 368.

a brilliant light filled my prison, and I saw before me an angel of God, who took me by the hand and led me forth, and delivered me from the death which has befallen all my companions, and which the ungodly determined to inflict on me upon the morrow. The angel transported me asleep to the gate of Münster, and that none may doubt my story, lo! the chains, wherewith I was laden by the enemies of Israel, still encumber me."

Some of the courtiers doubted the miracle, but not so the people, and the king gave implicit credence to his word, or perhaps thought the event capable of a very simple explanation, which had been magnified and rendered supernatural by the heated fancy of the mystic.

Graess became the idol of the people and the favourite of Bockelson. The king passed a ring upon his finger, and covered him with a robe of distinction, half grey, half green—the first the symbol of persistence, the other typical of gratitude to God.[1] Graess profited by his position to closely observe all that transpired of the royal schemes.

John Bockelson became more and more tyrannical and sanguinary. He hung a starving child, aged ten, for having stolen some turnips. A woman lost her head for having spit in the face of a preacher of the Gospel. An Episcopal soldier having been taken, the king exhorted him to embrace the pure Word of God, freed from the traditions of men. The prisoner having had the audacity to reply that the pure Gospel as practised in the city seemed to him to be adultery,

[1] Montfort., p. 40.

fornication, and all uncleanness; the king, foaming with rage, hacked off his head with his own hand.[1]

Provisions became scarce in Münster, and the inhabitants were driven to consume horse-flesh; and the powder ran short in the magazine.

The Diet of Coblenz assembled on the 13th December. The envoys of the Elector Palatine, the prince-bishops of Maintz, Cologne, and of Trier, the princes and nobles of the Upper and Lower Rhine and of Westphalia appeared. Francis of Waldeck, unable to be present in person, sent deputies to represent him.[2]

These deputies having announced that the cost of the siege had already amounted to 700,000 florins, besought the assembled princes to combine to terminate this disastrous war. A long deliberation followed, and the principle was admitted that as the establishment of an Anabaptist kingdom in Münster would be a disaster affecting the whole empire, it was just that the bishop should not be obliged to bear the whole expenses of the reduction of Münster. The Elector John Frederick of Saxony, though not belonging to the three circles convoked, through his deputies sent to the Diet, promised to take part in the extirpation of the heretics.[3] It was finally agreed that the bishop should be supplied with 300 horse soldiers, 3000 infantry, and that an experienced General, Count Ulrich von Ueberstein, should command them and take the general conduct of the war.[4]

---

[1] Kerssenbroeck, p. 110. [2] *Ibid.* p. 114.
[3] *Ibid.*; Sleidan, p. 419; Heresbach, p. 132. [4] Sleidan, p. 419.

The monthly subsidy of 15,000 florins was also promised to be contributed till the fall of Münster. It was also agreed that the prince-bishop should be guaranteed the integrity of his domains; that each prince, Catholic or Protestant, should use his utmost endeavours to extirpate Anabaptism from his estates; that the Bishop of Münster should request Ferdinand, King of the Romans, and the seven Electors, to meet on the 4th April, at Worms, to consult with those then assembled at Worms on measures to crush the rebellion, to divide the cost of the war, and to punish the leaders of the revolt at Münster.

Lastly, the Diet addressed a letter to the guilty city, summoning it to surrender at discretion, unless it were prepared to resist the combined effort of all estates of the empire.

But if the princes were combining against the Anabaptist New Jerusalem, the sectarians were in agitation, and were arming to march to its relief from all sides, from Leyden, Freisland, Amsterdam, Deventer, from Brabant and Strassburg.

The Anabaptists of Deventer were on the point of rising and massacring the "unbelievers" in this city, and then marching on Münster, when the plot was discovered, and the four ringleaders were executed. The vigilance of the Regent of the Netherlands prevented the adherents of the mystic sect, who were then very numerous, from rolling in a wave upon Westphalia, and sweeping the undisciplined Episcopal army away and consolidating the power of their pontiff-king.

It was towards the Low Countries that John of

Leyden looked with impatience. When would the expected delivery come out of the west? Why were not the thousands and tens of thousands of the sons of Israel rising from their fens, joined by trained bands from the cities, marching by the light of blazing cities, singing the songs of Zion?

Graess offered the king to hie to the Low Countries and rouse the faithful seed. "The Father," said he, "has ordered me to gather together the brethren dispersed at Wesel, at Deventer, at Amsterdam, and in Lower Germany; to form of them a mighty army that shall deliver this city and smite asunder the enemies of Israel. I will accomplish this mission with joy in the interest of the faithful. I fear no danger, since I go to fulfil the will of God, and I am sure that our brethren, when they know our extremity, and that it is the will of their king, will rise and hasten to the relief." [1]

John Bockelson was satisfied; he furnished Graess with letters of credit, sealed with the royal signet. The letters were couched in the following terms:—
"We, John, King of Righteousness in the new Temple, and servant of the Most High, do you to wit by these presents, that the bearer of these letters, Heinrich Graess, prophet illumined by the celestial Father, is sent by us to assemble, for the increase of our realm, our brethren dispersed abroad throughout the German lands. He will make them to hear the words of life, and he will execute the commandments which he has received from God and from us. We therefore

[1] Montfort., p. 40; Kerssenbroeck, p. 104 *et seq.*; Hast, p. 368.

order and demand of all those who belong to our kingdom to confide in him as in ourselves. Given at Münster, city of God, and sealed with our signet, in the twenty-sixth year of our age and the second of our reign, the second day of the first month, in the year 1535 after the nativity of Jesus Christ, Son of God."

Graess, furnished with this letter and with 300 florins from the treasury, left the city, and betook himself direct to Iburg, which he reached on the vigil of the Epiphany ;[1] and appeared before the bishop, told him the whole project, the names of the principal members of the sect at Wesel, Amsterdam, Leyden, &c., the places where their arms were deposited, and their plan of a general rising and massacring their enemies on a preconcerted day.

The bishop sent dispatches at once to the Duke of Juliers and the Governors of the Low Countries to warn them to be on their guard. They replied, requesting his assistance in suppressing the insurrection; and as the most effectual aid he could render would be to send Graess, he commissioned him to visit Wesel, and arrest the execution of the project.

Graess at once betook himself to Wesel, where he denounced the ringleaders and indicated the places where their arms and ammunition were secreted in enormous quantities. A tumult broke out; but the Duke of Juliers entered Wesel on the 5th April (1535), at the head of some squadrons of cavalry, seized the ringleaders, who were members of the principal houses in the place and of the senate, and on the 13th exe-

[1] Montfort., p. 40.

cuted six of them. The rest were compelled to do penance in white sheets, were deprived of their arms, and put under close surveillance.

Another division of the Anabaptists attempted to gain possession of Leyden, but were discomfited, fifteen of the principal men of the party were executed, and five of the women most distinguished for their fanaticism were drowned, amongst whom was the original wife of John Bockelson.[1]

In Gröningen, the partisans of the sect were numerous; orders reached them from the king to rise and massacre the magistrates, and march to the relief of the invested city. As the Anabaptists there were not all disposed to recognise the royalty of John of Leyden, an altercation broke out between them, and the attempt failed; but rising and marching under Peter Shomacker, their prophet, they were defeated on January 24th, by the Baron of Leutenburg, and the prophet was executed.

We must now return to what took place in the town of Münster at the opening of the year 1535.

Bockelson inaugurated that year by publishing, on January 2nd, an edict in twenty-eight Articles. It was addressed "To all lovers of the Truth and the Divine Righteousness, learned in and ignorant of the mysteries of God, to let them know how those Christians ought to live or act who are fighting under the banner of Justice, as true Israelites of the new Temple predestined for long ages, announced by the mouths of all the holy prophets, founded in the power of the Holy Ghost, by Christ and his Apostles, and

---

[1] Hast, p. 370; Bussierre, p. 403.

finally established by John, the righteous King, seated on the throne of David."

The Articles were to this effect :—

"1. In this new temple there was to be only one king to rule over the people of God.

2. This king was to be a minister of righteousness, and to bear the sword of justice.

3. None of the subjects were to desert their allotted places.

4. None were to interpret Holy Scripture wrongfully.

5. Should a prophet arise teaching anything contrary to the plain letter of Holy Scripture, he was to be avoided.

6. Drunkenness, avarice, fornication, and adultery were forbidden.

7. Rebellion to be punished with death.

8. Duels to be suppressed.

9. Calumny forbidden.

10. Egress from the camp forbidden without permission.

11. Any one absenting himself from his wife for three days, without leave from his officer, the wife to take another husband.

12. Approaching the enemy's sentinels without leave forbidden.

13. All violence forbidden among the elect.

14. Spoil taken from the enemy to go into a common fund.

15. No renegade to be re-admitted.

16. Caution to be observed in admitting a Christian into one society who leaves another.

17. Converts not to be repelled.

18. Any desiring to live at peace with the Christians, in trade, friendship, and by treaty, not to be rejected.

19. Permission given to dealers and traders to traffic with the elect.

20. No Christian to oppose and revolt against any Gentile magistrate, except the servants of the bishops and the monks.

21. A Gentile culprit not to be remitted the penalty of his crime by joining the Christian sect.

22. Directions about bonds.

23. Sentence to be pronounced against those who violate these laws and despise the Word of God, but not hastily, without the knowledge of the king.

24. No constraint to be used to force on marriages.

25. None afflicted with epilepsy, leprosy, and other diseases, to contract marriage without informing the other contracting party of their condition.

26. Nulla virginis specie, cum virgo non sit, fratrem defraudabit ; alioquin serio punietur.

27. Every woman who has not a legitimate husband, to choose from among the community a man to be her guardian and protector.

"Given by God and King John the Just, minister of the Most High God, and of the new Temple, in the 26th year of his age and the first of his reign, on the second day of the first month after the nativity of Jesus Christ, Son of God, 1535."[1]

[1] Kerssenbroeck, p. 132 *et seq.*

The object Bockelson had in view in issuing this
edict was to produce a diversion in his favour among
the Lutherans. He already felt the danger he was in,
from a coalescence of Catholics and Protestants, and
he hoped by temperate proclamations and protestations of his adhesion to the Bible, and the Bible only,
as his authority, to dispose them, if not to make
common cause with him, at least to withdraw their
assistance from the common enemy, the Catholic
bishop.

For the same object he sent letters on the 13th
January to the Landgrave of Hesse, and with them a
book called "The Restitution" (Von der Wieder-
bringung), intended to place Anabaptism in a favourable light.[1]

The Landgrave replied at length, rebuking the
fanatics for their rebellion, for their profligacy, and
for their heresy in teaching that man had a free will.[2]

This reply irritated the Anabaptists, and they
wrote to him again, to prove that they clave to the
pure Word of God, freed from all doctrines and traditions of men, and that they followed the direct
inspiration of God through their prophet. They also
retorted on Philip with some effect. The Landgrave,
said they, had no right to censure them for attacking
their bishop, for he had done precisely the same in
his own dominions. He had expelled all the religious
from their convents, and had appropriated their

---

[1] Kerssenbroeck, p. 128; Sleidan, p. 420; Hast, p. 373 *et seq.*;
"Acta, Handlungen," &c., f. 365 b. The king's letter began
"Leve Lips" ("Dear Phil").

[2] Sleidan, p. 421.

lands; he had re-established the Duke of Wurtemburg in opposition to the will of the Emperor; he had changed the religion of his subjects, and was unable to allege, as his authority for thus acting, the direct orders of Heaven, transmitted to him by the prophets of the living God. They might have retorted upon the Landgrave also, the charge of immorality, but they forbore; their object was to persuade the champion of the Protestant cause to favour them, not to exasperate him by driving the *tu quoque* too deep home.

With this letter was sent a treatise by Rottmann, entitled, " On the Secret Significance of Scripture."

Philip of Hesse wavered. He wrote once more ; and after having attempted to excuse himself for those things wherewith he had been reproached, he said, " If the thing depended on me only, you would not have to plead in vain your *just* cause, and you would obtain all that you demand ; but you ought ere this to have addressed the princes of the empire, instead of taking the law into your own hands ; flying to arms, erecting a kingdom, electing a king, and sending prophets and apostles abroad to stir up the towns and the people. Nevertheless, it is possible that even now your demands may be favourably listened to, if you recall on equitable conditions those whom you have driven out of the town and despoiled of their goods, and restore your ancient constitutions and your former authorities."[1]

Luther now thundered out of Wittemberg. Sleidan epitomises this treatise. Five Hessian ministers also

[1] Kerssenbroeck, p. 129 ; Sleidan, p. 421.

issued an answer to the doctrine of the Anabaptists of Münster, which was probably drawn up for them by Luther himself, or was at least submitted to him for his approval, for it is published among his German works.[1] It is full of invective and argument in about equal doses. A passage or two only can be quoted here :—

"Since you are led astray by the devil into such blasphemous error, drunk and utterly imprisoned you wish, as is Satan's way, to make yourselves into angels of light, and to paint in brightness and colour your devilish doings. For the devil will be no devil, but a holy angel, yea, even God himself, and his works, however bad they may be before God and all the world, he will have unrebuked, and himself be honoured and reverenced as the Most Holy. For that purpose he and you, his obedient disciples, use Holy Scripture as all heretics have ever done."[2]

"What shall I say? You let all the world see that you understand far less about the kingdom of Christ than did the Jews, who blame you for your want of understanding, and yet none spoke or believed more ignorantly of that same kingdom than they. For the Scripture and the prophets point to Messiah, through whom all was to be fulfilled, and this the Jews also believed. But you want to make it point to your Tailor-King, to the great disgrace and mockery of Christ, our only true King, Saviour, and Redeemer."[3]

[1] Luth. "Sämmtliche Werke," Wittenb. 1545-51, ii. ff. 367-375 ; "Von der Teuffelischen Secte d. Widerteuffer. zu Münster."

[2] *Ibid.* f. 367.   [3] *Ibid.* f. 369.

But this was the grievous rub with the Reformer—
that the Anabaptist had gone a step beyond himself.
"You have cast away all that Dr. Martin Luther
taught you, and yet it is from him that you have
received, next to God, all sound learning out of the
Scripture; you have given another definition of
faith, after your new fashion, with various additional
articles, so that you have not only darkened, but have
utterly annihilated the value of saving faith."[1]

In a treatise of Justus Menius, published with
Luther's approval, and with a preface by him, "On
the Spirit of the Anabaptists," it is angrily complained, that these sectaries bring against the
Lutheran Church the following charges:—"First, that
our churches are idol-temples, since God dwelleth not
in temples made with hands. Secondly, that we do
not preach the truth, and have true Divine worship
therein. Thirdly, that our preachers are sinners, and
are therefore unfit to teach others. Fourthly, that
the common people do not mend their morals by
our preaching." All which charges Justus Menius
answers as well as he can, sword in one hand against
the Papists, trowel in the other patching up the walls
of his Jerusalem.[2]

Melancthon also wrote against the Anabaptist
book, combating all its propositions, and to do so
falling back on the maxim, *Abusus non tollit sub-
stantiam*, a maxim completely ignored by the Reformers when they attacked the Catholics.[3] Thus

---

[1] *Ibid.* f. 373.   [2] *Ibid.* ii. ff. 298-325.

[3] *Ibid.* ii. ff. 334-363. Melancthon says that things had come
to such a pass in Münster, that no child knew who was its
father, brother, or sister.

Y

the new sect fought Lutheranism with precisely the same weapons wherewith the Lutherans had fought the Church ; and the Lutherans, to maintain their ground, were obliged to take refuge in the authority of the Church and tradition—positions they had assailed formerly, and to use arguments they had previously rejected.

In the treatise of the five Hessian divines, drawn up by Philip of Hesse's orders, the errors of the Anabaptists are epitomised and condemned; they are as follows :—

"1. They do not believe that men are justified by faith only, but by faith and works conjointly.

2. They refer the redemption of Christ alone to the fall of Adam, and to its consequences on those born of him.

3. They hold community of goods.

4. They blame Martin Luther as having taught nothing about good works.

5. They proclaim the freedom of man's will.

6. They reject infant baptism.

7. They take the Bible alone, uninterpreted by any commentary.

8. They declare for plurality of wives.

9. They do not correctly teach the Incarnation of Christ."[1]

This " Kurtze : und in der eile gestelte Antwort," is signed by John Campis, John Fontius, John Kymeus, John Lessing, and Anthony Corvinus.

It was high time that the siege should come to an end, so every one said ; but every one had said the

[1] "Acta Handlung." &c. f. 366 a.

same for the last twelve months, and Münster held out
notwithstanding.

An ultimatum was sent into the city by the general
in command, offering the inhabitants liberal terms if
they would surrender, and warning them that, in case
of refusal, the city would be taken by storm, and
would be delivered over to plunder.[1] No answer was
made to the letter ; nevertheless, it produced a profound impression on the citizens, who were already
suffering from want of victuals. A party was formed
which resolved to seize the person of the king, and to
open the gates and make terms with the bishop.[2]
Bockelson, hearing of the plot, assembled the whole
of the population in the cathedral square, and
solemnly announced to them by revelation from the
Father that at Easter the siege would be raised, and
the city experience a wonderful deliverance. He
also divided the town into twelve portions, and placed
at the head of each a duke of his own creation,
charged with the suppression of treason and the protection of the gates. Each duke was provided with
twenty-four guards for the defence of his person, and
the infliction of punishment on those citizens who
proved restive under the rule of the King of Zion.[3]
These dukes were promised the government of the
empire, when the kingdoms of Germany became the
kingdom of John of Leyden. Denecker, a grocer,
was Duke of Saxony ; Moer, the tailor, Duke of
Brunswick; the Kerkerings were appointed to reign

---

[1] Kerssenbroeck, p. 130.   [2] *Ibid.* p. 140.
[3] Sleidan, p. 419; Bullinger, l. ii. c. 9; Heresbach, p. 156;
Dorp. f. 498.

over Westphalia; Redecker, the cobbler, to bear rule in Juliers and Cleves. John Palk was created Duke of Guelders and Utrecht; Edinck was to be supreme in Brabant and Holland; Faust, a coppersmith, in Mainz and Cologne; Henry Kock was to be Duke of Trier; Ratterberg to be Duke of Bremen, Werden, and Minden; Reininck took his title from Hildesheim and Magdeburg; and Nicolas Strip from Frisia and Gröningen. As these men were for the most part butchers, blacksmiths, tailors, and shoe-makers, their titles, ducal coronets and mantles, and the prospect of governing, turned their heads, and made them zealous tools in the hands of Bockelson.

The king made one more attempt to rouse the country. He issued letters offering the pillage of the whole world to all those who would join the standard. But the bishop was informed of the preparation of these missives by a Danish soldier in Münster; he was much alarmed, as his *lantzknechts* were ready to sell their services to the highest bidder. He there-fore pressed on the circumvallation of the city, kept a vigilant guard, and captured every emissary sent forth to distribute these tempting offers. On the 11th February, 1535, the moat, mound, and palisade around the city were complete; and it was thenceforth im-possible for access to or egress from the city to be effected without the knowledge of the prince and his generals. The unfortunate people of Münster dis-covered attempting to escape were by the king's orders decapitated. Many men and women perished thus; amongst them was a mistress of Knipperdolling named Dreyer, who, weary of her life, fled, but was caught and delivered over to the executioner. When her turn came, the headsman hesitated. Knipperdolling, perceiving it, took from him the sword, and without changing colour smote off her head. " The Father," said he, " irresistibly inspired me to this, and I have thus become, without willing it or knowing it, an instrument of vengeance in the hands' of the Lord." [1]

The legitimate wife of Knipperdolling, for having disparaged polygamy, escaped death with difficulty ; she was sentenced to do public penance, kneeling in the great square, in the midst of the people, with a naked sword in her hands. [2]

Easter came, the time of the promised delivery, and the armies of the faithful from Holland and Friesland and Brabant had not arrived. The position of Bockelson became embarrassing. He extricated himself from the dilemma with characteristic effrontery. During six days he remained in his own house, invisible to every one. At the expiration of the time he issued forth, assembled the people on Mount Zion, and informed them that the deliverance predicted of the Father *had* taken place, but that it was a deliverance different in kind from what they had anticipated. " The Father," said he, " has laid on my shoulders the iniquities of the Israelites. I have been bowed down under their burden, and was well-nigh crushed beneath their weight. Now, by the grace of the Lord, health has been restored to me, and you have been all released from your sins. This spiritual deliverance is the most excellent of all, and

[1] Kerssenbroeck, p. 148.   [2] *Ibid.* p. 149.

must precede that which is purely exterior and temporal. Wait, therefore, patiently, it is promised and it will arrive, if you do not fall back into your sins, but maintain your confidence in God, who never deserts His chosen people, though He may subject them to trials and tribulations, to prove their constancy."[1] One would fain believe that John Bockelson was in earnest, and the subject of religious infatuation, like his subjects, but after this it is impossible to so regard him.

The princes, when separating after the assembly of Coblenz, had agreed to reassemble on the 4th of April. Ferdinand, King of the Romans, convoked all the Estates of the empire to meet on that day at Worms. The deputies of several towns protested against the decisions taken at Coblenz without their participation, and the deliberations were at the outset very tumultuous. An understanding was at length arrived at, and a monthly subsidy of 20,000 florins for five months was agreed upon, to maintain the efficacy of the investment of Münster. But before separating, a final effort to obtain a pacific termination to the war was resolved upon, and the burgomasters of Frankfort and Nürnberg were sent as a deputation into the city. This attempt proved as sterile as all those previously essayed. "We have nothing in common with the Roman empire," answered the chiefs of Zion ; "for that empire is the fourth beast whereof Daniel prophesied. We have set up again the kingdom of Israel, by the Father's command, and

---

[1] Kerssenbroeck, pp. 153, 154 ; Sleidan, p. 422 ; Bullinger lib. ii. c. 2 ; Heresbach, pp. 159, 160.

we engage you to abstain for the future from assailing this realm, as you fear the wrath of God and eternal damnation."[1]

The famine in Münster now became terrible. Cats, rats, dogs, and horses were eaten; the starving people attempted various expedients to satisfy their craving hunger. They ate leather, wood, even cow-dung dried in the sun, the bark of trees, and candles. Corpses lately buried were dug up during the night and secretly devoured. Mothers even ate their children. "Terrible maladies," says Kerssenbroeck, "the consequence of famine, aggravated the position of the inhabitants of the town; their flesh decomposed, they rotted living, their skin became livid, their lips retreated; their eyes, fixed and round, seemed ready to start out of their orbits; they wandered about, haggard, hideous, like mummies, and died by hundreds in the streets. The king, to prevent infection, had the bodies cast into large common ditches, whence the starving withdrew them furtively to devour them. Night and day the houses and streets re-echoed with tears, cries, and moans;—men, women, old men, and children sank into the darkest despair."[2]

In the midst of the general famine, John of Leyden lived in abundance. His storehouses, into which the victuals found in every house had been collected, supplied his own table and that of his immediate followers. His revelry and pomp were unabated, whilst his deluded subjects died of want around him.[3]

[1] Kerssenbroeck, p. 155; Hast, 394.

[2] Kerssenbroeck, p. 157 *et seq.*; Heresbach, pp. 151, 152; Hast, p. 395; Montfort., p. 46.   [3] *Ibid.* p. 157.

When starvation was at its worst, a letter from Heinrich Graess circulated in the town, informing the people that his miraculous escape had been a fable, and that he had rejected the follies of Anabaptism, disgusted at the extravagance to which it had led its votaries, and assuring them that their king was an impostor, exploiting to his advantage the credulity of an infatuated mob.[1]

This letter produced an effect which made the king tremble. He summoned his disciples before him, reproached them for putting the hand to the plough and turning back, and gave leave to all those whose faith wavered to go out from the city. "As for me," said he, "I shall remain here, even if I remain alone with the angels which the Father will not fail to send to aid me to defend this place."[2]

When the king had given permission to leave the city, numbers of every age and sex poured through the gates, leaving behind only the most fanatical who were resolved to conquer or die with John of Leyden.

Outside the city walls extended a trampled and desolate tract to the fosse and earthworks of the besiegers, strewn with the ruins of houses and of farmsteads. The unfortunate creatures escaping from Zion, wasted and haggard like spectres, spread over this devastated region. The investing army drove them back towards the city, unwilling to allow the rebels to protract the siege by disembarrassing themselves of all the useless mouths in the place. They refused, however, to re-enter the walls, and remained in the Königreich, as this desert tract was

[1] Montfort., p. 47.   [2] Kerssenbroeck, p. 161.

called, to the number of 900, living on roots and grass, for four weeks, lying on the bare earth. Some were too feeble to walk, and crawled about on all fours; their hunger was so terrible that they filled their mouths with sand, earth, or leaves, and died choked, in terrible convulsions. Night and day their moans, howls, and cries ascended. The children presented a yet more deplorable spectacle; they implored their mothers to give them something to eat, and they, poor creatures, could only answer them with tears and sobs; often they approached the lines of the camp, and sought to excite the compassion of the soldiers.

The General in command, Graff Ueberstein, sent information, on April 22nd, to the bishop, who was ill in his castle at Wollbeck, and asked what was to be done with these unfortunates who were perishing in the Königreich. The bishop shed tears, and protested his sorrow at the sufferings of the poor wretches, but did not venture to give orders for their removal, without consulting the Duke of Cleves and the Elector of Cologne. Thus much precious time was lost, and only on the 28th May, a month after, were the starving wretches permitted to leave the Königreich, upon the following terms: 1st. That they should be transported to the neighbouring town of Diekhausen, where they should be examined, and those who were guilty among them executed; 2nd. That the rest should be pardoned and dispersed in different places, after having undertaken to renounce Anabaptism, and to abstain from negotiations, open or secret, with their comrades in the beleagured

city.[1] These conditions having been made, the refugees were transported on tumbrils and in carts to
Diekhausen, at a foot's pace, their excessive exhaustion
rendering them incapable of bearing more rapid
motion. They numbered 200; 700 had perished of
famine between the lines of the investing army and
the walls of the besieged town. On the 30th May,
those found guilty of prominent participation in the
revolt were executed.

The prince-bishop might have spared his tears and
sent loaves. His hesitation and want of genuine
sympathy with the starving unfortunates serve to
mark his character as not only weak, but selfish and
cowardly.

Whilst this was taking place outside the walls of
Münster, John van Gheel, an emissary of Bockelson,
was actively engaged in rousing the Anabaptists of
Amsterdam. Having insinuated himself into the
good graces of the Princess Mary, regent of the
Netherlands, he persuaded her that he was desirous
of restraining the sectaries waiting their call to march
to the relief of Münster. She even furnished him
with an authorisation to raise troops for this purpose.
He profited by this order to arm his friends and lay a
plot for obtaining the mastery of Amsterdam. His
design was to make that city a place of rendezvous
for all the Anabaptists of the Low Countries, who
would flock into it as a city of refuge, when once it
was in his power, and then he would be able to
organise out of them an army sufficiently numerous
and well appointed to raise the siege of Münster.

[1] Kerssenbroeck, pp. 161-8.

On the 11th May he placed himself at the head of 600 friends, seized on the town, massacred half the guards, and one of the burgomasters. Amsterdam would inevitably have been in the power of the sectaries in another hour, had not one of the guard escaped up the tower and rung the alarm-bell. As the tocsin pealed over the city, the citizens armed and rushed to the market-place, fell upon the Anabaptists and retook the town-hall, notwithstanding a desperate resistance. Crowds of fanatics from the country, who had received secret intimation to assemble before the walls of Amsterdam, and wait till the gates were opened to admit them, finding that the plan had been defeated, threw away their arms and fled with precipitation.[1]

Van Gheel had fallen in the encounter. The prisoners were executed. Amongst these was Campé whom John of Leyden had created Anabaptist bishop of Amsterdam. His execution was performed with great barbarity; first his tongue, then his hand, and finally his head was cut off.[2]

We must look once more into the doomed city.

In the midst of the general desolation John Bockelson and his court lived in splendour and luxury. Every one who murmured against his excesses was executed. Heads were struck off on the smallest charge, and scarcely a day passed in May and June without blood flowing on Mount Zion. One of the most remarkable of these executions was that of Elizabeth Wandtscherer, one of the queens.

[1] Kerssenbroeck, pp. 73, 74 ; Hast, p. 37 ; Montfort., p. 58 *et seq.*   [2] Montfort., pp. 68, 69.

This woman had had three husbands ; the first was dead, the second marriage had been annulled, and Bockelson had taken her to wife because she was pretty and well made.

She was a great favourite with her royal husband, and for six months she seemed to be delighted with her position ; but at length, disgusted with the unbridled licence of the royal harem, the hypocrisy and the mad revelry of the court, contrasted with the famine of the citizens, a prey to remorse, she tore off her jewels and her queenly robes, and asked John of Leyden permission to leave the city. This was on the 12th June. The king, furious at an apostacy in his own house, dragged her into the market-place, and there in the presence of his wives and the populace, smote off her head with his own hands, stamped on her body, and then chanting the " Gloria in excelsis " with his queens, danced round the corpse weltering in its blood.[1]

However, the royal magazines were now nearly exhausted, and the king was informed that there remained provisions for only a few days. He resolved to carry on his joyous life of debauchery without thought of the morrow, and when all was expended, to fire the city in every quarter, and then to rush forth, arms in hand, and break through the investing girdle, or perish in the attempt.[2] This project was not exe-

[1] Kerssenbroeck, pp. 176-7 ; Dorpius, f. 498 b ; Sleidan, p. 422, says she was executed for having observed to some of her companions that it could not be the will of God that they should live in abundance whilst the subjects perished from want of necessaries. Hast, p. 395 ; Heresbach, p. 145.

[2] Kerssenbroeck, p. 177.

cuted, for the siege was abruptly ended before the moment had arrived for its accomplishment.

Late in the preceding year, a soldier of the Episcopal army, John Eck, of Langenstraten, or, as he was called from his diminutive stature, Hansel Eck, having been punished as he deemed excessively or unjustly for some dereliction in his duty, deserted to the Anabaptists, and found an asylum in the city, where John Bockelson, perceiving his abilities and practical acquaintance with military operations, made him one of his captains.

But Hansel soon repented bitterly this step he had taken. Little men are proverbially peppery and ready to stand on their dignity. His desertion had been the result of an outburst of wounded self-pride, and when his wrath cooled down, and his judgment obtained the upper hand, he was angry with himself for what he had done. Feeling confident that the city must eventually fall, and knowing that small mercies would be shown to a deserter caught in arms, however insignificant he might be in stature, Hansel took counsel with eight other discontented soldiers in his company, and they resolved to escape from Münster and ask pardon of the bishop.

They effected the first part of their object on the night of the 17th June, and crossed the Königreich towards the lines of the investing force. The sentinels, observing a party of armed men advancing, with the moon flashing from their morions and breast-plates, fired on them and killed seven. His diminutive stature stood Hansel in good stead, and he, with one other named Sobb, succeeded in escalading the ramparts unobserved, and in making their way to the nearest fort of Hamm, where the old officer, Meinhardt von Hamm, under whom he had formerly served, was in command. Hansel and Sobb were conducted into his presence, and offered to deliver the city into the hands of the prince-bishop if he would accord them a free pardon; but they added that no time must be lost, as it was but a question of hours rather than of days before the city was fired, and the final sortie was executed.[1]

Meinhardt listened to his plan, approved of it, and wrote to Francis of Waldeck, asking a safe-conduct for Hansel, and urging the utmost secrecy, as on the preservation of the secret depended the success of the scheme.

The safe-conduct was readily granted, and the deserter was brought to Willinghegen concealed amidst game in a cart covered with boughs of trees. Willinghegen is a small place one mile outside the circumvallation. The chiefs of the besieging army met here to consider the plan of Hansel Eck. The little man protested that with 300 men he could take the city. He knew the weak points, and he could escalade the walls where they were unguarded. Four hundred soldiers were, however, decided to be sent on the expedition, under the command of Wilkin Steding, "a terrible enemy but a devoted friend;" John of Twickel was to be standard-bearer, and Hansel was to act as guide; and the attempt was to be made on

[1] Kerssenbroeck, p. 179 *et seq.*; Sleidan, p. 427; Montfort., p. 71; Heresbach, p. 162 *et seq.*; Hast, p. 395 *et seq.*; Dorpius, f. 499.

the eve of St. John the Baptist's day.[1] However, the
bishop and Count Ueberstein, desirous of avoiding
unnecessary effusion of blood, summoned the inhabitants to surrender, for the last time, on the 22nd
June.

Rottmann replied to the deputies that "the city
should be surrendered only when they received the
order to do so from the Father by a revelation."

Midsummer eve was a hot, sultry day. Towards
evening dark heavy clouds rolled up against the wind,
and a violent storm of thunder, lightning, and hail
burst over the doomed city. The sentinels of
Münster, exhausted by hunger, and alarmed at the
rage of the elements, quitted their posts and retreated
under shelter. The darkness, the growl of the wind,
and the boom of the thunder concealed the approach
of the Episcopal troops. The 400, under Steding,
guided by the deserter, marched into the Königreich
between ten and eleven o'clock, and met with no ob-
stacles till they reached the Holy-cross Gate. Here
they filled the ditch with faggots, trees, and bundles
of straw; a bridge was improvised, the curtain of
palisades masking the bastion was surmounted,
ladders were planted, and without meeting with the
least resistance, the 400 reached the summit of the
walls. The sentinels, whom they found asleep, were
killed, with the exception of one who purchased his
life by giving up the pass-word, "Die Erde." The
soldiers then advanced along the paved road which
lay between the double walls, captured and killed the
sentinels at every watch tower, and then, entering the

[1] Kerssenbroeck, p. 169 ; and the authors before cited.

streets, crossed the cemetery of Ueberwasser, the River Aa by its bridge, and debouched on the cathedral square, where the faint flashes of the retreating lightning illumined at intervals the gaunt scaffolding of the throne and gallery and pulpit of the Anabaptist king, looking now not unlike the preparations for an execution.

The cathedral had been converted into the arsenal. Hansel led the Episcopal soldiers to the western gates, gave the word "Die Erde," and the guards were killed before they could give the alarm. The artillery was now in the hands of the 400.[1]

The Anabaptists had slept through the rumble of the thunder, but suddenly the rattle of the drum on their hill of Zion woke them with a start. They sprang from their beds, armed in haste, and rushed to the cathedral square, where their own cannons opened on them their mouths of fire, and poured an iron shower down the main thoroughfares which led from the Minster green. But they were not discouraged. Through backways, and under the shelter of the surrounding houses, they reached the Chapel of St. Michael, which commanded the position of the Episcopal soldiers, and thence fired upon them with deadly precision.

Steding turned the guns against the chapel, but its massive walls could not be broken through, and the balls bounded from them without effecting more than a trivial damage. The Anabaptists pursued their advantage. Whilst Steding was occupied with those who held the Chapel of St. Michael, a large number

---

[1] Kerssenbroeck, p. 176 *et seq.* ; and the authors before cited.

assembled in the market-place and marched in close ranks upon the cathedral square.

The 400, unable to withstand the numbers opposed to them, were driven from their positions, and retreated into the narrow Margaret Street, where they were unable to use their arms with advantage. Steding burst open the door of a house, and sent 200 of his men through it; they issued through the back door, filled up a narrow lane running parallel with the street, and attacked the Anabaptists in the rear, who, thinking that the city was in the hands of the enemy, and that they were being assailed by a reinforcement, fled precipitately.

By an unpardonable oversight, Steding had forgotten to leave a guard at the postern by which he had entered the city. The Anabaptists discovered this mistake and profited by it, so that when the reinforcements sent to support Steding arrived, the gates were closed, and the walls were defended by the women, who cast stones and firebrands, and shot arrows amongst them, taunting them with the failure of the attempt to surprise the city; and they, uncertain whether to believe that the plot of Hansel Eck had failed or not, remained without till break of day, vainly attempting to escalade the walls. The Anabaptists, who had fled in the Margaret Street, soon rallied, and the 400 were again exposed to the fury of a multitude three times their number, who assailed them in front and in rear, and they were struck down by stones and furniture cast out of the windows upon them by the women in the houses.

Nevertheless they bravely defended themselves for

z

several hours, and their assailants began to lose courage, as news of the onslaught upon the walls reached them. It was now midnight. King John proposed a temporary cessation of hostilities, which Steding gladly accepted; and the messengers of Bockelson offered the 400 their life if they would lay down their arms, kneel before him, and ask his pardon. [1]

The soldiers indignantly rejected this offer, but proposed to quit the town with their arms and ensigns. A long discussion ensued, which Steding protracted till break of day.

At the opening of the negotiations, Steding bade John von Twickel, the ensign, hasten to the ramparts with three men, as secretly as possible, and urge on the reinforcements. Twickel reached the bastions as day began to dawn, and he shouted to his comrades without to help Steding and his gallant band before all was lost. The Episcopalians, dreading a ruse of the besieged to draw them into an ambush, hesitated; but Twickel called the watchword, which was *Waldeck*, and announced the partial success of the 400.

Having accomplished his mission, Twickel returned to his comrades within, cheering them at the top of his voice with the cry from afar, "Courage, friends, help is at hand!"

At these words the remains of the gallant band of 400 recommenced the combat with irresistible energy They fell on the Anabaptists with such vehemence that they drove them back on all sides; they gave no

[1] Kerssenbroeck, p. 385; Heresbach, pp. 162-6; Montfort., p. 72; Hast, p. 396 *et seq.*

quarter, but breaking into divisions, swept the streets, meeting now with only a feeble resistance, for the soldiers without were battering at the gates. In vain did the sectarians offer to leave the town, their offer came too late, and the little band drove them from one rallying point to another.[1]

Rottmann, feeling that all was lost, cast himself on their lances and fell. John of Leyden, instead of heading his party, attempted to fly, but was recognised as he was escaping through the gate of St. Giles, and was thrown into chains.

In the meantime the reinforcement had mounted the walls, beaten in the gates, and was pouring up the streets, rolling back the waves of discomfited Anabaptists on the swords and spears of the decimated 400. Two hundred of the most determined among the fanatics entrenched themselves in a round tower commanding the market-place, and continued firing on the soldiers of the prince. The generals, seeing that the town was in their power, and that it would cost an expenditure of time and life to reduce those in the tower, offered them their life, and permission to march out of Münster unmolested if they would surrender.

On these terms the Anabaptists in the bastion laid down their arms. The besiegers now spread throughout the city, hunting out and killing the rebels. Hermann Tilbeck, the former burgomaster, who had played into the hands of the Anabaptists till he declared himself, and who had been one of the twelve elders of Israel, was found

[1] Kerssenbroeck, pp. 188, 189.

concealed, half submerged, in a privy, near the gate
of St. Giles, was killed, and his body left where he had
hidden, "thus being buried," says Kerssenbroeck,
"with worse than the burial of an ass." When the
butchery was over, the bodies were brought together
into the cathedral square and were examined. That
of Knipperdolling was not amongst them. He was,
in fact, hiding in the house of Catherine Hobbels, a
zealous Anabaptist ; she kept him in safety the
whole of the 26th, but finding that every house
was being searched, and fearing lest she should
suffer for having sheltered him, she ordered
him to leave and attempt an escape over the
walls.[1]

On the 27th all the women were collected in
the market-square, and were ordered to leave the
city and never to set foot in it again. But just as
they were about to depart, Ueberstein announced that
any one of them who could deliver up Knipperdolling
should be allowed to remain and retain her possessions.
The bait was tempting. Catherine Hobbels stepped
forward, and offered to point out the hiding-place of
the man they sought. She was given a renewed
assurance that her house and goods would be respected,
and she then delivered up Knipperdolling, who had
not quitted his place of refuge. The promise made
to her was rigorously observed ; but her husband, not
being included in the pardon, and being a ringleader
of the fanatics, was executed.[2] The women were
accompanied by the soldiers as far as the Lieb-Frau

[1] Kerssenbroeck, p. 195.
[2] *Ibid.* p. 196; Heresbach, p. 166.

gate; they took with them their children, and were ordered to leave the diocese and principality forthwith.

Divara, the head queen of John of Leyden, the wife of Knipperdolling, and three other women, were refused permission to leave. They were executed on the 7th July.

Münster was then delivered over to pillage; but all those who had left the town during the government of the Anabaptists were given their furniture and houses and such of their goods as could be identified.

All the property of the Anabaptists was confiscated, and sold to pay the debts contracted by the prince for defraying the expenses of the war. The division of the booty occasioned several troubles, parties of soldiers mutinied, and attempted a second pillage, but the mutineers were put down rigorously.

Several more executions took place during the following days, and men hidden away in cellars, garrets and sewers were discovered and killed or carried off to prison. Among these were Bernard Krechting and Kerkering.[1]

On the 28th June, Francis of Waldeck entered the city at the head of 800 men. The sword, crown, and spurs of John of Leyden, together with the keys of the city, were presented to him. [2]

The prince received, as had been stipulated, half the booty, and the articles and the treasure deposited in

[1] Kerssenbroeck, pp. 198-200. Dorpius says, "In the capture of the city, women and children were spared; and none were killed after the first fight, except the ringleaders."—f. 399.

[2] Montfort., p. 73.

the town-hall and in the royal palace, which amounted to 100,000 gold florins.[1]

Francis remained in Münster only three days. Having named the new magistrates, and organised the civil government of the city, he departed for his castle of Iburg. On the 13th July he ordered a Te Deum to be sung in the churches throughout the diocese, in thanks to God for having restored tranquillity ; and the Chapter inaugurated a yearly thanksgiving procession to take place on the 25th June.[2]

On the 15th July, the Elector of Cologne, the Duke of Juliers, and Francis of Waldeck, met at Neuss to concert measures for preventing a repetition of these disorders. The leading Protestant divines wrote, urging the extermination of the heretics, and reminding the princes that the sword had been given them for this purpose.

On the same day, the diet of Worms agreed that the Anabaptists should be extirpated as a sect dangerous alike to morals and to the safety of the commonwealth, and that an assembly should be held in the month of November, to decide upon defraying the cost of the war, and on the form of government which was to be established in the city.[3]

The diet met on the 1st November, and decided,— That everything should be re-established in Münster on the old footing, and that the clergy should have their property and privileges restored to them. That all who had fled the city to escape the government of

---

[1] Kerssenbroeck, Heresbach, p. 168 ; Hast, p. 400.
[2] *Ibid.* p. 200.   [3] *Ibid.* p. 201.

the Anabaptists should be reinstated in the possession of their offices, privileges, and houses. That all
the goods of the rebels should remain confiscated to
defray the expense of the war. That the princes of
neighbouring states should send deputies to Münster
to provide that the innocent should not suffer with
the guilty. That the fortifications should be in part
demolished, as an example ; but that Münster should
not be degraded from its rank as a city. That the
bishop and chapter and nobles should demolish the
bastions within the town as soon as the city walls
had been razed. That the bishops, the nobles, and
the citizens should solemnly engage, for themselves
and for their successors, never to attempt to refortify
the city. Finally, that the envoys of the King of the
Romans and of the princes should visit the said town
on the 5th March, 1536, to see that these articles of
the convention had been executed.

All these articles were not observed. The bishop
did not demolish the fortifications, and the point was
not insisted upon.

As for the civil constitution of Münster, its privileges and franchises, they were not entirely restored
till 1553.

Francis of Waldeck now set to work repairing and
purifying the churches, and restoring everything as it
had been before. Catholic worship was everywhere
restored without a single voice in the city rising in
opposition. The people were sick of Protestantism,
whether in its mitigated form as Lutheranism, or in
its aggravated development as Anabaptism.

But Lutherans of other states were by no means

satisfied. The reconciliation of the great city with the Catholic Church, from which half its inhabitants had previously separated, was not pleasant news to the Reformers, and they protested loudly. "On the Friday after St. John's day," wrote Dorpius "in midsummer, God came and destroyed this hell and drove the devil out, but the devil's mother came in again. . . . The Anabaptists were on that day rooted out, and the Papists planted in again."[1]

It is time to look at John of Leyden and his fellow-prisoners: they were Knipperdolling and Bernard Krechting. There could be no doubt that their fate would be terrible. It was additional cruelty to delay it. But the bishop and the Lutheran divines were curious to see and argue with the captives, and they were taken from place to place to gratify their curiosity.

When King John appeared before Francis of Waldeck, the bishop asked him angrily how he could protract the siege whilst his people were starving around him. "Francis of Waldeck," he answered, "they should all have died of hunger before I surrendered, had things gone as I desired."[2] He retained his spirits and affected to joke. At Dulmen the people crowded round him asking, "Is this the king who took to himself so many wives?" "I ask your

---

[1] "Hernach auff freitag S. Johanstag mitten in Sommer, kommet Gott und zerstöret die Helle, und jaget den Teuffel heraus, und komet sein Mutter wider hinein . . . und sind die Widerteuffer an obgemeltem tag ausgerottet worden, die Papisten aber wider eingepflantzet."—Dorp. f. 399 (by misprint 499).

[2] Dorp. ff. 399 a, 400 a, b.

pardon," answered Bockelson, " I took maidens and made them wives."[1]

It has been often stated that the three unfortunates were carried round the country in iron cages. This is inaccurate. They were taken in chains on horseback, with two soldiers on either side ; their bodies were placed in iron cages and hung to the steeple of the church of St. Lambert, after they were dead.

At Bevergern the Lutheran divine, Anthony Corvinus, and other ministers " interviewed " the fallen king, and a long and very curious account of their discussion remains.[2]

" First, when the king was brought out of prison into the room, we greeted him in a friendly manner and bade him be seated before us four. Also, we asked in a friendly manner how he was getting on in the prison, and whether he was cold or sick? Answer of the king : Although he was obliged to endure the frost, and the sins weighing on his heart, yet he must, as such was God's will, bear patiently. And these and other similar conversations led us so far—for nothing can be got out of him by direct questions— that we were able right craftily to converse with him about his government."

Then followed a lengthy controversy on all the heretical doctrines of the Anabaptist sect, in which the king exhibited no little skill. The preachers having brought the charge of novelty against Ana-

[1] Dorp. f. 399 b.
[2] Luther's " Sämmtliche Werke." Wittenb. 1545-51. Band. ii. ff. 376-386.

baptism, John of Leyden very promptly showed that those living in glass houses should not throw stones, by pointing out that Lutheranism was not much older than Anabaptism, that he had proved his mission by miracles, whereas Luther had nothing to show to demonstrate his call to establish a new creed.

The discussion on Justification by Faith only was most affectionate, for both parties were quite agreed on this doctrine—surely a very satisfactory one and very full of comfort to John of Leyden. But on the doctrine of the Eucharist they could not agree, the king holding to Zwingli.[1]

"That in this Sacrament the faithful, who are baptised, receive the Body and Blood of Christ believe I," said the king; "for though I hold for this time with Zwingli, nevertheless I find that the words of Christ (This is my Body, This is my Blood) must remain in their worth. But that unbelievers also receive the Body and Blood of Christ, that I cannot believe."

The Preachers: "How that? Shall our unbelief avail more than the word, command and ordinance of God?"

The King: "Unbelief is such a dreadful thing, that I cannot believe that the unbelievers can partake of the Body and Blood of Christ."

The Preachers: "It is a perverse thing that you should ever try to set our faith, or want of faith, above the words and ordinance of God. But it is evident that our faith can add nothing to God's

---

[1] "Denn wiewol ichs fur dieser zeit mit dem Zwingel gehalten," &c., f. 384.

ordinance, nor can my unbelief detract anything therefrom. Faith must be there, that I may benefit by such eating and drinking ; but yet in this matter must we repose more on God's command and word than on our faith or unbelief."

The King : "If this your meaning hold, then all unbelievers must have partaken of the Communion of the Body and Blood of Christ. But such I cannot believe."

The Preachers : "You must understand that our unbelief cannot make the ordinance of God un-availing. Say now, for what end was the sun created ?"

The King : "Scripture teaches that it was made to rule the day and to shine."

The Preachers : "Now if we or you were blind, would the sun fail to execute its office for which it was created?"

The King : "I know well that my blindness or yours would not make the sun fail to shine."

The Preachers : "So is it with all the works and ordinances of God, especially with the Sacraments. When I am baptised it is well if faith be there ; but if it be not, baptism does not for all that fail to be a precious, noble, and holy Sacrament, yes, what St. Paul calls it, a regeneration and renewal of the Holy Ghost, because it is ordered by God's word and given His promise. So also with respect to the Lord's Supper; if those who partake shall have faith to grasp the promise of Christ, as it is written, *Oportet accedentem credere,* but none the less does God's word, ordinance, and command remain, even if my faith

never more turned thereto.   But of this we have said
enough."[1]

The preachers next catechised John of Leyden on
his heresy concerning the Incarnation.   He did not
deny that Jesus Christ was born of Mary, but he
denied that He derived from her His flesh and
blood, as he considered that Mary being sinful, out of
sinful flesh sinful offspring must issue.

The catechising on the subject of marriage follows.

The Preachers : " How have you regarded marriage, and what is your belief thereupon ? "

The King : " We have ever held marriage to be
God's work and ordinance, and we hold this now,
that no higher or better estate exists in the world than
the estate of matrimony."

The Preachers : " Why have you so wildly treated
this same estate, against God's word and common
order, and taken one wife after another ?   How can
you justify such a proceeding ? "

The King : " What was permitted to the patriarchs
in the Old Testament, why should it be denied to us ?
What we have held is this : he who wished to have
only one wife had not other wives forced upon him; but
him who wished to have more wives than one, we left
free to do so, according to God's command, Be fruitful
and multiply."

This the preachers combat by saying that the
patriarchs were guiltless, because the law of the land
(*die gemeine Policey)* did not then forbid concubinage,
but that now that is forbidden by common law, it is

[1] *Ibid.* f. 384 b.

sinful.[1] Then they asked the king what other texts he could quote to establish polygamy.

The King : " Paul says of the bishop, let him be the husband of one wife ; now if a bishop is to have only one wife, surely, in the time of Paul, laymen must have been allowed two or three apiece, as pleased them. There you have your text."

The Preachers : " As we said before, marriage is an affair of common police regulation, *res Politica.* And as now the law of the land is different from what it was in the time of Paul, so that many wives are forbidden and not tolerated, you will have to answer for your innovations before God and man."

The King : " Well, I have the consolation that what was permitted to the fathers cannot damn us. I had rather be with the fathers than with you."

The Preachers : " Well, we prefer obedience to the State."[2]

Here we see Corvinus, Kymens, and the other ministers placing matrimony on exactly the same low footing as did Luther.

Having " interviewed" the king, these crows settled on Knipperdolling and Krechting in Horstmar, and with these unfortunates they carried on a paper controversy.

The captivity of the king and his two accomplices lasted six months. The Lutheran preachers had

[1] Wei zweiveln nicht wenn ein bestendig Policey und Regiment gewesen were, wie itzt est, es würden sich die Vetter freilich aug der selbigen gehalten haben.

[2] Predicanten : So wöllen wir in diesemfäll viel lieber der Oberkeit gehorsam sein, f. 386 b.

swarmed about him and buzzed in his ears, and the poor wretch believed that by yielding a few points he could save his life. He offered to labour along with Melchior Hoffmann, to bring the numerous Anabaptists in Friesland, Holland, Brabant, and Flanders into submission, if he were given his liberty ; but finding that the preachers had been giving him false hopes and leading him into recantations, he refused to see them again, and awaited his execution in sullen despair.

The pastors failing to convert the Anabaptists, and finding that the sectaries used against them scripture and private judgment with such efficacy that they were unable in argument to overcome them, called upon the princes to exterminate them by fire and sword.

The gentle Melancthon wrote a tract or letter to urge the princes on ; it was entitled, " Das weltliche Oberkeiten den Widerteuffern mit leiblicher straffe zu wehren schüldig sey. Etlicher bedenken zu Wittemberg gestellet durch Philip Melancthon, 1536. Ob Christliche Fürsten schüldig sind der Widerteuffer unchristlicher Sect mit leiblicher straffe und mit dem schwert zu wehren." He enumerates the doctrines of the unfortunate sectarians at Münster and elsewhere, and then he says that it is the duty of all princes and nobles to root out with the sword all heresy from their dominions ; but then, with this proviso, they must first be instructed out of God's Word by the pure reformed Church what doctrines are heretical, that they may only exterminate those who differ from the Lutheran communion.

He then quotes to the Protestant princes the example of the Jewish kings: "The kings in the Old Testament, not only the Jewish kings, but also the converted heathen kings, judged and killed the false prophets and unbelievers. Such examples show the office of princes. As Paul says, the law is good that blasphemers are to be punished. The government is not to rule men for their bodily welfare, so much as for God's honour, for they are God's ministers; let them remember that and value their office."

But it is argued on the other side that it is written, "Let both grow together till the harvest. Now this is not spoken to the temporal power," says Melancthon, "but to the preachers, that they should not use physical power under the excuse of their office. From all this it is plain that the worldly government is bound to drive away blasphemy, false doctrine, heresies, and to punish in their persons those who hold to these things .... Let the judge know that this sect of Anabaptists is from the devil, and as a prudent preacher instructs different stations how they are to conduct themselves, as he teaches a wife that to breed children is to please God well, so he teaches the temporal authorities how they are to serve God's honour, and openly drive away heresy."[1]

So also did Justus Menius write to urge on an exterminatory persecution of the sectaries; he also argues that "Let both grow together till the harvest,"

[1] "Das weltliche Oberkeit," &c., in Luth. "Sämt. Werke." 1545-51, ii. ff. 327-8.

is not to be quoted by the princes as an excuse for sparing lives and properties.[1]

On the 12th January, 1536, John of Leyden, Knipperdolling, and Krechting were brought back to Münster to undergo sentence of death.[2]

A platform was erected in the square before the townhall on the 21st, and on this platform was planted a large stake with iron collars attached to it.

When John Bockelson was told, on the 21st, that he was to die on the morrow, he asked for the chaplain of the bishop, John von Siburg, who spent the night with him. With the fear of a terrible death before him, the confidence of the wretched man gave way, and he made his confession with every sign of true contrition.

Knipperdolling and Krechting, who were also offered the assistance of a priest, rejected the offer with contempt. They declared that the presence of God sufficed them, that they were conscious of having committed no sin, and that all their actions had been done to the sole glory of God, that moreover they were freely justified by faith in Christ.

On Monday the 22nd, at eight o'clock in the morning, the ex-king of Münster and his companions were led to execution. The gates of the city had been closed, and a large detachment of troops surrounded the scaffold. Outside this iron ring was a dense crowd of people, and the windows were filled with heads. Francis of Waldeck occupied a window immediately

---

[1] " Von dem Geist d. Widerteuffer." in Luth. "Samt. Werke." 1545-51, ii. f. 325 b.

[2] Kerssenbroeck, p. 209 ; Kurtze Hist. f. 400.

·opposite the scaffold, and remained there throughout the hideous tragedy.[1] As an historian has well observed, " Francis of Waldeck, in default of other virtues, might at least have not forgotten what was ·due to his high rank and his Episcopal character ; he regarded neither —but showed himself as ferocious as had been John Bockelson, by becoming a spectator of the long and horrible torture of the three criminals."[2]

John and his accomplices having reached the town-hall, received their sentence from Wesseling, the city judge. It was that they should be burned with red-hot pincers, and finally stabbed with daggers heated in the fire.[3]

The king was the first to mount the scaffold and be tortured.

"The king endured three grips with the pincers without speaking or crying, but then he burst forth into cries of, " Father, have mercy on me! God of mercy and loving kindness!" and he besought pardon ·of his sins and help. The bystanders were pierced to the heart by his shrieks of agony, the scent of the roast flesh filled the market-place ; his body was one great wound. At length the sign was given, his tongue was torn out with the red pincers, and a ·dagger pierced his heart.

Knipperdolling and Krechting were put to the torture directly after the agonies of the king had begun.

---

[1] Kerssenbroeck, p. 210 ; Kurtze Hist. f. 400.

[2] Bussierre, p. 462.

[3] Kerssenbroeck, p. 211 ; Bullinger, lib. ii. c. 10 ; Montfort., p. 74 ; Heresbach, pp. 166-7 ; Hast, pp. 405-6 ; Kurtze Historia f. 400.

Knipperdolling endeavoured to beat his brains out against the stake, and when prevented, he tried to strangle himself with his own collar. To prevent him accomplishing his design, a rope was put through his mouth and attached to the stake so as totally to incapacitate him from moving. When these unfortunates were dead, their bodies were placed in three iron cages, and were hung up on the tower of the church of St. Lambert, the king in the middle.[1]

Thus ended this hideous drama, which produced an effect throughout Germany. The excess of the scandal inspired all the Catholic governments with horror, and warned them of the immensity of the danger they ran in allowing the spread of Protestant mysticism. Cities and principalities which wavered in their allegiance to the Church took a decided position at once.

At Münster, Catholicism was re-established. As has been already mentioned, the debauched, cruel bishop was a Lutheran at heart, and his ambition was to convert Münster into an hereditary principality in his family, after the example of certain other princes.

Accordingly, in 1543, he proposed to the States of the diocese to accept the Confession of Augsburg and abandon Catholicism. The proposition of the prince was unanimously rejected. Nevertheless the prince joined the Protestant union of Smalkald the following year, but having been complained of to the Pope and the Emperor, and fearing the fate of Hermann von Wied, Archbishop of Cologne, he excused himself as best he could through his relative, Jost Hodefilter,

[1] Kerssenbroeck, p. 211 ; Kurtze Hist. f. 401.

bishop of Lübeck, and Franz von Dei, suffragan bishop of Osnabrück.

Before the Smalkald war the prince-bishop had secretly engaged the help of the Union against his old enemy, the "wild" Duke Henry of Brunswick. After the war, the Duke of Oldenburg revenged himself on the principality severely, with fire and sword, and only spared Münster itself for 100,000 guilders. The bishop died of grief. He left three natural sons by Anna Polmann. They bore as their arms a half star, a whole star being the arms of Waldeck.

Authorities : Hermann von Kerssenbroeck ; Geschichte der Wiederthaüffer zu Münster in Westphalen. Münster, 1771. There is an abbreviated edition in Latin in Menckenii Scriptores Rerum Germanicaum, Leipsig, 1728-30. T. iii. pp. 1503-1618.

Wie das Evangelium zu Münster erstlich angefangen, und die Widerteuffer verstöret widerauffgehöret hat. Darnach was die teufflische Secte der Widerteuffer fur grewliche Gotteslesterung und unsagliche grawsamkeit . . . . in der Stad geübt und getrieben ; beschrieben durch Henrichum Dorpium Monasteriensem ; in Luther's Sammtliche Werke. Wittemb. 1545-51. Band ii. ff. 391-401.

Historia von den Münsterischen Widerteuffern. *Ibid.* ff. 328-363.

Acta, Handlungen, Legationen und Schriften, &c., d. Munsterischen sachen geschehen. *Ibid.*, ff. 363-391.

Kurtze Historia wie endlich der König sampt zweien gerichtet, &c. *Ibid.* ff. 400-9.

D. Lambertus Hortensius Monfortius, Tumultuum Anabaptistarum Liber unus. Amsterdam, 1636.

Histoire de la Réformation, ou Mémoires de Jean Sleidan. Trad. de Courrayer. La Haye, 1667. Vol. ii. lib. x. [This is the edition quoted in the article.]

Sleidanus : Commentarium rerum in Orbe gestarum, &c. Argent. 1555 ; ed. alt. 1559,

I. Hast, Geschichte der Wiederthaüffer von ihren Entstehen in Zwickau bis auf ihren Sturz zu Münster in Westphalen Münster. 1836.

Lightning Source UK Ltd.
Milton Keynes UK
UKHW031933120421
381871UK00009B/1912